Flight

Flight

The Story of Virgil Richardson, A Tuskegee Airman in Mexico

Ben Vinson III

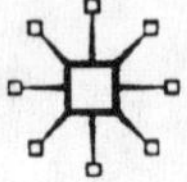

FLIGHT

First published 2004 by
PALGRAVE MACMILLAN™
175 Fifth Avenue, New York, N.Y. 10010 and
Houndmills, Basingstoke, Hampshire, England RG21 6XS
Companies and representatives throughout the world

PALGRAVE MACMILLAN is the global academic imprint of the Palgrave Macmillan division of St. Martin's Press, LLC and of Palgrave Macmillan Ltd. Macmillan® is a registered trademark in the United States, United Kingdom and other countries. Palgrave is a registered trademark in the European Union and other countries.

ISBN 1–4039–6618–4 hardback

Library of Congress Cataloging-in-Publication Data
Vinson, Ben.
Flight : the story of Virgil Richardson, a Tuskegee airman in Mexico / by Ben Vinson, III [and] Virgil Richardson.
p. cm.
Includes bibliographical references (p.) and index.
ISBN1-4039-6618-4 (hc : alk. paper)
1. Richardson, Virgil, 1916– 2. United States. Army Air Forces. Fighter Group, 332nd. 3. World War, 1939–1945—Aerial operations, American. 4. Unites States. Army Air Forces—Airmen—Biography. 5. United States. Army Air Forces—African Americans—Biography. 6. Actors—United States—Biography. 7. African American actors—Biography. 8. African Americans—Mexico—Biography. 9. United States—Ethnic relations—History—20th century. 10. Mexico—Ethnic relations—History—20th century. I. Richardson, Virgil, 1916– II. Title.

E745.V56 2004
973'.0496073'0092—dc22
[B] 2004044539

A catalogue record for this book is available from the British Library.

Design by Newgen Imaging Systems (P) Ltd., Chennai, India.

First edition: November 2004
10 9 8 7 6 5 4 3 2 1

Printed in the United States of America.

For Virgil—In Home of His Memory
December 14, 1916–May 15, 2004

Contents

Acknowledgements

All books have a history. *Flight* is intertwined in the lives and experiences of more people than I can possibly list. Of course, tremendous gratitude goes to Mr. Virgil Richardson and his family, who patiently put up with me for many days on end, for my endless needs for "a ride," and for my too many probing questions about the innerworkings of their lives. In particular, I would like to thank Morris, Lois, Deborah, Charles, and Evette Richardson for their kindness and hospitality. Vincent De Lusia is responsible for hosting the conference that brought me into contact with Virgil, and Omar Farouk-Roque helped conceive of this project in its earliest stages. The guidance, support, and insight of Herbert S. Klein, Louis Pérez, Jr., Richard H. Kohn, Caryl "Caz" Phillips, Duchess Harris, Gabriel Haslip-Viera, Paul Eiss, Peter Coclanis, Jacqueline Hall, Rosalind Rosenberg, Herbert Sloan, JoAnn Gustafson, and William "Sandy" Darity, Jr. all proved instrumental to the research and writing of the final manuscript. In Mexico, the friendship and comments of Annadale Snider, Olivia Livera, William Somersille, and Alicia Mejia opened up new avenues of research. My dedicated student team worked endlessly, sometimes seeing no sense in their work and numbing their eyes, ears, and hands by reviewing tapes and transcribing. Thank you, Julie Gilgoff and Tanya Dantus, for your incredible efforts. In Mexico City, Fabiola Melendez was magnificent in tracking down obscure photographs, documents, and records. I would also like to thank the *New York Times Book Review*. An author's query published there led to some very interesting correspondence that helped shape this book. A very special thanks is extended to my fantastic parents, Ben Vinson, Jr. and Lillie M. Hill Vinson. Both rolled up their sleeves on this project. My father accompanied me into the National Archives and fished through a sea of documents for information on Virgil's life. With his trained soldier's eye, he also carefully read and gave constructive comments on the first full draft of the manuscript. My mother not only traveled to West Columbia, Texas, but she also assisted with several rounds of interviews. Her endless charm placed Virgil at ease, even at moments when it seemed like he was too tired to answer any further questions.

Early versions of this work were presented at a number of workshops and colloquia. In particular, I would like to thank the Race(ing) Research, Researching Race: Demography and Inequality Seminar at UNC-Chapel Hill; the Black Atlantic History Seminar sponsored by the Center for Historical Analysis at Rutgers University; the Barnard Forum on Migration; and the Mellon Career Enhancement Retreat sponsored by the Woodrow Wilson Foundation at Princeton, for the opportunity to share my research.

Financial support has been made possible through a Mellon Foundation Career Enhancement Fellowship, a Ford Foundation Postdoctoral Fellowship, a UNC-Chapel Hill Fellowship for Faculty Diversity, and a Barnard College Summer Travel Grant. I will forever cherish the friendships I made while working on this book at UNC-Chapel Hill. I also extend warm thanks to my colleagues at Barnard College, whose early encouragement persuaded me that the project was a good idea. To my new colleagues at Penn State, I extend hearty thanks for helping me see the book through to its completion.

The project could not have been finished without the moral support of my "Monday Cowgirl," Yolanda Fortenberry, who read drafts and literally rode this project through right to the finish line. Her loving support means the world to me. Finally, to Jaime Rodriguez, Rhonda Sharpe, Mrs. Bernadette Merlin, Nédgé Guercin, and my friends at Cooper Square and Remington Ridge—here is the final product *at last*!

State College, PA, 2004

Introduction
From the Eyes of an Historian

It was barely nine but it was already forbiddingly hot, as only the morning of a Texas June could be. I shut the door of the gray Silverado, thanking Morris for the six-minute ride. Stuffing a blueberry muffin into my mouth, I picked up my tripod, camera bag, tape recorder, and notebook. Then I hastened along the manicured lawn to the front of a single-story, red brick, condo-style apartment. Despite the heat, someone was lingering outside, taking advantage of the last bearable hour before the sun began reaching for its midday peak. I could feel his eyes following me as I made my way toward unit no. 9. I casually turned to look around and smiled his way as I approached the door. As he stroked the white stubble from his chin, he probably wondered who I was and what I was doing at the Brooks Manor Assisted Living complex.

I gave the door a loud knock. Almost instantly, a shuffling sound could be heard from within, as if someone was rustling papers and pulling chairs away from a table. Then came that familiar, commanding voice, "Hello, who is it?"

"It's me, Ben, from Barnard College." He knew who it was. We had just talked about a half-hour earlier and I'd seen him peeping from his curtains when Morris pulled up behind the house. "Wait! Hold on a minute there, Ben." With the assistance of his cane, he began his three-legged walk to the door.

Honestly, I didn't want to wait a second longer. A full ten months had passed since I'd last seen Virgil. We'd been introduced in Minnesota where we were co-panelists at a conference held at Minneapolis Community and Technical College. Although Virgil was a layman, the tone of the two-day event on the African presence in Mexico was academic. The opening day's morning sessions featured historical and anthropological papers—partly read, partly ad-libbed—on the Afro-Mexican experience from colonial to modern times.

Refreshingly, the afternoon session promised to be different. Virgil was the first presenter. Standing nearly six feet tall and bedecked in a sport coat and tie, Virgil eased toward the auditorium's stage. Each step forward, paced by the assistance of his brown cane, seemed deliberate and well thought through, yet fluid enough to provide an air of distinction to his gait. Virgil thanked the student aide as he took up a seat beside me. Using the tip of his forefinger to prop up his glasses, he leaned over the microphone and tapped it a couple of times. A series of dull thuds filled the room. Leaning over some more, he said, "Testing, testing, One, Two, Three, testing." His rich baritone voice, that of a seasoned actor and radio host, caught the attention of everyone. Chattering students grew silent, and those milling around outside began filing back in. The camera crew inserted a tape. Virgil Richardson began telling us the story of his experience as an African American expatriate who lived 47 years in Mexico.

From tightly closed eyes that at times squinted and winced in the effort of recollection, Virgil provided snippets of life in New York as a struggling actor, and took pains to discuss his initial arrival in Acapulco and Mexico City during the summer of 1950. All of us were captivated by the amazing detail of his memories. He was describing not just events, but the color of furniture, the intricate features of landscapes, and the mood of lost friends and acquaintances. The delight that ran through his face showed us that he wasn't just talking, but reliving life as it flashed before him. After a quick hour, it was obvious he needed more. Antsy historians, myself included, waited anxiously to get more details after the Q&A. Stored in his mind was a wealth of information that could illuminate a rich and relatively unknown chapter of African American history south of the Rio Grande.

So it was with great anticipation that I couldn't wait for Virgil to open the door on that sweltering summer day. Since our initial meeting, I'd also learned that he'd been a co-founder of the American Negro Theater in Harlem, a radio personality on WNEW (New York), and had flown 63 combat missions as a Tuskegee Airman during World War II. Virgil had also been stationed in England as a member of the U.S. Army battalion located in the port of Bristol. After the war, upon experiencing a score of racial incidents and enduring the trials of a failing marriage, Virgil fled to Mexico, eventually vowing to live there permanently. He continued acting, finding roles in the low-budget *Tarzan* and *Sheena* movies filmed in Mexico City during the 1950s and 1960s. He starred in *Su Excelencia* (1966), taking a Spanish-speaking role opposite the great Mexican film star Cantinflas. He combined his acting career with other work, including positions as a teacher, writer, and professional film dubber. In the 1970s, he also developed an instructional aide to help language students master the fundamentals of Spanish and English grammar. The successful tool, a grammar clock, was sold throughout Mexico City in the 1980s.

I also learned that Virgil was part of a sub-current of the black diaspora,[1] a member of a small clique of black military servicemen who retired in Mexico.

African American G.I.'s began branching out internationally after World War II, with many taking advantage of the G.I. bill to improve their education. Mexico offered a cheap alternative to crowded U.S. schools. Some servicemen, after they got their degrees, decided to remain in the country. In the 1960s and 1970s, black vets from the Korean and Vietnam wars added to the mix. Even wounded soldiers found a new lease on life south of the border, settling, marrying, and thriving in the wonderful Mexican climate.[2]

But Virgil was unique from the rest because he was a former Tuskegee Airman. This group of elite fliers occupies a special place in the mythology of America. They were among the "talented tenth" of their generation, whose pedigree among blacks was unquestioned, and whose patriotic service to their country would eventually earn wide respect and praise. Especially true for the early graduates, nearly all held college degrees and some had even attended graduate school. Lodged as they were amidst the black middle- and upper-middle classes, after the war many of the 450 pilots who served overseas came home and translated their air victories into domestic success.[3] Some remained military officers, climbing steadily through the ranks. Others made contributions in fields such as law, education, medicine, public service, and business. Some of the less successful returned to jobs as mechanics, teachers, clerks, and small business owners—all of which were respectful positions. The road wasn't easy for any of the fliers, and they continually confronted racism and discrimination, as did the other blacks of their era. But the majority persevered with determination in their long-term mission of conquering the battle of race relations on the domestic front.

A handful of Tuskegee Airmen chose to try their luck abroad. Those who had wanted to stay home to use their flying skills as commercial pilots found their hopes quickly dashed by Jim Crow. James Plinton, Jr. was among the discontented. Just a couple of years after V-Day, he relocated to Haiti, where he became an aviator and part owner of an airline specializing in interisland transportation. In addition to his dry cleaning business (reportedly among the first on the island), he was poised to make a fortune in the Caribbean.[4] Other former Tuskegee Airmen, like Walter Palmer, left the United States because they found that they could live off of their pensions more comfortably abroad. Palmer, who had been a civil servant in New York City after World War II, tried living in California in the late 1950s before finally moving his family to Guadalajara in 1958. Earning 15 to 18 percent interest on savings in a Mexican bank, he realized that he didn't have to work at all for the seven years his family remained abroad.[5] Meanwhile, Tuskegee aviators like Jack Willis and Bill Jackson chose to retire out of the country only after they had scored substantial success at home. Bill Jackson, a B-25 pilot in the 477th Composite Group, attended dental school after the war and went on to become one of the first black dentists to open an office in downtown Chicago. Having practiced for over 32 years, in 1983 he was persuaded to visit Mexico for vacation by another Airman, George Anderson. Bill fell in love with the country and ended up buying two homes there, one near Guadalajara and the other in Puerto Vallarta. More than 20 years later, Bill still lives in Puerto Vallarta today. Living in the same city is Jack Willis, who flew in the 332nd Medium Bomber Group. He and his wife moved to Mexico in the early 1990s, after he'd logged a full career in the United States and had served as the director of the Caribbean Institute for Computer Technology. Mexico represented Willis's second long-term move to a Spanish-speaking country, since he'd lived for nearly three years in Puerto Rico while working for the Caribbean Institute.[6]

The life history of Virgil Richardson offers a detailed glimpse into the rare world of such Tuskegee expatriates. Of the surviving Tuskegee Airmen who are known to have lived in Mexico, none remained abroad for as long as Virgil, nor were any as thoroughly ensconced in the Mexican and U.S. expatriate social scene. He had a unique opportunity to view the lives of other blacks in Mexico, and to comment upon his own complicated search for a place in history and a place to call "home." Jim Crow America made his wartime homecoming difficult; Mexico's unique history of race relations made the adjustment easier in a foreign land.

I confess that I had no idea what I was getting into when I walked through Virgil's front door. As I set up my video camera and tripod in the living room, all I had to guide me was an initial set of questions designed to probe Virgil's life from his childhood through 1997, which was the year he decided to return to the United States. Maybe there would be an article in all of this information, maybe a biography, or maybe nothing at all. I set aside ten days for initial interviewing. On most days, we worked for between eight to ten hours, stopping only to eat lunch (provided by Meals on Wheels), short afternoon walks, and dinner (a healthy diet of pizza, soda, and beer); in the evenings we paused for *Jeopardy*, *Wheel of Fortune, Sex in the City*, Houston Astros baseball games, and to listen to tapes of the *Spice Girls*.

Given my training as a Latin American historian, as well as my research interests in the experiences of blacks outside the United States, the interviewing process took on a dichotomous character. Generally, the questions that I asked about Virgil's life prior to his departure for Mexico tended to be comprehensive, but very open-ended. As a result, Virgil was free to recount his life prior to 1950 largely on his own terms. Because of the patterned crispness of the narrative, its flavor, and its colorful characters it became quite clear to me that what I was hearing were a series of stories that he had grown accustomed to telling over time. Many revolved around World War II and his training at Tuskegee, which comprise a large portion of this book; however, certain major life transitions were also poignantly remembered. These included the initial days of his arrival in New York City and the circumstances leading up to his self-imposed exile from the United States. A short question on any of these points could lead to answers that were easily 15 minutes long or more.

By and large, I let these stories unfold uninterrupted, or with small breaks to ask minor questions of clarification. Later, from the comfort of my office or upon the desks of an archive, I checked the details as much as possible for historical accuracy. The remarkably few aberrations from historical "truth" were sometimes insightful, since they revealed how Virgil processed certain events, or demonstrated how much information he was exposed to during their happening. For instance, when Virgil first arrived in New York City in 1938, he was told that the person who encouraged him to move there and who'd offered him a place to stay, V. F. Calverton, had recently died. This left him devastated and wondering what to do. In truth, Calverton did not pass away until 1940. But Virgil had no way of knowing this at the time, and this brush with adversity positively influenced his resolve and determination to succeed in the urban environment.

My own involvement in Virgil's memory recollection process became much more aggressive as we began discussing his life in Mexico. Almost from the beginning of this phase of questioning it was clear that Virgil had already ordered his thinking about this period of his life into a series of stories prepared for recall. However, the type of questions for which I sought answers involved deeper reflection on his feelings about Mexico as a racial environment. I asked him to contemplate his treatment by Mexicans, to describe his feelings about race, and to discuss his life in relation to other blacks that he knew in Mexico City during the 1950s and 1960s. What I encountered, surprisingly, was difficulty in acquiring information on these themes. Later, I realized that Virgil had left the United States in large part because of issues related to race. It had been liberating for him to live in an environment that was so radically different from America in racial terms. Part of Mexico's charm was that he did not have to think about color as he had before. Consequently, asking Virgil to entertain the possibility that Mexico was anything less than an accepting place for blacks was simply too much, and contradicting to reality—or at least reality as he perceived it to be.

In navigating my barrage of questions, Virgil relied heavily upon "memory loops." That is, to address issues that he had not contemplated before he resorted to using his databank of well-remembered stories to help him think through what was less familiar. Awkward pauses perforated the interviews as he struggled to remember a name, a face, or a feeling. It was not unusual for us to suddenly find ourselves blending events and situations—talking about up to three or four time sequences simultaneously. Frequently, we revisited stories repeatedly to get at something new. Then suddenly, a thundering laugh and a broad smile showed that Virgil seemed genuinely excited by the recollection of something that he'd long forgotten.

With Virgil, there was never enough time to get the full story. The ten days of intense interviewing was just the beginning of what was to become several trips to Texas, and countless phone conversations, over a three-year period. My research team, including several of my students from Barnard College and Columbia University, helped me process the material, think through the results, and conduct supplementary interviews with Virgil's friends in Mexico City. Together, we tried to make sense of the now-transcribed silences. Poring over the story, we discovered that some key holes existed in the narrative. What about Virgil's relationship with his wife? What were the circumstances of his divorce? In Mexico City, one of our informants alluded to possible connections to the political left. Exactly what was the nature of these connections—indeed, did they exist? Unfortunately, even after extensive archival work, we could never get satisfactory answers to these questions. Their absence, however, does not undermine the value and power of his story.

Slowly, this project blossomed into a book, but one that was increasingly taking an unusual shape. When searching for the right voice with which to pitch the narrative, I experimented with writing *Flight* as an ordinary biography. But in the process, the story began losing its energy and expression. The biography format compromised the human touch that made Virgil's account initially so compelling. At the same time, the book couldn't work as a transcription. There were too many time shifts, too many historical gaps, and too many logic-related issues for this to be successful. Therefore, what you have before you is a historical memoir. Like a biography or autobiography, the book takes a chronological approach, navigating us from Virgil's childhood into his adult years. Like a memoir, the book pauses on key life moments for reflection and explanation. With a historian's hand, I have played a pivotal role in ordering the memories from the transcription into something that "works" chronologically. In certain areas (alluded to in the footnotes) Virgil's memory has been supplemented with archival research to provide added depth to the story. So as not to saturate the first-person narrative, the book closes with a separate chapter, providing contextual material detailing the history of black travel to Mexico during the nineteenth and twentieth centuries. Of special concern here is demonstrating how African Americans and Mexicans thought about one another, showing how Mexico contemplated its own black heritage, and uncovering the way in which African Americans became embedded in the political debates that erupted between the United States and its southern neighbor. Much of this information, especially about African Americans living in Mexico after the 1930s, is being compiled and narrated for the first time. The information on the nineteenth and early twentieth centuries, meanwhile, synthesizes a disparate, yet exciting body of scholarship that sometimes only mentions blacks in passing. In its effort to be both analytical and descriptive, the book's closing chapter offers crucial material toward understanding how Virgil's story fits into larger patterns of African American migration south of the border, and speaks broadly to the growing scholarly literature on the Black Diaspora. It also helps us to ponder a frequently overlooked place of black refuge during the era of Jim Crow: Latin America. Much is known about Europe as a site of African American exile, but the tale is still unfolding for areas south of the Rio Grande. Finally, to make problematic areas of the text and Virgil's memory fit together, the voice adopted in the book is a blended one—Virgil's and mine. While much of the prose you read in the narrative section is Virgil's, it is edited. Virgil, however, has generously commented upon the final versions of this text to ensure that it has been rendered according to his experiences, memory, and, ultimately, his voice.

Chapter 1

Virgil: Before the War

My mother and father first met in a romantic accident. She had come to Texarkana, Texas to meet one of her cousins, but had confused the dates. Nobody was there to greet her when she stepped off the train. After waiting for what seemed like an eternity in the hot sun, a man appeared, sitting up tall on the back of a white horse. He politely asked why she was standing there alone. She explained her situation. After comforting her, he suggested that her family might come for her next day and that, in the meantime, he would gladly take her to his sister's house to spend the night. He then dismounted and helped her up onto his horse. The pair started talking along the way home.

Papa was a farm boy. Mama had attended college and was employed as a country schoolteacher, making 45 dollars a month. Because most of her students needed to help their families during the cotton harvest season, she worked for only part of the year, during the months of October through April.

Mama's family could trace their roots back to India. Her grandfather, Joe Green Cotler, was originally from Bombay and had been brought to America by his mother, an indentured servant. Listening to mama tell the story, Grandpa Green's mother was so fiery and troublesome that her contractors decided to let her go early. Grandpa Green himself went on to become a large landowner, with nearly 600 acres in Arkansas. He built a big log house and a church on his property. Razorbacks ran about freely on the land, and Grandpa Green would constantly chase after them with his dogs. One day, he fell into a ditch and froze to death while walking around his domain. He was nearly 105.

I still remember Grandpa Green from when I was a boy. He once invited all of his children and grandchildren over for a special breakfast. There were about

50 people seated around the table. There were so many different skin shades among us that you could tell Grandpa Green must have been married at least twice. His first wife was white or mulatto, since a group of my cousins was light-skinned—they were what we called "yellow" back then. Later, grandpa married my mother's grandmother, who was part black and part American Indian. My father, too, was part American Indian, so I have some East Indian and American Indian blood in me, although I don't know exactly how much.

I was born in Center Point, Arkansas on December 14, 1916, but raised in Texarkana because my parents chose to leave Arkansas shortly after they were married. Papa had initially followed mama to Center Point in order to help her father and brothers raise cotton, which was in great demand at the time. Cotton prices had shot up to 60 cents a pound during World War I, but when talk of armistice came, prices dropped to 20 cents a pound.[1] There seemed to be little future in cotton, so, in 1918, papa decided to move us back to Texarkana. He found some rooms for us in a big house next to Hopewell Church. We shared this house with two other people. Then papa got a railroad job and became a skilled worker making about 75 cents an hour with lots of overtime. That was a fabulous amount of money at the time. But when the Great Depression hit, all railroad workers lost their overtime pay.

Papa eventually bought his own house and began adding rooms—a bedroom for my sister, Clementine, and a screened-in back porch for us six boys. Our family also owned a cow. Not too long after my parents got married, my grandfather, Jim Clardy, gave it to mama as a gift. We were virtually the same age, the cow and I. When I finished high school at 18, the cow was also 18! Until I was a senior, one of my chores was to milk her every morning and take her out to graze. I would milk her again in the evening, right about suppertime.

We had a yard too, with a nice garden and over 200 chickens. Between the cow, the chickens, and the garden we ate very well during the Depression. Even hoboes would stop by our house looking for food. Mama would always find something to give them—a quart of milk, some cornbread, whatever.

Mama was determined that I would attend college. We had a neighbor, also named Virgil. His mother lived about a block or two away from Wiley College, in Marshall, Texas.[2] Somehow, Virgil mentioned to mama that his mother, Mrs. Simpson, had a room for rent. Mama arranged for me to get it. She also wrote a letter to the college president, Dr. Dogan, somehow convincing him that I would be a credit to Wiley if I got a scholarship.[3] Not too much later, I went off to school and began living with Mrs. Simpson. She didn't have the amenities that we had back in Texarkana, like a bathroom, running water, a shower, or even lights. But for five dollars a month, Mrs. Simpson did my laundry and cooked. My family mailed me groceries so that she could fix them. Papa sent flour, corn meal, beans, black-eyed peas, and things like that. He also sent me money. Eventually, after I'd been at Wiley for a while, Mrs. Simpson said, "Virgil, you tell your mother not to send us anything else, because these rich people that I work for have me throwing away filet mignon, steaks, and pork chops. I'll just bring it home because I'm sick of throwing it away."

I made the honor roll during my first two years at Wiley. My sister became a student there during my second year, so now there were two of us there. Two of my brothers also ended up going to Wiley.

My parents struggled to keep us in school. Wiley was what they called a "silk stocking college." That is, during the 1920s, the co-eds would wear silk stockings during the week and even more formal attire on Sundays.[4] That didn't mean tuxedos for men, but they were still sharply dressed. By my sophomore year I had become painfully aware that I didn't have enough clothes. All the guys from Dallas and Houston brought big wardrobe trunks with them to Wiley. They had *everything*. At the time, it was popular to wear brushed-wool sweaters and white buckskin shoes. They had all of this. There was even one guy who would change his clothes twice a day!

To help me with clothes and expenses, mama made some special arrangements with Wiley's president, allowing me to get a job as a waiter. Not only did I earn an income, but I also received some basic lessons about life. For instance, I'd always thought that pretty girls didn't have big appetites, but you sure learn otherwise waiting tables at a college!

Wiley had one of the best football teams of any Negro school in the country. We had beaten virtually everyone in the area except for the team from Langston. They had all this oil money—they would ride down from Oklahoma on the Langston bus with huge, 250-pound guys. Then they would beat the hell out of us! One of our greatest rivals, though, was Bishop College. Wiley's campus was located on one hill in Marshall, Texas, called Methodist Hill. Bishop stood on another; Baptist Hill. Wiley was a Methodist school and Bishop was a Baptist school. The games between us always generated tremendous excitement, not just because of football, but because of the religious rivalry between Methodists and Baptists.

Wiley also had a good jazz band called the Wiley Wild Cats. We had sororities and fraternities too—I was a Kappa. On the other hand, Bishop's strict Baptist tradition forbade them from having Greek organizations. They had a good theological seminary and a strong music department, but no sororities and fraternities. Wiley was far more prestigious than Bishop, in my opinion. Our fine library, the Carnegie Library, was one of the strongest among the black schools. We also had a large number of Ph.D.s on the faculty and our president, Dr. Dogan, despite being a tiny brown-skinned man, was a brilliant fundraiser.

He was always traveling to places like Minnesota and Wisconsin seeking money. More nationally prominent schools like Fisk, Howard, and Wilberforce may have had larger endowments than we did, but even they were not as good, in my opinion.

James Farmer, Jr., the civil rights activist who became the founder of the Congress of Racial Equality (CORE) and who eventually received the Medal of Freedom (1998) from President Clinton for his life achievements, was a classmate and acquaintance of mine.[5] His father, Dr. James Farmer, Sr., also taught religion and philosophy at the college.[6] Dr. Farmer was a fool. Although he had a Ph.D. from Boston University and had taken courses at Harvard, he was always talking nonsense to the girls in his classes. "Oh, you yellow [light-skinned] gals who wanna get grades to make your sororities, you girls just sit up here in the front row and open up your legs so that I can see the Christmas Tree. You'll get your A's." I can still see the girls now, embarrassed that he was being such a clown. All of this was done while his son was sitting right there in class!

Dr. Farmer was often seen walking around town, talking to himself. We attended church with him a couple of times a week. He dared to read from his notebook instead of the Bible—as if his own words were more important than the word of God! Despite his antics, Farmer was a well-respected intellectual and spoke at numerous philosophical conferences.

I was involved in the sciences when I started out at Wiley. I was a science major and a biology minor. I also studied chemistry and mathematics. Back then, seemingly the only career that a young black man could think of for making money was in medicine—chemistry and medicine. Contemplating a career in medicine caused me to study Latin in high school. I didn't just study the language; I mastered it. I was the best student in my high-school Latin class. In college, after taking some French, I switched to German. I couldn't twist my mouth in the way that is needed to speak French, and I knew that German was a great scientific language. Many of the world's famous scientists were German. So, as with Latin, I set about mastering the language, despite my teacher's terrible accent and his tendency to send a stream of spit out of his mouth each time he pronounced "Ich." Surprisingly, I found German to be much like English, and in a very short time I was becoming fluent.

I wasn't involved in college athletics. Although I had played basketball in high school, the competition in college was too great. We had some of the best athletes in the country. We had Packinghouse Adams from St. Louis, O'Neil from Gary, Indiana, Pat Patterson from Chicago, and "Showboat" Barnes. They were like the "Four Horsemen" of Notre Dame. I'm sure these men thought they were equal to anybody in the United States.

Dr. Botner, a music teacher, and Melvin B. Tolson, my college mentor and freshman English teacher, encouraged me to try some new extracurricular activities. Dr. Botner gave me a few singing lessons and suggested that I try out for his a cappella choir. To tell the truth, I was tone deaf and couldn't carry a tune, but I did have a good speaking voice, so Dr. Botner put me in the choir anyway. I rumbled along, doing my best. Dr. Botner even encouraged me by saying that if I continued, I could end up being another Paul Robeson!

Tolson, the great poet who wrote "A Gallery of Harlem Portraits," and who eventually became the poet laureate of Liberia, coached the debating team.[7] He persuaded me to try out for it. Tolson always had a winning squad and would take it up to the "Nordic" colleges of Wisconsin and Minnesota. My friend James Farmer made the team easily and became one of the lead debaters. He was a *very* glib speaker. I didn't have that same glib delivery, so I didn't make the final cut. But in the process, I discovered that I did have a talent for memorization. This facilitated learning scripts. I could remember a whole play, including each and every part in the play. If there was any miscue, I could ad lib. While these talents didn't serve me as a prospective debater, they did serve me well as an actor. I soon started performing in a few college plays. In one of my earliest roles, I played the villain in a rendition of Rudolph Besier's *The Baretts of Wimpole Street*.

The thing that changed my whole outlook on life, or rather, I should say my outlook on the future, was a play called *The Road to Damascus*, written by a classmate of mine named Clemens. We performed *Damascus* in the spring of 1938, along with two other Wiley student plays. Tolson arranged for V. F. Calverton to come and judge us. We were all delighted; Calverton was a respected New York critic and the editor of a magazine called *Current History*.[8] I ended up acting in two plays, *The Pot Boiler*, which was about a gunman, and *Damascus*. A light-skinned girl named Reba Mattox played the role of my stepdaughter in *Damascus*. With radiant skin and impeccable hair, she was truly a beautiful piece of work; she'd been the campus queen the previous year. My character was a drunkard who pursued her, smacking her about the stage. Tolson had taught us in rehearsals precisely how and when I should strike. She was supposed to lift up her hand so that the slap would be simulated. But when Calverton visited, Reba decided that she would try to steal the scene by actually absorbing the blows. When I hit her—for real—her freckles got redder and redder, darker and darker—heightening the effect of my own performance. I went backstage to remove my gray wig and makeup when the play was over. A few minutes later, the woman playing [the mother of Reba's character] came back and rushed up to me, shouting excitedly, "Virgil, Mr. Calverton is talking about *you!*"

I wasn't quite sure how to react or what to do. I'd certainly hoped that he'd like the show, but it seemed that he was really taken by my acting. I thought to myself that it might be time to take a little curtain call, so I stepped back onstage for some applause. Gazing out into the audience, I thought I caught a glimpse of Calverton, smiling. Later, he approached me. Sure enough, Calverton thought that I had tremendous talent. While he didn't like the first two student plays he'd seen, he thought *Damascus* was well written and that I shined as the best actor he'd had the chance to observe during his visit. It was a real compliment.

I saw Calverton on campus again the next day. This time he was staggering around, with the hot stench of liquor on his breath. He'd shown himself to be a notorious drunkard and a flirt during his brief stay. Incorrigibly, he was hitting on Wiley women even though he'd come to town with his girlfriend.[9] During this second meeting, Calverton gave me his card and invited me to come to New York for some additional training. I was to look him up in Greenwich Village once I arrived in the city. He promised to arrange to get me into the Federal Theater, which was being run by the Works Progress Administration (WPA).[10] On the back of his card he scribbled: "Have Mr. Richardson come to see me."

Calverton was right. I needed some real, professional training. I'd never even seen a professional play before in my life! It took some thinking, but I eventually decided to take Calverton up on his offer. Shortly after graduation, I came to realize that I didn't want to go back to working the menial jobs that I'd worked to get through college. The Depression wasn't over yet and finding good employment was difficult. My sister, who graduated after me, was far luckier. She quickly got a job with a Negro insurance company and was later transferred to Louisiana, where she started a family. When I graduated there were a few teaching jobs available, but they were primarily in country schools that paid just 30–50 dollars a month. I didn't want that. Some high school coaching positions were open as well, but I couldn't dream of getting one of these. As I said earlier, I didn't play football in college.

I thought seriously about returning home to Texarkana, but there were just too many people in my family there for me to want to stay around. My father ended up purchasing me a round-trip pass to New York City. Meanwhile, Tolson wrote me a letter of introduction to the secretary of the New York City YMCA, 135th St. Branch. Tolson had lived in the city when he studied at Columbia and still had some contacts there. I got to the city in the summer of 1938.

I arrived in the sweltering heat of July and caught the subway from Grand Central Station to 135th street. I got a room in "The Annex," which was part of the Harlem YMCA at the time. The Y's main building was across the street and was clearly the tallest building in the community. It stood 14 stories high and had a paneled lobby, a cafeteria, a little theater, a swimming pool, and a gymnasium. After setting down my bags, I showered and put on a sports shirt that I had recently bought; then I went down to Greenwich Village. I got off at Fourth Street and began asking how to get to Calverton's house. Finally, I found the address and rang the doorbell. A heavy-set man in a dark suit and tie came to the door. "My name is Virgil Richardson," I said. "Mr. Calverton told me to come here as soon as I got to New York." I eagerly handed him the card. He took it, looked at it, and said, "I'm sorry, but my brother died of a heart attack yesterday." He quickly shut the door.[11] I don't even know whether I told him that I was sorry to hear the news. But I was devastated. I didn't know anyone in New York City.

I went to Washington Square Park and sat down on a park bench to think about what the hell I was going to do. I didn't have many options. Some luck to have my benefactor die just the day before! I sat there looking around with a blank stare. People passed by, some noticing me, others not. As I started leaning back in the seat, my hand brushed up against some newspapers. People are always leaving newspapers lying around on the park benches in New York. I picked up the *Daily News* and the *Daily Mirror*. It so happened that one of them was turned to the theater section. I read an ad for William DuBois's *The Birth of Haiti*, a WPA production. After returning to my room at the Y, I went back downtown to see the play. I don't know which theater I went to, but seeing the production changed my perspective. In watching Canada Lee play Christophe, the great Haitian revolutionary who had helped black slaves free themselves from the French, I thought to myself, "This theater thing is mine!" I had never seen a black person perform in anything like this before. Canada Lee, who had been a boxer and had lost an eye, was magnificent in the part![12] That's when I decided that I was going to stay in New York.

But without Calverton, one of the trustees of the WPA Theater Project, I didn't have an entrée into the Federal Theatre anymore. Fortunately, I still had my letter from Tolson. When I went back to the Y, I pulled it out and handed it to the secretary. He looked it over and suggested that we walk down to the YMCA's Little Theater and meet with Pat Avery to see about the possibility of getting some acting work. Pat was a small man, maybe about five-foot-eight, and an only child from Philadelphia. He sure was a dude! He had a neatly trimmed, thin mustache and was immaculately dressed. At the time, he was directing the New Theater in Harlem and was on the WPA Theater Project. He was also doing Broadway plays such as *When Ladies Meet* by Claire Booth Luce.[13] She was the playwright who eventually became the U.S. ambassador to Italy, and who married Henry R. Luce, the cofounder of *Time* magazine. Somehow, Pat and I started talking about college. I told him that I had gone to

Wiley. That's when we discovered that we were fraternity brothers—both of us were Kappas. This helped break the ice. We made some more small talk before discussing business.

Pat was very realistic about the profession. "In the first place, actors only work 20 weeks out of the year," he said. Pat made it clear that even if I could land some parts, I wasn't going to earn a living in New York on acting alone. Very soon after, I got myself a job in a Strauss Discount Auto Store, where they put seat covers on cars and changed tires. This was up near the Bronx County Court House. They paid me two dollars a day plus tips.

It wasn't long before I started acting. One of my earliest roles was in one of Pat's plays called *Night Must Fall*. To my surprise, it was produced! The play was a three-act, psychological mystery about an introverted man who walked around town with a hatbox. Every time night fell, he had a yearning desire to kill someone. I played the part of Mr. Bellsize, a Secret Service inspector who tracked him down for killing a woman. This was the kind of stuff that we did. Of course it was free, and nothing close to the caliber of Canada Lee.[14]

I soon did another play written by a guy named Abraham Hill. He was from Georgia and had gone to Lincoln University, where he'd studied playwriting and eventually became the Director of Dramatics. Hill was also part of the WPA's Federal Theater Project (he had been an administrative assistant to the office of the national director) and had written several scripts about lynching. One was called *Hell's Half Acre*, directed by an Italian named Joseph Ornato. I was with an acting troupe called the Unity Players at the time, and we did this play up in the Bronx Theater so that we could get some coverage.

The play was powerful. It opened with a scene that must have gripped our audiences. The mutilation of a black body—shot, pummeled, hanged, slashed, dragged—was performed on stage for all to see. The rage and cruelty of the white perpetrators behavior made them seem more like beasts than humans. Gradually, the audience learned that the lynching was taking place in retribution for an alleged assault on a white woman, Ms. Daisy Culpepper. But as the play continued to unfold, the real truth came out. The victim, Rufus Brown, had not really attacked Daisy. Her boyfriend had persuaded her to denounce Brown because he stood in the way of their getting married. With him out of the picture, not only could they get engaged, but Daisy would also be able to inherit Brown's money. The play took an unexpected twist when the lynchers were indicted for their actions, brought to trial, and found guilty. Astonished, the play's black characters thought true justice had been reached. Loopholes, however, allowed the perpetrators to escape harsh punishment. As the play closed, all the blacks that had been bold enough to testify against the lynchers had their homes burned to the ground. Amid the blazes, the town of Tuckerstown, where the play was set, literally became "Hell's half-acre."[15] Night after night, our performance forced audiences to think about the American justice system.

I eventually moved out of the YMCA and started living with Pat and his wife, Viola. Although they had a little girl, they still had a spare room and agreed to rent it to me, provided that I help them eat their extra food. This was no problem. Viola liked to cook and made a great leg of lamb on Sundays. There were always leftovers, since Pat didn't eat much. He was vain about his figure. Meanwhile, Viola was in nursing school and was watching her weight as well. She was constantly strapping on tight girdles. So there was always plenty of food around for me.

While I was acting I never forgot Pat's words of counsel. I tried to keep a steady day job. In September of 1938, I began working as a stockroom clerk for Mammoth Hosiery Company down on 23rd Street, making between 16 and 18 dollars a week. That was excellent money! To put it in some perspective, my rent was only about five dollars a month at the time. Not too long after I started this new job, one of the men in the stockroom left his position to work for the bookkeeper. Since they needed someone else to take his place, I passed along Pat's name. Pat still had his position with the WPA, so now he had two paychecks. The commute, though, was hell. At 7 P.M. Pat had to be at the Little Theatre in the basement of the YMCA. We would get off work at Mammoth around 5 o'clock. Then we would go all the way from 23rd Street to 219th Street in the Bronx where we lived. Then it was back to 135th Street by 7 P.M. With three salaries coming in (Viola worked at Harlem Hospital), Pat was able to buy a car, a very small Studebaker. Sometimes Viola would take the car. When Pat had it we wouldn't take the 241st Street train to work. Instead, we'd hop on the Eighth Avenue train to 42nd Street.[16] The next stop was Penn Station. Then we'd get a local train to 23rd Street. This would save time. Working at Mammoth Hosiery, I learned to walk and run really fast because regardless of which route we took, running was essential to getting to work on time. Pat and I regularly sprinted five or six blocks a day.

After about a year of working at Mammoth, the company decided to move to Camden, New Jersey. They offered me an increased salary to relocate with them, but I didn't go. Moving to New Jersey would have meant distancing myself from New York, and I was becoming very involved with the theater scene. Besides, I had a good living situation that I was not interested in changing.

As I said, I was making good money at Mammoth. Right before they relocated I was earning over 20 dollars a week, but I had virtually nothing to show for it. Some of my money paid for acting classes. I'd started theater school in 1939, studying under Nadya Ramonov, a Russian master who taught the famous techniques developed by Konstantin Stanislavski.[17] It was Stanislavski's modern theater concept that eventually helped Sidney Poitier and many others to become successful. I was hoping that these lessons would make me great as well. Nadya focused on certain aspects of the craft, such as improvisation, affective memory, imagination, rhythm, dynamics, and characterization. She gave special emphasis to gesture, posture, and body movement as it related to character and emotion.[18] Besides working on my acting technique, I also worked hard on developing my speaking voice. At the New Theater School I studied under Doris Sorrell, the head of the Voice Division. She was a consultant with the National Theater, and one of the best speech coaches in New York. Among her clients was Helen Hayes, arguably one of the most successful actresses of her time, having starred in Broadway productions like *Caesar and Cleopatra* and *Mary Queen of Scots*.[19] Sorrell had also worked with Amelia Ramano of *Big Blow* and Ella Gerber of *Pins and Needles*, two important stage productions. I already had a good speaking voice, but with Sorrell's help, I made tremendous progress.

By 1940, I had started to build an impressive résumé. I had received acting training at Wiley College Little Theater, the New Theater School, and at City College (New York). After leaving Wiley, I'd managed to win a Texas scholarship for further study in dramatics, which I was using to help underwrite my expenses at the New Theater School. I'd also starred in a number of amateur and semiprofessional plays, including *Hell's Half Acre*. I'd even written a play of my own, a political satire that was produced by the Amalgamated Clothing Workers Union.[20]

My circle of friends had started to grow ever since my arrival in New York. By the fall of 1938, I had met Francis Wills, Aida Harrison, and Odessa Vaughn. Francis, who'd studied speech at Hunter College and who'd graduated about the same time that I'd finished Wiley, performed with me on stage occasionally. Francis was also Langston Hughes's secretary. Aida and Odessa worked as social workers for the welfare agency. Odessa was a stunningly beautiful woman who was married to a man named Vaughn. He sang in one of the quartets that performed in Harlem and had a memorable, deep, rhythmic voice. I also became friends with Abe Hill, the celebrated black playwright whose play I'd starred in.[21]

On Sunday afternoons during the spring of 1940 I started meeting with a group of about five or six other actors and playwrights to strategize the future of black theater. It must have been the month of May when we first gathered. The meetings were held at Abe's parent's house. Sitting around Mrs. Hill's dining room table was Vivian Hall, a respected actress and shrewd businesswoman who'd been trained at New York University's School of Commerce. Fred O'Neal was also at the table. Like myself, he'd come from elsewhere to try to make it big in New York City theater. His initial career breakthrough came when his family moved from Mississippi to St. Louis in 1920. In 1927, O'Neal went on to found the Aldrige Players, a highly successful acting group. But he struggled in New York. Arriving in 1936, he found it hard to get parts and lived for a time on a meager diet of fish and potatoes. Later, of course, O'Neal would go on to be one of America's premiere black actors, starring in movies such as *Pinky*, *Anna Lucasta*, and *Cotton Comes to Harlem*. He also eventually became the president of the Associated Actors and Artists of America. But he was relatively unknown in 1940. Austin Briggs Hall, the Haitian-born singer and violinist, was probably better known at the time, at least on the music scene. He sat with us at the Hill's house too, as did James Jackson, the South Carolina native who'd costarred with me in *Hell's Half Acre*.

Mrs. Hill's dining room became the setting for our extravagant dreams. Here, we fantasized about creating a type of alternative theater that was experimental and that sought to raise the profile of blacks in the world of stage. Up until then, many of the roles that blacks received were stereotypical and denigrating. We were frequently written into scripts as bumbling minstrels, providing moments of comic relief. At other times, we were featured as underdogs, criminals, or exotic and lazy. There were few serious roles, even despite the impact of the Harlem Renaissance and the powerful performances delivered by actors like Paul Robeson and Canada Lee. While these two were among the best-known black actors at the time, there were hundreds more, many of them now forgotten, who were working hard to change the image of blacks in theater.

It may seem ironic, but the Depression actually offered a special time of opportunity for black theater workers. Franklin Roosevelt's New Deal policy, which sought to provide jobs to scores of unemployed people, also had a branch for the theater, known as the Federal Theater Project. Launched in 1935, it employed nearly 10,000 white theater workers in 40 states, and almost 900 blacks. About half were actors. The rest were writers, directors, producers, and designers. Roosevelt's project probably offered more to blacks than it did to whites. Whites simply got access to the same type of jobs that they would have normally had if there hadn't been a Depression. Blacks, though, were getting a chance to try their hands at directing, writing, and a whole range of other creative positions that they were usually restricted from in professional circles. The Federal Theater itself was also very conscious about not trying to typecast blacks into roles that were demeaning and stereotypical. It was through the Federal Theater Project that Langston Hughes' great work *Mulatto* was produced, as well as Georgia Douglas Johnson's *A Sunday Morning in the South*. Other important hits included *Vodoo McBeth* (a rendition of Shakespeare's masterpiece set in Haiti) and Eugene O'Neil's folk drama about African American life, *All God's Chillun' Got Wings*.

Within the Federal Theater Project there were many ethnic "units." In other words, there were special performance groups specifically designated for Irish Americans, German Americans, and blacks. The 22 "Negro units," as the black groups were called, were spread out all over the country. The most important ones operated in places like Chicago, New York, New Haven, and Los Angeles. But if one had to point out a single, prominent group among the black units, the most famous would have been the Federal Negro Theater, based out of Harlem's Layfayette Theater. Its first director, Rose McClendon, immediately gave the unit a high profile. She was one of the most acclaimed black actresses of the 1920s and 1930s, having starred opposite Robeson and boasting stage credits such as *Porgy*, which earned her a Morning Telegraph Acting Award in 1927. But to give the Federal Negro Theater even more credibility, McClendon agreed to step down and share the group's leadership with white directors. Orson Welles and John Houseman joined her, adding to the Theater's legendary success.[22]

In 1938, a series of hearings called by Texas congressman Martin Dies spelled the end of Roosevelt's Federal Theater Project. Dies accused the theater of being a cesspool of communism and moved to destroy it in June of 1939. Hundreds of black actors found themselves suddenly unemployed. Unfortunately, thanks to segregation and racism, it wouldn't be until much later, in the 1950s and 1960s, that many blacks would be able to return to jobs in serious works for the stage, like those produced by the Federal Theater.

Abe Hill, who had initially joined the Federal Theater as a playreader, (screening plays to make sure they were not stereotypical), didn't want to lose the momentum of the revolution in black theater that Roosevelt had helped ignite. He wasn't alone. All of us who gathered at Abe's parents' house were driven by similar passions. Together, sweating in the late-spring heat, the six of us argued, compromised, and hammered out the bylaws of what was to become the American Negro Theater (ANT). As founding members, we appointed ourselves to be the group's Executive Committee. Vivian, the only woman among us but also the best trained in matters of finance, became the theater's secretary and treasurer. She didn't have much bookkeeping to handle in those early gatherings. Although we realized that money would be critical to our long-term success, as a group we were only able to muster a grand total of six cents to launch the American Negro Theater. It was all we could spare.

By the end of May we began sending out cards to attract others to come to an ANT organizational meeting. People didn't have easy access to phones back then, so we had to rely on the mail for a lot of our communication.[23] On June 5, 1940, a group of 29 convened to finish shaping the structure of the group. We were really diverse in terms of our professional experience. Some, like Abe Hill and Fred O'Neal, had been in the theater business a long time. Howard Augusta, who joined us in June, had even been in seven motion pictures, and had directed, acted, and written plays in both New York and Philadelphia. Others of us were amateurs and semiprofessionals. Collectively, we were definitely too green to be on Broadway, but seasoned enough to offer a real, "civilized" stage performance to our audience.

Being based in Harlem, we found it important to provide our audience with experiences that reflected the reality of the community. We conceived of ourselves to be very much a "people's theater," and we rejected the impulse to provide elaborate fantasies on stage that were simply out of touch with the people. We wanted to offer commentary, interpretation, and criticism of common life. Our early repertoire, I think, reflected that mission. We also brought out many new theatergoers to enjoy works of stage. From the beginning, we understood that New York City, with seven million inhabitants, and Harlem, with its population of 350,000 blacks, potentially offered one of the largest black audiences in the world.

Those of us who designed the American Negro Theater were also bent on making sure that it was a "collective." We didn't want any stars. We emphasized that each member should subordinate their individual ambitions for the greater good of the group. Regardless of experience and talent, no one actor or actress was to constantly play the lead in our productions. Instead, different types of parts were to be rotated from play to play, so that every member had an equal opportunity at being the lead. As a "collective" we also shared the responsibilities of directing and producing. To remain as independent as possible from outside influences, we also established the ANT as a nonprofit cooperative, based solely on income from annual subscriptions, contributions, and endowments. This way, we did not have to worry about being pressured to perform or produce works that ran against our underlying mission.

From the beginning, the ANT was not wedded to any single acting style. We found it important to experiment with various techniques of group theater because we were searching for something completely new. We were striving to unlock a deeply imbedded, inherent "Negro quality," one that would ultimately prove to be the essence of black acting. Of course, we didn't claim to know what that special "quality" was, nor am I sure that the American Negro Theater ever discovered it. Regardless, we continually strove to discover what it might be. Many of us were convinced that it was somehow based upon the "rhythm" and "naturalness" that seemed to be fundamental aspects of black character.

We also understood that there was something special about the history of black struggle, something tragic about the 300 years of social conflict that blacks had experienced, which made black theater extremely rich. We were equally convinced that if we could tap into this "Negro temperament" we could demonstrate that it applied to blacks internationally. We could also show how this temperament would be valuable in helping people of all races better understand themselves.

In our minds, the New York seat of the American Negro Theater was just the beginning of something much grander. We envisioned that the ANT would eventually fan out to other cities. When this happened, New York would serve as the parent group for the rest.[24]

On July 10, 1940, barely a month after our first large organizational meeting, the ANT produced its first work, a variety show, at the Library Theater on 135th Street in Harlem. While far from a financial success, the show did demonstrate our artistic abilities and got good reviews. I did a couple of skits. In one, I played the ghost of Hamlet's father from the first act of Shakespeare's *Hamlet*. In the other, I performed the role of "the Republican" in a piece written by Abe Hill, called *Republicans Woo Negroes*. Here, I acted opposite Stanley Green and Howard Augusta.[25]

After getting our feet wet with the variety show, we started rehearsing another one of Abe's plays, a satire called *On Striver's Row*.[26] Striver's Row still exists in Harlem—on 139th Street between Seventh and Eighth Avenue. In the 1930s, there were nice brownstone homes lined up along the street and it used to be *cleeean*!! The curbs were always painted white, the snow was always shoveled, and everything else was immaculate. The plot centered on a real estate agent named Mr. Van Striven (played by Fred O'Neal) who was having a "coming out" party for his daughter (played by Ruby Dee). The Van Striven's considered themselves to be a very middle-class black family, and, true to their name, they were "striving" to be more. Their young girl had a boyfriend who arrived at the party in a tuxedo. But in reality she loved another man, a waiter, played by James Jackson. He was working at the party as a server. You can begin to see here how the play involved all kinds of twists on proper social norms and class expectations.

O'Neal's character was trying to sell property to a woman who was a maid. She had recently won the Irish sweepstakes and had all this money! She also had a boyfriend, a cab driver named Joe Smothers, played by Kenneth Manigault. In order to disrupt the party, an enemy of Mrs. Van Striven, a character named Mrs. Envy, invited Joe and the maid to the party. This is where the play got cookin'! Joe was a real "Joe the Jiver" type, a true character of the era. These types of guys stood around on the streets of Harlem wearing Stacy Adams shoes, wide-brimmed felt hats, pants so tight they grabbed your skin, and zoot suits. They had long coats and key chains that ran all the way down to their knees. They were called "Harlem Hipsters." On Thursdays and Fridays, these sweet-talkers could be found in the Savoy Ballroom, where they took their dates, especially maids, who typically had these nights free. Kenneth did a remarkable job playing Joe because his personality was so completely different from the role he acted on stage. During performances, Kenneth would strut around, snapping his fingers and delivering lines like "I'm Jim Pool from Liverpool!" Right after his girlfriend entered the stage, Kenneth would say something like, "Nickel snapping taxi driver, I'm Joe the Jiver!" It was hilarious! The couple started doing the Lindy Hop and the whole place became a mess! The show was superb, running for a record 50 performances, longer than any other show had ever run in Harlem. It quickly became a hit because we attracted mostly white people. To get more blacks, we resorted to giving tickets away to kids on the street in hope that they would pass them on to their parents. Sometimes it was embarrassing to look out into the audience and see 50 whites and only 5 blacks.[27] I had two roles in the play, an acting part as Professor Hennypest, and the show's assistant director. I took a short break from *Striver's Row* when an opportunity came about for me to take the lead role of Victor Mason in the Negro Playwright's production of *Big White Fog*. Originally starring Canada Lee, this play was about a frustrated Garveyite who ultimately met his death.[28] This was my big Broadway debut. I was also stepping into Canada Lee's shoes, the man who inspired me to remain in New York.

✈ ✈ ✈

In 1940, the World's Fair was held in New York City.[29] To supplement my acting gigs, I began working for the WPA in the spring. My job consisted of going around to various primary schools in Harlem, taking children to see the fair. Quite truthfully, I would have been much happier dealing with older students, but my job was to chaperone the younger ones. During the summer, I also started putting my teaching certificate from Wiley College to good use; I began teaching at Aviation High School in the Bronx. Because I had taken acting classes and speech training, when the fall courses started I was identified as someone who could teach remedial English and reading at a new girl's school, William F. Taft High School, in the Bronx. I really don't remember how it was that this new school came into being, but the man in charge of the English department (his name was Chomby, or something like that) gave me an interview. That's how it happened, that's how I started teaching at a white girls' school.

I soon discovered that there were very few blacks that were teaching in New York City at the time, even in Harlem. In fact, from 1938 to 1941 I met just one black woman teacher. In any case, here I was, teaching young white girls. Despite their age, I found them to be rather bold and provocative. They were truly having a ball with me; I was the only black teacher in their school. They would always try to turn me on. Some would stay after class and put their books on the desk where I was seated. Some would rub their tits up against my shoulder. That's when I really came to notice that a few of these girls were not so little, particularly the Italian girls. I also found that when they wore black, these same girls, many of whom were just 18, could look a lot older, like they were at least 22.

By the time I started teaching I'd moved back to Harlem from the Bronx. After *Striver's Row* ended, I was cast as the lead in the ANT production of *Natural Man*, a play based on the John Henry legend about a railroad-driving man who would not let a steam drill outperform him. As fortune would have it, I never did act in this play because in March of 1941, I was drafted into the army. Stanley Green took over my part.[30] I didn't know it, but my life was about to change dramatically.

Chapter 2

In the Army Now

I can't forget the days leading up to my departure from Manhattan. The American Negro Theater threw a party for me the night before I left, at which I was given a shaving kit, a diary, and some other useful gifts. The next morning, I reported to the Armory on Park Avenue. There were a lot of guys hanging around, many of them dressed up in zoot suits looking like Joe the Jiver! New recruits were supposed to take the oath of allegiance. As I recited mine, I looked at the other guys. Their eyes were closed. I don't know if they were scared, proud, or resentful for being in the army. Perhaps it was a mixture of the three. After the ceremony we were escorted from Fifth Avenue to 42nd Street. Jeeps and MPs scrambled around, clearing the streets. Meanwhile, crowds of people were chanting "The Yanks *ain't* coming, the Yanks *ain't* coming!" There was a strong antiwar movement during these times.

I eventually boarded the train from Penn Station to Fort Dix, New Jersey. We disembarked and marched down the ramp to the induction ceremony. There was a rail in the middle of the walkway. A black sergeant stood on one side while a white sergeant stood on the other. As we approached, the black sergeant shouted "Goats to the right!" That was the cue for black recruits to line up on the right hand side.

The guy fidgeting in front of me put something in my hand. "What's this?" I asked. "Here, take it, it's lye soap," he said. "If you chew this your heart starts beating fast, and they won't pass you—you won't pass the exam." I took it, looked at it, and then threw it away. I wasn't interested in playing any tricks to get out of the army.

We proceeded to march over to a building where we were examined. It was March, and it was cold. I was wearing lots of layers so I first removed my overcoat and pants, then my shirt and underwear. Next, I bent over and they stuck a finger up my ass. They were looking to see if I discharged any blood. After this, they gave me some new underwear—long johns in fact—a pair of pants, a shirt, jacket, overcoat, and a cap. Except for a blue pinstripe suit, I'd left all my other clothes at home, so now this was all that I had. After the exam, I noticed that the guy who had given me the soap was not in line. He was standing off to the side, grinning. I guess his clever trick had worked.

Galoshes and a raincoat were part of the gift pack as well. You learned pretty quickly not to use the raincoat because it was rubberized and made you sweat. But I do remember putting those shoes to good use. It was very muddy outside, and although they had constructed wooden walkways for people not to get dirty, it was hard to avoid some mud. Around 9 P.M. thousands of people began lining up for food. Almost everyone in my area was black. We took our newly issued mess kits with us, got our dinner, and brought it back to our tents. We ate, talked, and then got some sleep.

The next day, after breakfast, I heard someone shouting "Virgil!!" I spun around and looked. Lo and behold there was Harold Cruz, a man whom I had met at the YMCA Little Theater. He called me over, "Hey man, what are you doing here?" Apparently, he'd already been at the fort for about six months. I wasn't sure, but it seemed like he had volunteered. He asked me if I played any football or basketball. If you were a good athlete, you could become part of an insider's circuit. Base commanders were interested in having good basketball and football teams and were willing to offer special privileges to excellent players. My skills, however, had not been tested since high school.

My stay in the camp was nowhere near as long as Cruz's. After just four days I boarded the troop train—we were in Pullman cars, of course. Astonishingly, this was the first time I had ever ridden a Pullman car. They sat two-to-four to a seat, a little crowded if you ask me. For sleeping, there were berths available for the passengers. After getting on board and situating my belongings, I started noticing a splendid odor filling the car. Back then I used to smoke a pipe, and the odor I smelled was the rich, full aroma of good pipe tobacco. I tracked the odor down and sat next to the man with the pipe. "Good morning, my name is Virgil," I said. "Good morning," he replied, a black man with an affected British accent. Later, we would nickname him "Churchill." We exchanged pleasantries and in the process he told me that he was a law student from New York. It turned out that he was from a well-to-do family; his father was a medical doctor in the city. His sister was a student in the Royal Drama Academy of London, but when Hitler started pounding England with bombs, Churchill was sent over to bring her back home. She didn't come easily. She'd fallen in love with a Royal Air Force (RAF) fighter pilot and didn't want to leave. It's funny. As Churchill started telling me the story, I suddenly realized that I'd actually met his sister during the auditions for *Natural Man*. She wanted to play a leading role, but the director wouldn't let her read for it. I ended up walking her home a couple of times and the two of us came close to kissing. That's when she confessed that she was engaged to an RAF pilot. Kissing wouldn't be fair to him, she said. Listening to Churchill on the train, I started putting all of this together in my mind.

Churchill and I rode together for about four days, finally ending up in Texas at Camp Walters, near Mineral Springs. The town was remarkably small. On one side of the street was a resort where the elderly came to cure their rheumatism. On the other side stood a barbershop, a hotel, and a liquor store. In the distance stood a sort of hill, standing 200 or 300 feet high. Really it was a huge, red-clay mound that the soldiers used for target practice. We would later nickname it "Mt. Texas." Everything else in the area was just dirt. The wind whistled from the north as we got off the train. To get out of the cold, we quickly threw our barracks bags on a truck and boarded a bus bound for camp.

We were sorted into platoons when we arrived. Mine had a sergeant who'd been stationed at Fort Huachuca, Arizona. This was a sort of penal colony that had been used to house black soldiers who'd rioted in Houston after World War I.[1] It was amazing to me to see how quickly soldiers could rise in rank once they were stationed there. A private could jump to being a sergeant within the blink of an eye! The first sergeant in our platoon was probably one of those. His name was Daniels, but we called him "Dirty Red" because he had reddish skin and a liver mark on his face. He had originally gone into the army during World War I to become a cavalryman, but shortly after joining he discovered that he had hay fever. He ended up becoming a chauffeur for the colonels who were stationed at Fort Huachuka. Daniels always spoke very properly, using the third person when he conversed with his superiors. "Does the *Captain* want this?" he would say, or "Does the *Colonel* need that?" When he stood at attention, he *really* stood at attention. He pulled in his stomach real tight, clinched his buttocks real hard, stiffened his neck and arms. He was a model soldier in this sense.

Daniels had been first sergeant for a long time. But during our stay at Camp Walters, he was finally promoted to top sergeant and given another stripe. I didn't immediately realize it, but this eventually meant good news for me, too. Churchill and I were standing at ease one day during reveille. The sergeant said something to us, but I didn't hear him. Churchill nudged me excitedly and said "Virgil, now you'll have a chance to write your novel!" I looked at him, agitated at first, but then with glazed eyes. "What?" I said. A while ago I had told Churchill that I wanted to write a book about our time in the military called *A Year and a Day in the USA Army*. I was still wondering what Churchill was talking about when he nudged me again. This time I managed to hear the sergeant saying, "Does anyone here know how to type?" I perked up, then raised my hand. I had started learning how to type in college. I improved in New York using Pat Avery's typewriter. Apparently, in his new position as head sergeant Daniels was going to need a clerk, and I was proficient. "Can you come to the orderly room?" he said. I followed him there. I was handed some materials to copy. I nimbly typed what I was given. The sergeant seemed impressed, "You are one of them ten-fingered typists!" he said. So that's how I started my new position as clerk. All official documents needed to be copied six times. This was one of my duties.

My other tasks included making out sick reports, taking men to the company clinic, and picking up mail at the post office. On paydays, I made out the payroll. Twenty-one dollars a month, can you believe it? That's all we were getting. I made almost four times that amount at Mammoth Hosiery in New York.

What I really wanted to use my time for as a clerk was to type letters to Aida Harrison, the daughter of Harlem radical Hubert Harrison, who eventually became my wife in 1942.[2] We'd met through the American Negro Theater. She was an usher who eventually became the ANT's house manager and its chairman of local production. I was an actor. We started talking back then, but it really wasn't until I'd left New York that our relationship grew stronger. I have our letters to thank for that. Aida wrote me frequently during my stay in Camp Walters, sending papers and clippings on the ANT. Mrs. Roosevelt had a column called "My Day" in the *New York Herald Tribune*, I think. I recall reading a piece that she'd written on the ANT's production of *Natural Man*, giving it wonderful praise. Her review provided the group with tremendous publicity. Soon, every theater critic on Broadway started seeing the play, and, apparently, all subsequent ANT productions. I showed some of these clippings to Sergeant Daniels.

I stayed at Camp Walters until June 5. By that time, I had applied for the Air Corps and was waiting to hear a response. Air Corps cadets started off making 75 dollars a month. That inspired me to apply, along with some encouragement from Sergeant Daniels. It all started one day when some circulars were sent to the orderly room. A blonde-haired, blue-eyed guy showed up, with a parachute lifted up to his buttocks and his fingers tucked into his straps. Daniels looked at him, then over at me and said, "That's something you should think about Private Richardson, you know, General Davis' son is going to study flight at Tuskegee Institute."[3] General Davis was the first black general in Army history. I had never in my life thought about flying an airplane. I had barely seen one in the air. But I gave it some serious thought and submitted my application shortly afterward.

I can't remember exactly when it was, but I eventually went to Fort Worth to take the physical exam for admission to Tuskegee. Anyone who'd graduated from college didn't have to do anything else to qualify but pass the physical exam. Walking into the room, however, I could almost feel prejudice fill the air. It didn't take long for me to realize that I wasn't going to be passing anything that day. Unfortunately, I've also always had trouble with my eyes—I have great difficulty crossing them. This didn't help my situation. They gave me an eye exam that tested my depth perception. I was supposed to line up some weights parallel to each other as they dangled from strings. Since I couldn't cross my eyes, I couldn't quite get it right. I didn't get accepted into the Air Corps right away, but this didn't discourage me from continuing to try again several weeks later.

When I returned to Camp Walters, I was surprised to find that the members of my former company were gone—Churchill, Sergeant Daniels, even our captain. I was soon attached to another company, and after three days, I ended up being stationed in Oakland, California. Instead of being placed in the infantry-training center, I became a part of the port battalion. I was one of the newest members of the 394th Quartermaster Corps, Company A.

It didn't take long for me to reapply to the Air Corps. During the first week of August, I went to take the physical exam again, this time at Fort Ord, located just a few miles north of Monterey. While the change in testing site certainly lessened the prejudice, I also didn't want my eye problem to interfere with my eligibility again, so I diligently practiced crossing my eyes, with and without a pencil. I did this for days on end and thankfully it worked! I passed the exam routinely and got a letter from Washington in early September saying that I would be sent to Tuskegee when there was an opening in the next class. I took a furlough at the end of the month, thinking that I would become an air cadet shortly thereafter.

The months passed quickly. Before I knew it, we were approaching December, 1941. I'll never forget the day that the Japanese attacked Pearl Harbor. I was riding on the back of a fire truck, fulfilling my childhood dream of being a fireman (I had been reassigned from desk duty) when I heard the news. "The Japanese attacked Pearl Harbor, the Japanese attacked Pearl Harbor!" a radio blared. As we circled around, I noticed that other guys in the battalion were playing cards. Suddenly, they looked at each other like they'd just seen ghosts. Nobody could believe it! Then, surprise and panic spread everywhere. People started scurrying, their emotions reflecting a mixture of fear and anger.

We assembled down at the port later in the evening, searching for Japanese submarines that might have been deployed near the San Francisco Bay Bridge. We knew that the Japanese had used some miniature subs at Pearl Harbor, and it was quite likely that they could've sent some our way, too. The army had been preparing the port for war for some time now, and a great deal of construction activity was still going on. Tall light poles jutted into the air, providing illumination for the workers at night. But during this time of crisis, bright light was the last thing that we wanted, since it revealed our position. For some reason, though, they couldn't seem to turn the lights out. A few of our guys, armed with Winchester shotguns, took aim and started shooting. This didn't work either. Finally, we managed to get some rocks together. Hurling them up into the air, we cracked the glass lamps and bulbs.

I got into a boat and we started rowing around in the bay, looking for enemy subs. As we approached the bridge, the naval patrol caught sight of us and sped over. "You get your arses out of here or you'll get them shot off!" someone shouted over the beam of a searchlight. "Thank God for that!" I thought. You see, I've never been able to swim. I don't know what the hell I was doing out there! The frenzy of the moment seized me, pushing me to do things that put me in harm's way.

Some days later we were outfitted with carbines, and not too long after that my company commander called me into his office to say that I would soon be sent overseas. I was nervous. Fortunately, the War Department had issued a circular saying that men who had signed up for the Air Corps could not be enlisted for duty abroad. So I didn't go. The rest of my unit was shipped off though, seeing action in the South Pacific. I was the only one of my group who remained behind.[4]

I was reassigned to another port battalion, the 399th. The same thing happened all over again after several more months of service. In June, my new unit was alerted to prepare for an assignment in Europe. Still patiently waiting to enter Tuskegee, I promptly notified the adjutant that I was enrolled in the Air Corps and could not leave the country.[5] He responded with anger and surprise. "Richardson, I think you'll be going with us," he said sternly. I would later learn that he went through my file and removed my letter of qualification for the Air Corps. Thankfully, I still had a copy in my possession and showed it to him as proof. But he responded nastily, "How do I know that this is not a *forged* copy, Richardson?" I knew that there was one more copy of the order on record, sitting in a cabinet somewhere at Fort Ord. However, nothing helped. Against my will, and against the directives of the government, I was now bound for Europe.[6]

My company was relocated to Fort Dix en route to England in the summer of 1942. Desperate to see Aida, who I'd married in February while in Oakland, I decided to go AWOL.[7] I fled to the Bronx, where I gave Aida details about my predicament. She assured me that she was going to find a way to contact Eleanor Roosevelt so that she could resolve the situation. Aida had met Mrs. Roosevelt briefly during the ANT's production of *Natural Man*. Still an usher, Aida had seated the president's wife and attended her during the performance. She did her job so wonderfully that Mrs. Roosevelt asked for her name when she left. While it is definitely a stretch to say that the two enjoyed any kind of friendship, Mrs. Roosevelt's kindness toward Aida, along with her openness and sensitivity to issues regarding blacks, made Aida feel that she was approachable.

But before writing Mrs. Roosevelt, Aida contacted E. F. Morrow, a businessman and politician who worked for the NAACP. He instructed her to get in touch directly with Judge William Hastie, the Civilian Aide to the Secretary of War (and a black, Harvard-trained lawyer). Within days she had a response. Unfortunately, there was nothing the War Department could do to prevent my being shipped overseas. There was a long waiting list for Tuskegee. They thought it would be almost a year before I could join. I was instructed to continue serving in the 399th Quartermaster Corps until further notice.

After spending time with Aida, I returned to my company. Since I'd abandoned camp for only one night, thankfully no one even realized that I'd left.

We boarded a ship bound for Bristol on what became a difficult, 13-day voyage. The ship was thick with soldiers. There were so many that they generated an intense heat below deck, making it hard to get any rest. I decided to sleep on deck, leaning against one of the davits used to launch our lifeboats. For company, I had a novel with me called *The Sun Was My Undoing*. I don't remember it too well, but I think it had to deal with a white man who went to the West Indies and fell in love with a black woman. It was ironic since, as I would soon find out in England, many of our black troops were falling madly in love with white women, much to the chagrin of their superiors. Whereas it was fine for a white man to take a black lover, a black man, at least a black American, couldn't do the same.

When we got to Bristol we were greeted by some middle-aged women who were serving tea and crumpets. What a delight that was for us, especially after having endured a grueling voyage. Our headquarters battalion remained stationed in the city, but my company was moved to a place called Henbury Lane. There we were bivouacked at a large manor house, actually a castle of sorts, with two floors. I was one of a group that was quartered in an old birdhouse. Don't get the wrong impression. This was not a small space by any means, since the birdhouse had several rooms, running water, and heat. The duke who once owned the castle had a wife who loved birds and owned many different species. She treated them like royalty. I didn't much mind living there.[8]

We ate our meals in a tent outside the castle and we all shared a common bathroom. The bathhouse shocked everybody since it was the first time that we had ever encountered a bidet. Sitting on them is much like sitting on a toilet, but the soldiers were surprised that when they went to flush, they gave themselves an enema instead!

We served under Lieutenant Schone while we were in England. A white, Jewish officer in charge of an all-black company, Schone's dream was to go across the English Channel to fight Hitler. He wanted to be in a combat unit, not an idle port battalion of blacks whose main responsibility was unloading ships. But he had to make the best of the situation he was in. Schone had to deal with us.

Schone and his unit were like the yard birds of the battalion. Because of Schone's efficiency, the commanding officer used him to bring other officers up to par, and to perform many of the menial tasks that others couldn't (or didn't want to) do. Schone consistently maintained the cleanest kitchen, managed the best records, and was keenly competent with company funds. A great deal of Schone's success, though, should have been credited to Sergeant Springer, who was always keeping him out of trouble. Springer meticulously saw to it that the company had the best-kept barracks and mess hall. He also helped make sure the troops were in order.

I was in charge of a Military Police (MP) squad that was responsible for patrolling the streets of downtown Bristol, making sure that the guys did not get too drunk and disorderly. I rode around in a jeep and deployed men. It wasn't long before I received a promotion. Back in Oakland I had already been promoted to the rank of corporal. In Bristol, I became a staff sergeant.

After getting off duty at five o'clock, the black MPs would frequent the pubs located downhill from where we were stationed. English pubs were not like American bars. I remember seeing baby carriages parked outside during the day. Inside, women were sipping on warm beer (the English do not like ice) while their babies waited impatiently. About a block away from our post was a radar battalion manned by British women. They would frequently join us in the bar and we would have a wonderful time. Helped by free-flowing liquor, many black soldiers took a white lover.

The adjutant of our unit was appalled by our close fraternization with white women. To help put an end to it, he told the female commander in charge of the radar battalion that all black soldiers bore venereal diseases and should not get anywhere near British women. Convinced, she stopped her soldiers from frequenting the pub. Deeply angered by these events, one of the women called her uncle, a member of the British war ministry. He thundered back at the commander, saying that according to his knowledge, all black soldiers were routinely checked for venereal disease before leaving the United States. Therefore, if they had any illnesses, they must have contracted them from *her* charges. That was the end of that! White women returned to the pub and into the arms of their black lovers. On a dark evening, or in the shadows of an afternoon, one could spy members of our port battalion making love to British women on blankets in the grass.

At about ten or eleven o'clock one night, the air raid siren sounded. Most of the men were already in bed. I had recently returned from town myself. The pubs closed at ten during wartime and I had just brought my men back from Bristol and was getting ready to go to sleep. Suddenly the sirens went off, scaring the hell out of me and everybody else at camp. I frightfully began recalling images of a previous air raid that I'd witnessed, in which about 70 German bombers attacked from formation. I wasn't sure if we were being hit with another large raid. People flooded out of the manor house, some carrying flashlights. I rushed out in my pajamas. I overheard men yelling at each other, saying, "Fool, put out that flashlight!" Meanwhile, throughout the ordeal Lieutenant Schone loudly repeated the words of FDR, "There is nothing to fear but fear itself!" Some men started laughing at his attempted bravery. Insulted, Schone fired back, "Stop that laughing!" Sergeant Springer, perhaps amused himself, replied, "Why can't the men laugh if they want to?"

Thankfully, shortly after arriving to Bristol we'd dug a number of slit trenches (six feet deep and about three feet wide) where we could seek shelter in case of an air raid. Men were starting to hurry toward these trenches carrying their gas masks and helmets. A member of my squad ran alongside me, a man named Curly. He was an older guy, well past draft age, and was bald except for a noticeable curl of hair on top of his forehead. We dashed into the trenches and together we looked up into the air. Searchlights were combing the skies. Curly, always a comedian, said to me, "If you tell your buddies up there not to drop bombs on us, I promise you that you will be going home tomorrow." Ever since he had learned that the adjutant had refused to accept my Air Corps papers as acceptable proof for being exempt from duty in Europe, he used every opportunity to tease me. His favorite line involved telling me that the adjutant had not just removed the Air Corps papers from my file, but had probably chewed, eaten, and discharged them.

Finally, the searchlights spotted the enemy bomber. The ground rattled and shook as guns pounded into the air. Curly ducked his head down and said "Oh sergeant!!!!!" Meanwhile, I was determined to get a better look at what was happening, since I was trying to get into the Air Corps and wanted to see firsthand what air combat was all about at every opportunity. As I took glimpse at the plane, more rounds of gunfire sliced into the sky. After a few more shots, the plane was hit and burst into a cloud of flames. When it was over, the siren stopped and the lights were turned off. Shortly thereafter, we received the "all-clear" sign. People in my trench started murmuring, asking if anyone had seen anybody get out of the plane. No one had. We returned to the manor house and finally went to sleep.

Sometime between 5:00 and 5:30 the next morning the charge of the quarters came over and woke me up, saying, "Lieutenant Schone wants to see you immediately." In a daze, I fumbled around looking for my watch, then I got dressed in a hurry to meet Schone. "Sergeant Richardson," he said, "pack your belongings—you're going back to the States!" I was shocked. Curly's teasing the night before had become prophetically true. Ever since I'd met Schone, he'd been very sympathetic to my cause. Sergeant Springer, however, had kept him from butting in. But somehow, a decision had been made to send me back and I was grateful. What Schone didn't know was that my luggage was already packed. I had a small trunk where I kept all of my correspondence. My clothes were stuffed into a barracks bag. I ran back and grabbed everything, piled it into the jeep and went down to Bristol headquarters. When I arrived, the sergeant in charge said, "Oh God, the inspector general has just been here! He told the adjutant that, 'You will stay a first lieutenant for the duration of the war for what you've done to Richardson; this man has been shipped all the way around the world for no good reason.' " Feeling a sense of vindication, I took copies of my orders from the sergeant. None other than Inspector General Robert E. Lee III himself had signed the papers!

I left Bristol and returned to Liverpool to wait for the first available transportation back to the States. While stationed in the port, I noticed that black soldiers here fraternized heavily with white women, too. They met their British girlfriends at the shattered railroad station, off the interurban train that connected the port and the main city. Upon greeting with hugs and kisses, the men would take the girls next door to the dance hall to teach them the Lindy Hop. They had a fantastic time!

The U.S. Navy was infuriated at seeing blacks and white women intermingling so openly and freely. I remember one night vividly. A group of sailors came up to the station determined not to let the white girls inside to meet their beaus. Then they lined up in front of the dance hall with their .45s and clubs. What happened next was both startling and saddening. One thing you have to remember is that during those days men and women carried gas masks to protect themselves from a possible gas attack. I recall the women grabbing their masks and flailing them in front of the sailors in anger. It was a real standoff! As I looked on, I heard someone say to me "Listen sergeant, you'd better come with me." I half turned around, getting get ready to leave, when a white army officer jumped up on top of the steps, armed, and yelled "You boys should be ashamed of yourselves!" He was talking to the black soldiers. Suddenly, there was a gunshot. The officer buckled over and went tumbling down the stairs. The next day, after the incident, the papers in Liverpool read: "White Yanks, Black Yanks Open Second Front. One White Man Dead." The headline was full of double meaning. In 1942, the Russians had been asking for the Allies to open up a second front to take some pressure off of them and to stop the Germans. This is certainly not what they had in mind.

While the clash between white and black soldiers alarmed the colonel who was in command in Liverpool, there was another scandal taking place that was far more disturbing, especially since it compromised his chances at getting a promotion. One of the main responsibilities of port battalions was unloading ships. All kinds of valuable materièl were brought into Liverpool, including spam, nylon stockings, steak, pork, powdered milk, ham, and powdered eggs. Cleverly, black soldiers made a private industry out of these shipments. They would secretly haul bricks and other heavy objects up to the incoming American ships. Once in the cargo hold, they would wait for the right moment to replace the goods with these bricks and rocks. Then they cut the ropes of the carry-all to make sure that it was weak enough so that a slight jostle would cause it to slip, fall, and eventually break. A winch lifted cargo out of the hold. When the weak ropes got over the side of the ship, suddenly the cases would start tumbling into the water. Two cases of nylon, three cases of ham, ten cases of spam, five cases of powdered eggs—all of this and more was considered lost at sea. But in reality, it was just worthless stones. Later, the black soldiers would take all of the goods that they had stolen from the cargo hold and sell them on the black market to British clients.

Only black soldiers were involved in this enterprise because they were exclusively assigned to the port battalions. When the colonel discovered their activities, he cursed the soldiers using every name under the sun—sons of whores, sons of bitches, and all that kind of stuff. One day, a group of black sergeants burst into my barracks, tearing off their stripes in anger and shouting, "Nobody's gonna call my mama a whore!" They wanted to demonstrate their disgust by resigning their noncommissioned status and signing a group letter of resignation. Since they knew I could type, and since I had a typewriter, they asked me to prepare the letter for them. I told them, "Look, if you all sign your names to the same letter, it becomes a mutiny. But I can make you ten copies of the same letter. I have carbon paper. If you individually sign your copies it won't be a mutiny." Unfortunately, I couldn't reason with them. One of the guys angrily pulled out a knife, raised it to my neck, and said: "It's no skin off your ass [to type the letter] since you are going home!" I began nervously hacking away at the keyboard. But since they didn't follow my advice, I later learned that they were each given 10 to 20 years in Leavenworth Prison.

I was called into the office the next day, where the captain told me that the last of the paperwork for my return to the States had finally arrived. "Well, now you're going back to become an officer. Of course, you are already a gentleman," he said. I smiled. He asked me to be silent for 30 days about what was happening in Liverpool. Throughout the war there were so many problems between black and white soldiers that the army eventually started an officer training school in England in order to more rapidly increase the number of black officers serving abroad. The army reasoned that if black enlisted men reported to superiors of their own color, many of the squabbles, such as the mess in Liverpool, could be avoided.

The following day I climbed into a motorboat that sped me out to the U.S.S. *America*, arguably the fastest ship afloat at the time—so fast that it didn't need an escort. We headed back to New York and docked in just five days. I played poker throughout most of the trip. On the fifth day I remember going onto the upper deck in what they call "officer's country" and looking out at the Statue of Liberty, which was glistening in the sun. I felt great returning home; in fact, the sensation I felt was true euphoria. We disembarked at the Brooklyn Naval Yard, where I became temporarily attached to a work battalion. I asked the first sergeant for a pass so that I could stay with my wife. I gave him a telephone number and our address in case he wanted to send me a telegram when my orders came in.

Three weeks later, around the end of October, the telegram finally arrived, along with a ticket for Washington, D.C. I remember stepping outside the train station in D.C. and seeing the silhouette of the Washington Monument in the background. It was evening, but still early enough so that I could see. The city was not lit up, though, because we were at war. I changed over to a Pullman car bound for Tuskegee. On board, I got to know a porter. He'd been in World War I and wanted to know some of the places that I'd been. I told him that I was coming back from England. He started asking me about other things, and I told him the story about the British girls and the black soldiers in Liverpool, but not too much. After a while, I started inventing a bunch of fabrications for him to leave me alone.

He woke me up at 6:30 A.M. the next morning and told me to shave and get ready since it was nearly time to get off. I was surprised that we had already arrived, and when we stopped, I looked outside. It didn't seem like I was in the right place. I reminded him that I was going to Tuskegee. But he said, "We don't go to Tuskegee, we go to Cheehaw." That was another train station in Alabama. Again, I was surprised because everybody knew Tuskegee and the famous Tuskegee Institute. It was an important place. Surely, the train would stop there. I was wrong. The porter put down the footstool and I hopped off the train. I waived to him as the train pulled out and moved on to Montgomery.

I started towards the door. It took me a second before I realized that I was moving toward the exit marked "white." I turned around and made my way toward the "colored" sign. You can't imagine what a depressing sight this was for me. As I looked around the station I saw a black woman with her poor children seated near a pane of windows, sort of crouching. While they had plenty of belongings, they didn't have any proper luggage with them at all. Their stuff was crammed into paper bags and boxes. Pausing, I walked over to the baggage window and asked about my own luggage. All I had with me was my barracks bag and a homemade file box where I kept my correspondence. Unable to locate my things, the ticket master finally said, "Hey, that might be your bag over there!" He had just tossed my stuff anywhere, and now, water was dripping off of it. I picked up the luggage and did my best to control my anger. I boarded a bus that ran from Cheehaw directly to the Army Flying School. I got off at headquarters—a building shaped like a wing at the top of the airfield complex.

Chapter 3

Days at Tuskegee

I didn't realize it before I arrived, but the upperclassmen in advanced training hazed the underclassmen at Tuskegee. They would come over and make us recite a whole lot of foolishness. We memorized things like "*What is a dodo bird, and what's a cow? She walks, she talks, and she's full of chalk. The lacteal fluid that comes from her udders is delectable to the nth degree!*" We repeated such nonsense. And we would have to shout "Yes sir!" and "No sir!" to the upperclassmen when they questioned us, as if they were our senior superiors. If you didn't answer their questions properly they would make you sit on a little red imaginary stool until sweat streamed down your face, your legs cramped and your whole body was aching. When we walked around the airbase, we'd have to run and spread our arms out like wings. We were hazed.

I belonged to class 43-E. Most of my classmates had never been in the army before. I'd joined in March of 1941. It was now October of 1942. So I had some experience over the rest of the guys.

I learned early that the upperclassmen and officers were very concerned about what was happening in England. I volunteered to tell them about my experiences because none of them, not even the officers, had been overseas. I was also one of the only blacks there that had lived through or witnessed an air raid.

Learning to fly at Tuskegee was a marvelous and unique opportunity. Most whites in America didn't believe that blacks had the reflexes or intelligence to fly planes. This included the president himself. They were all wrong. Back in the 1940s, a civilian pilot training program (CPT) had been started at a number of colleges, offering instruction on small planes called Piper Cubs with long fragile wings. Since five black schools were allowed to join by the time I arrived at Tuskegee, I noticed that a lot of people in my class had flown before. The head flight instructor, Chief C. Alfred Anderson, had been flying since the early 1930s. In fact, I believe he was the first black licensed pilot. He received his flight training in Chicago, where blacks had established a prominent flying club.[1] In the mid-1930s, Chief Anderson and his copilot also became the first blacks to fly round-trip across the country.

Mrs. Roosevelt embarrassed all of white America when she took it upon herself to come down and visit Tuskegee in 1941. To the dismay of many, she even dared to go up in a biplane with Chief Anderson. Suddenly, the congressmen in Washington got worked up. Imagine, a white woman "caught up" in the air with a black pilot! Whether they liked it or not, though, her actions forced whites throughout the country to accept Tuskegee and its pilots, although many still referred to us disparagingly as "Eleanor Roosevelt's niggers."

Mrs. Roosevelt continued taking up the cause of black pilots even after they were commissioned as officers. Some whites worked hard to prevent black pilots from being sent into combat. Even after being trained, many were found performing trivial tasks in the States. However, after Mrs. Roosevelt's visit, she returned to Washington and lobbied vocally for the first black fighter squadron, the 99th, to be sent to duty in North Africa. Thanks to her letters and the fuss she raised, Benjamin O. Davis, Jr. took the 99th overseas in 1943. They were attached to a white fighter group, the 33rd, which was based in Tunisia. But despite serving together, everything still remained segregated.

We didn't have a tremendous amount of airspace at Tuskegee, only about 30 square miles. It seemed crowded for us to train there, even dangerous. Our men flew P-40s at altitudes ranging from 15,000 to 20,000 feet. Early trainer biplanes were flown up to 8,000 feet, which was their limit. Basic trainers were used until 10,000 feet. Advanced trainers operated higher than that. Eventually, we were sent to Florida for gunnery practice. The facilities at Tuskegee really differentiated us from white pilots. They went to one airfield for primary training, another for retraining, a different field for basic training, and another for advanced training. Then they moved to yet a different location for fighter training. We did almost everything right at Tuskegee.

Because I had already been in the army for a while, they bumped me up a class so that I only had to do one month of pre-flight training. Then I went to primary training, where a man named Henderson became my instructor. Since the planes in primary had open cockpits, you had to wear leather suits and sheep-skinned boots over your shoes to help fight the cold. For every 1,000 feet that the plane climbed, the temperature dropped one degree. We also wore parachutes. On my first flight Henderson said, "Would you like to go with me to make a weather check?" I was stupid. I climbed into the back of the plane, which had a wooden propeller and a 90-horsepower engine. I was wearing all of my gear. Henderson said, "Allright now, buckle up!" Then we began zigzagging the planc. Since the plane sat on two wheels, the only way that the student in back could see what was ahead was by zigzagging. Henderson proceeded to maneuver us into takeoff position. I saw a yellow "T" on the grass field, which served to guide pilots in the proper direction during their takeoffs and landings. "Allright Mr. Richardson," Henderson said (they started calling you "Mr." when you began flying, not before). "I want you to follow me through on the rudder pedals. . . ."

So that's how we took off. The next thing I remember I was up in the air. I felt like I was riding the tail of a kite! We went up to 2,000 feet. I was now holding on for dear life. "Oh Lord!" I said, "Just let me make it back to the ground! I'll never ever leave it again!" It was horrible. Then we climbed up higher to 4,000 feet. As we approached that altitude Henderson noticed that bad weather was moving in. Speaking through a tube, he said, "Alright now, we're going down, I'm following through." I couldn't respond since there was only one-way communication on the plane. He could see me though, through his rearview mirror. I was holding onto the side of the plane real tight.

In that trainer, you don't have any instruments to tell you how fast you are going. All you have is an altimeter and a needle and ball that tell you when you're skidding. That's it. You just have to *feel* it. You fly by the seat of your pants at primary level, and by the sound of the struts and wires. When you try to land, the struts and wires are among the only things that indicate your speed. You have to use your ears carefully, noticing changes from high to low frequency. When you get down very close to the ground you cut the throttle and hopefully the plane lands smoothly. Well, we managed to land and I wanted to jump out and kiss the ground. Henderson said, "We'll try again tomorrow."

Lower primary training took place in the mornings and upper primary trained in the afternoons. Those who weren't flying were in ground school, which included Morse code instruction. There was also physical training directed by the former coach of Tuskegee's football team, now a captain in the army. After a hard day's work, we boarded the bus and returned to Tuskegee Institute, where we slept in the dormitories. The campus was located about 13 miles away from the flying school. At that time there were no men studying there, since most of them had volunteered for the army. It was just women, studying nursing and other interesting professions. Our bus rides back were often filled with song. I taught some of my classmates a tune that I had learned in England: "*I've got a sixpence, jolly jolly sixpence, to last me all my life! Two pence to save, and two pence to spend, and two pence to send home to my wife. Poor wife! Oh I've got no cares to grieve me. I've got no pretty little girls to deceive me, I'm happy as a king, as we go rolling on, rolling on.*" The Air Corps also taught us to sing, "*Off you go into the wild blue yonder, climbing high into the sun. . . . We live in fame and go down in flames, nothing can stop the Army Air Corps!*" We could get really energized singing these songs and flying.

We ate our dinners at Tuskegee Institute's dining hall. The cooks prepared special meals for us, which we ate in a private dining room. Typically, we feasted on chicken, steak, and vegetables—our dinners tended to be very high in protein. In order to get to our special cafeteria, we had to march through the main dining area. We certainly made an impression on the women, dressed up as we were in our cadet uniforms, our officer's blouses, and brown shoes. We sashayed down the aisles as if we were royalty! The prettiest girls you could imagine were there to serve us. One woman whom we saw regularly was "Wash-Out Rose." She was simply gorgeous, but, unfortunately, every guy that she liked ended up "washing out," which meant that they had to give up their officer's uniform and return to the army to become a mechanic or a private. Most men washed out while training on the PT trainer (the biplanes we used up to 8,000 feet), which we dubbed the Maytag Washing Machine. Failure rates on the PT ran as high as 50 percent.

After supper you could write letters or read books if you wanted to. There were always plenty of good books to read. We awoke at six in the morning, got dressed, made our beds (tight enough to bounce a quarter), had breakfast, got on the bus, and eventually made it back to "the flying line," as they called it. On my second and subsequent flights with Henderson, we started practicing some really daring things, such as flying upside down, stalls, and spins. I suppose these were all part of the routine. You had to learn to spin the airplane and how to recover from a stall. You had to learn how to climb and then zigzag. It took me a while to overcome some of my fears, especially when the plane stalls . . . then you come down spinning! That is scary. Henderson was a nice enough man and really helped me through my training. To tell the truth, though, I was worried because I didn't want to get washed out. Some guys who'd washed out had been flying for years, so I had real reason to be concerned.

Chief Anderson finally gave me a check ride with him. He instructed me on what he wanted, "Turn right! Turn left! Two stalls! Power on! Power off! Two spins!" He'd say, "OK, before landing, find out which way the wind is blowing and then go down and land." Then he'd say, "OK, go back up." When I finally finished with Chief Anderson, he handed me over to another young instructor, an ex-football player from Tuskegee who looked like he weighed about 300 pounds. His name was Daniel "Chappie" James. He was really too big to be in a plane, but somehow he taught me. Chappie went on to become a full-fledged fighter pilot himself in a class after mine. In time, his military career became remarkably distinguished. Chappie was promoted to four-star general in the mid-1970s, the first black to be awarded such rank.[2]

I had two or three more instructors until Mr. Henderson got me again. One day he took me up, landed, and then said, "Now, you take it out." I looked at him disbelievingly, then said to myself, "Oh Lord, I've DONE it!" This was it. I was about to embark upon a solo flight.

I took the plane up and did all the things that I was supposed to do, just the way they were supposed to be done. When I landed, I climbed out of the cockpit with some pep in my step. I thought, "Now I can keep my goggles on the front of my helmet!" Until you made your first solo flight, cadets wore their goggles facing the back of their helmets. Placing them on the front was the sign of a true pilot. This was a tremendous moment for me. I ran across the street to the photo studio and had my picture taken with my goggles facing forward. I sent copies back home to my wife.

Since I had no problems in lower and upper primary, I moved on to basic training. Here, we used the BT 13-A, which had steel propellers and two long, wide wings. As you were flying you could look out and see the wings flapping in the wind. Some cadets did very stupid things, such as flying under the bridge to show off their daring. I was smart enough not to get involved with any of this. I did acquire a new friend in basic, another guy named Richardson. Our nametags carried our first initials; I was V. J. Richardson, and he was E. E. Richardson, otherwise know as "Double E." He became my closest buddy, or my "Boon Coon," as blacks used to say back then. He was from Philadelphia and impressed us all with his talents on the pool table, and with his hotshot piloting.

In basic training you also practice night flying. In the dark you could see the exhaust fire coming out of your engine. While up in the air you could also see for hundreds of miles, all the way down to the Gulf Coast. We had to plan our flights from Tuskegee to Chattanooga, Tennessee. We returned by going through Atlanta. We took off for Chattanooga in daylight using contact navigation—looking for water towers, railroad signs, highways, and so forth. On our way back we resorted to flying the light line, since it was already night.

Unfortunately there was a shortage of maps, so a certain number of pilots flew one night while others would fly on another. I was slated to fly on the second night; however, at the last minute, Bernie Jefferson, the great All-American football star who was training with us, got sick. I was immediately told to prepare to take his place. When Capt. Green sent for me I was relaxing in the day room, where "Double E" was teaching me how to play pool. I had not yet studied any of the maps for making the round-trip flight. Regardless, I had to move quickly because light was fading.

When I arrived in Chattanooga all I could see was a dirt field on the side of a mountain. Because there were no lights, I could barely make it out and I certainly couldn't see any planes on the ground. I called for instructions. "It's under your left wing," the instructor said. I made a steep turn and finally I could see the other planes. After landing, I had no time to review the chart and calculations prepared by Jefferson. The instructor gave me a cup of coffee—I stayed on the ground just long enough to drink it—and then I was on my way back to Tuskegee. I was the last one to leave. I was unprepared.

I flew the light line to Atlanta. The light line is like Morse code in lights. A distinct pattern flashes for each city and airport—Atlanta's lights flash an "A." Anyway, I started to make my turn for Tuskegee, flying at about 5,000 feet. After being in the air for nearly two hours I didn't see the lights for Tuskegee! I figured that I should head back to Atlanta. Along the way, I ended up in the clouds with bad weather moving in. So I turned around again and flew for what seemed like another two hours. Something was definitely wrong. I had no idea which way the wind was blowing and I was also losing altitude. I decided to take the plane all the way down to 1,000 feet so that I could at least follow a train or car to some small town in Alabama. Sure enough, I saw a postage stamp sized light and went in closer. It turned out to be a small airport. I dipped lower and began "dragging the field"—that is, I began maneuvering to see if there were any telephone poles or power lines in my way. Someone in a car noticed me and started driving toward the airport so that I could have more light. Of course I had lights on my plane, but the driver was making sure that I could see where I was going. I circled back over the airport and began landing. There was a fence surrounding the airfield that I barely cleared on my approach. After getting out of the plane, I asked the man in charge where I was and if I could call Tuskegee. He looked a little surprised that a black man was flying the plane. I glanced over toward the car that had helped me and saw a white woman sitting in the front seat. I phoned Tuskegee and told them that I was in Canton, about 20 miles away, and that everything was fine. They asked to speak to the man running the airport and told me to give them another call in the morning. Meanwhile, the woman in the car ran up to me and said, "I knew that you were in trouble, I'm so happy to see you!" "Oh, my cook will just go *crazy* when I bring you home and show her a black cadet!" Since I had nowhere to go, I decided to take her up on her offer to stay the night. We walked over to her car. I was about to reach for the front door when the guy from the airport casually opened the back for me. We started for Canton.

The woman kept turning her head back as she tried to talk and drive. Finally, she said, "Oh! For goodness sake, come on up here, this is stupid, we'll both get killed!" When we arrived at her house her cook was indeed overjoyed to meet me. "Oh Lord!" she shouted, "Ain't my son gonna love to meet you!" After talking with the ladies for a while, I went home with the cook, at whose home I spent the night. Her son took me out for a drink or two, and the next morning around seven o'clock the white woman, who was a schoolteacher, came by to pick us up. When I returned to the airfield I immediately called Tuskegee. My instructor asked, "Can you take off?" "Of course I can take off," I replied.

I found that I had missed a math test when I got back, which unfortunately they wouldn't allow me to make up. The officer in charge of cadets decided that I would have to drop back a class and take another course called Instrument Training. "Double E," who was half a class behind, caught up with me at this point. Instrument training was conducted in a midget plane called a Link Trainer, operated by compressed air. You did everything with this trainer, including 90-, 80-, and 360-degree turns. Surprisingly, this simulator was no larger than a coffee table and could replicate speeds of about 200 miles an hour. The Army mainly used it for teaching pilots how to fly "blind."

I deeply regretted having to call my wife to tell her that I had lost my class, but the truth is that I got more flying time as a result. Finally, I proceeded to advanced training, using the North American AT-6. We then started gunnery practice at Eglin Field in Florida. Here, big powerful planes picked up a windsock from the runway and took it into the air. A cable carried the sock about 100 yards behind the plane. We dived in on it over the sea, firing our guns. Our bullets punctured colored holes into the sock. Two or three planes would shoot simultaneously, each with different colored bullets. After our training was complete, we returned to Tuskegee. By this time I had completed nearly 220 hours of flight training; 60 in primary, over 70 in basic, and now over 80 hours in advanced training.

"Double E" and I made it through successfully right up until the day before graduation. All ready for our ceremony, we were sent to the base with officers' uniforms, our bars, a green shirt, overcoat, pink pants, a green coat, and our cap. As I said earlier, though, "Double E" had a reputation for being a hotshot pilot. Remarkably, the day before graduation he washed out. It wasn't until 40 years later that I found out why. Apparently, he had been flying in a "V" formation; that is to say, he was flying side by side with his instructor. During flight, he was signaled to make a left turn. Instead, he went under the instructor's wing and accidentally hit the top of it. When they landed, he washed out![3]

My wife came down to stay with me a month before graduation. I hadn't seen her for several months, so I was overjoyed that she was there. My parents and youngest brother also came, but they arrived much later than Aida. Unfortunately, there weren't too many black people in Tuskegee at the time, and the few who were there had rented all of their spare rooms to other families who were visiting for the ceremony. Because my parents couldn't find a place to stay, they came to Tuskegee just for the day—all the way from Texarkana, Texas! It didn't matter much because they were still happy to come.

On a hot morning at the end of June 1943, Lieutenant Colonel Noel Parrish presented us with our commissions. Then we were issued our wings. I couldn't help but smile. As the Army Post Band struck up the "Star Spangled Banner," I could see my father beaming from ear to ear. After the ceremony, I took Aida up for a ride in the airplane so that she could see what it was like to fly. I didn't do anything fancy, just some simple turns. It was delightful! But the most lasting impression that day was probably made on my little brother, Charles. Seeing me get my pilot's wings and being around the environment of the military base inspired him to become a career soldier, which I later thought was a terrible thing.

Chapter 4

From Tuskegee Back to War

Tuskegee Airmen received a lot of attention during those days, especially when dressed in uniform. Many of the stares we got from whites outraged us. I had a friend in the 99th who became General Davis's wingman. One day he told me a story about what he did on a train from Washington, D.C. to Tuskegee. When people started looking at him, he pretended to remove a needle from the lapel of his jacket. He simulated threading it, then tying it. After that, he carefully placed it near his nose with his left hand, and pulled it out with his right. It looked like he was thumbing his nose at people (which he was), but he was doing it so cleverly that he could easily deny what he was doing.

After graduation, Tuskegee teemed with pilots, hundreds of pilots, too many pilots! The army had to do something with us! Before we could go on a vacation though, we had to fly ten hours on the P-40. This was a real combat aircraft, used by Americans in missions all over in World War II. They were used to defend Pearl Harbor, to fight in Italy, the Philippines, in North Africa—just about everywhere. The P-40 was also one of the mainstays of the 99th, our all-black unit. Thankfully, we didn't train on them in the cramped airspace at Tuskegee. Instead, we were transferred to Selfridge Field in Michigan, located about 40 miles outside of Detroit. Of course, Selfridge Field had initially been built for whites and had a long, proud history stretching back to World War I. It was the first aerial gunnery school in the country and was also a place where World War I mechanics received their training. High-ranking officers continued living at Selfridge. It had an officers' club, officer's quarters, and a barracks.

I wanted Aida to spend some time with me in Michigan, so I got in touch with a friend of mine, Dempsey Morgan, who had washed out and was living in Detroit. He made all the necessary arrangements ahead of time and found a room for me with a family. When Aida came, she stayed there. Meanwhile, I split my time between Detroit and Selfridge Field. When I had to do night flying, I slept in the officer's quarters. All other days I stayed in Detroit. Dempsey kindly picked me up in the mornings up and drove me back to the base.

I first arrived at Selfridge by train, along with a group of other black officers. When we stepped through the gates people started staring at us in shock, they couldn't imagine what the hell was happening. There had been a race riot some weeks earlier—they said it was the Poles against the blacks. I later learned that the Detroit area was a hotbed for racial strife. That June, some black teenagers had gotten into a fight with some whites and it quickly escalated into a citywide conflict. Rumors were also flying that a black man had raped and killed a white woman. At the same time, blacks were infuriated because allegedly, some whites had thrown a black woman and her child over a bridge. I don't know what of this was true, but in retaliation, Detroit's whites began streaming into the black section of town and started attacking every black person in sight. Only the presence of the army calmed the violence. Needless to say, such events created a tense atmosphere around Selfridge Field. We could feel the tension as we marched into the camp with our orders. Perhaps it was for this reason that they kept us sitting by idly in the officers' quarters for days on end without any responsibilities. There must have been as many as 200 of us.

Colonel Selway, the white officer in charge of the base, wanted to have complete control over us. Truth be told, he could barely maintain control over himself. Having been a test pilot some years earlier, Selway had managed to break just about every bone in his body. He walked around the base with a cane. An assistant followed close behind, carrying a bottle of whiskey. Liquor supposedly helped the colonel treat his pain. Selway had the audacity to have us barred from visiting the officer's club, which was supposed to be open to all officers, regardless of color. But being the racist he was, he made it clear that if we were even seen there, we were to be arrested immediately.

Finally, we started our training. After flying the P-40L and P-40N, we began training with the P-39 Airacobra. It was a dramatic change for us since the P-39 had many novel features. First of all, you entered the cockpit through a door, as if you were getting into a car. The plane's motor was located behind the pilot, and there was a propeller shaft that came from the motor, under the pilot's seat, to the three-blade metal propeller. P-39s were equipped with a 37-millimeter cannon in the propeller hub. There were also two .50-caliber machine guns in each wing, and two more in the nose. That was substantial armament! The plane had wide, tricycle landing gear and was a joy to fly, since there was no torque—no pulling to the left, as in the P-40. We enjoyed flying them, at least initially. The down side to the P-39 was that there was what they called a "servo tab" on the wings, which served the purpose of relieving the stick load when you were turning. This was dangerous at low speeds since you didn't have a feeling for your plane. This is why we started landing at 150 miles per hour, instead of at 110 miles per hour. There was plenty of airspace and maneuvering room at the base to do this. Interestingly, we weren't alone training on the P-39s. There were female pilots using them too, part of the Women's Army Corps. It was as surprising for us as it was for others to see these white women coming in and taking off their helmets, with their hair flowing in the wind.

The army had taken over a resort in Oscoda, Michigan, where there was a runway in place for our planes to use. There was also a ground gunnery range that we used to practice machine guns and cannon. When we fired at ground targets, placards raised behind dirt mounds indicated our hits. Consequently, the next time we veered around, we would know exactly where our bullets had struck. For some reason, however, we discovered that after one or two rounds our cannons wouldn't fire again.

Our training in Oscoda lasted for about a week. Since it was a former resort, there were some really nice cabins available for married couples. I decided to bring Aida. I don't think I can describe the joy I felt of having my wife with me. But what made it even more magical was that she was now pregnant. We had made the decision to have a baby during her month-long visit at Tuskegee.

In November 1943, perhaps the largest mission of black flyers that had ever been assembled in the United States left Selfridge Field for Fort Dix, New Jersey. We weren't exactly celebrated. We received a cool reception upon landing. A visibly agitated ground crew was startled to see so many black pilots. There were 48 planes in all. We were supposed to return to Selfridge that same day, taking a route that would lead us through Niagara Falls, but bad weather caused us to delay our flight for a day. I took advantage of the time to visit New York. My wife had already returned by this point and I was anxious to see her again. Others from our group went into the city as well, since many had never seen Manhattan.

The following morning, a man named Tresvel, one of only a handful of black graduates from West Point, led our three squadrons to Niagara Falls.[1] Snow flurries intensified as we started for Selfridge Field. The weather forecasts predicted even more snow near Detroit. Once again, we found ourselves delayed. We returned to Niagara to weather the storm.

Despite the stiff enforcement of racial segregation in the hotels surrounding the area, we found a place to spend the night. It was thanks to the president of Bell Aircraft that one of the hotels in Buffalo was forced to take us in. Unfortunately, given the supposed "lack of space," we were told that not all of us could sleep in rooms. Some would be forced to spend the night in the swimming pool. Cots were set up for us to sleep there.

I *really* became aware of how conspicuous we were when we entered the hotel. Impeccably dressed in our uniforms with wings and caps, we walked right through the lobby and filed into the dining room. People raised their forks, sat with mouths agape, and stared at us with disbelieving looks. Frozen in their chairs, we remained in motion. Most of us eased over to the bar. Little by little, disgusted guests started leaving the dining room. Soon, we found that we had the bar completely to ourselves.

I don't know why this particular episode felt different than the rest, but it did. Our guys were used to being stared at in Detroit. Most of them were not married and frequented the bars and nightclubs in Paradise Valley.[2] They received a good many looks here. But since this was primarily a black area, the types of stares weren't the same, we didn't get the type of attention we got in Buffalo.

When we made it back to Selfridge Field our time there was nearly up. In a matter of days, we received orders to depart for Camp Patrick Henry, Virginia, and boarded a troop train that ran through Chicago. Somehow, news of our journey reached the public. I remember droves of blacks lining up along the tracks, waving at us with smiles, laughs, and cheers. At last we were en route to Italy, where the 99th, the first black fighter squadron, was already stationed. As far as I could tell, our countrymen, at least the black ones, were proud.

There were probably 120 pilots (40 per squadron) among us, plus intelligence officers and a chaplain. Colonel Davis was traveling with us too. He had fought in the 99th but had returned to Michigan to take charge of the new fighter group, called the 332nd. A white captain headed the service group, consisting of black mechanics. They were responsible for changing engines and handling other technical tasks.

When we arrived at our destination, trucks picked us up and delivered us to Camp Patrick Henry. I was riding with Chaplain Petrey, who seemed elated that I was not very religious. Although he was a strikingly handsome man, I had trouble taking my eyes off the scar on his neck, which seemed to reveal that he'd "been around" a bit himself before "finding God." I later learned that he'd once been a football coach—so he'd definitely "been around," as they say. I'm not sure about this, but the scar may have come from a woman who'd slashed him with a razor blade in a fit of anger.

A fog and mist covered the trucks ahead of us as we pulled into camp. Petrey looked over and said to me in a low voice, "Now we are descending into Hades." It was an eerie introduction. I looked around and noticed a group of Italian POWs walking in raincoats. They were in charge of the upkeep at Camp Patrick Henry, such as maintaining the grounds and picking up foliage.

Through his rear view mirror, our black truck driver saw me watching them and said, "Oh, these Italians have all sorts of privileges. Italian civilians living in town come out to the base and take them on leave. Sometimes they stay the whole weekend, coming back on Monday mornings."

It seemed to me that the Italians prisoners had the run of the base! They had access to the PX [army "Post Exchange"] which was exclusively reserved for white officers. Black officers, by contrast, certainly didn't have any place to shop. Naturally, we felt some resentment. How was it that POWs, soldiers who had supported a fascist government, could get better treatment than U.S. Army officers?

Among the disgruntled was a black master sergeant named Geltzer, a communications chief. I think he'd gone to MIT and was involved in a number of scientific inventions, such as developing the wire recorder. He'd also been a chess champion in the state of Massachusetts. Geltzer decided one day that he was going to try getting into the PX. As he started entering, an MP told him "Hey, where do you think you're going?" "You can't get in here!" A POW who understood English was listening to the exchange and said in Italian, "I think it is written in the Bible that someday Ethiopia shall spread her wings and rule the earth!" Another Italian rebutted, "Ethiopia should just spread its wings and fly away!" This second comment was meant as derogatory. In so many words, the Italian prisoner was saying that blacks didn't merit existence and should just disappear.

None of this sat well with Geltzer, who spoke some Italian and understood what they were saying. Enraged, he thrust himself at the POW. The MP grabbed him before it got too violent and hauled him off. One of our guys saw the incident and rushed back to the barracks for his carbine. "Geltzer's in trouble," he shouted, while returning to rescue him. Chaplain Petrey and I were playing bridge with some of the others. We jumped up to see what was happening. I remember hearing a siren blaring, and then seeing droves of men with carbines flooding towards the PX. Geltzer, meanwhile, was being hustled away to an open area. At this point, the chaplain was fuming. I don't think I'd ever seen a man of the cloth so angry before. As his fists clenched ever tighter, I could see that he wanted to attack the MPs himself. I grabbed him before he did something stupid. I pulled him close to my bed, snatched a bottle of rum that I had hidden under the covers, and gave him a shot of it to calm him down. It helped bring him to his senses. There wasn't much to be gained in confronting the MPs.

Soon the growls of a half-track, equipped with a .50-caliber machine gun, could be heard roaring in the rain. A tank rolled in and parked at another end, effectively sealing off the area. By this time, there must have been nearly a hundred MPs swarming near the PX. Captain Tresvel, who was in charge of us while Colonel Davis was attending a briefing in Washington, managed to call our squadron officers together and helped persuade our men to stand down. In effect, we spent our first night at Patrick Henry in the midst of a standoff. Later in the evening, a few trucks were dispatched from headquarters to take the men to the mess hall, but none of us wanted to go because we would be escorted by armed white MPs. When Colonel Davis returned from Washington, he found his troops held prisoner. With the guns of the tank, the MPs, and the half-track turned on us, we effectively became American POWs on American soil.

Fortunately, our stay at Camp Patrick Henry was brief. Maybe a night passed after Geltzer's incident before we were ordered to be ready to board the train that would take us to the port of embarkation. The following morning we were set to go at 5 A.M., as instructed. The rain had eased, but it was still drizzling. The MPs marched Geltzer to the back of our formation, consisting of nearly 1,000 black soldiers. He'd spent the night in a tent hoisted in the mud, with just one blanket. As they escorted Geltzer towards the rear, Tresvel called his squadron to stand at attention in a show of respect and solidarity.

The white commander of the service group, however, made us stand in the rain for another three hours that morning, with a tank barrel and machine guns aimed at us. We all knew that he was trying to punish us for the previous day's insurgency. When we piled into the train, everyone was mad and upset, but there was absolutely nothing we could do about it.

A white man was standing under a shelter, playing a familiar melody when we pulled into port. It was the old, World War I, George M. Cohan tune, "*Over there, over there. Send the word, send the word over there—That the Yanks are coming, the Yanks are coming, the drums rum-tumming. . . .*" One by one, we began boarding a Liberty ship. I remember walking up the plank in the rain, giving my name, rank, and serial number. We were off to Europe.

Chapter 5

Atlantic Sound

It stormed the night we left the pier. The sea was especially rough. Everybody was exhausted and still angry about having had to stand in the rain for three hours, waiting for the train. We tried to relax in the common areas and vent some steam. Cards always help do that. I was virtually broke, though. I only had 25 cents in my pocket. A man named Daniels, who later became the commanding officer of my squadron, joined me, putting in 25 cents of his own. Together, we made that half-dollar earn us 135 dollars!

We stayed at sea for 31 days, from the first of January until the end of the month. On the second day, the waters calmed considerably. I went up on deck and looked around. As far into the horizon as I could see there were ships—cruisers with planes on them, destroyers, and seemingly hundreds of transports. As powerful as we were, this great convoy was just inching along the water. The U.S.S. *Arkansas*, which had seen action in World War I, was sailing with us. Since it could only do ten knots an hour, the rest of the fleet had to slow its pace.

There was a ship in our convoy that would pull up along side of us and play a song by one of the great jazz artists of the era. A young black man from their crew would burst out, singing the melody, "*Grab your coat and get your hat, leave your worries on the doorstep. Just direct your feet to the sunny side of the street. Can't you hear the pitter pat? And that happy tune is your step, life can be so sweet on the sunny side of the street.*" Some of the guys on my ship went crazy when they heard the tune. They would sing and some would dance. Although this was war, we took advantage of moments like these to have a good time, which boosted our morale.

I continued to be a successful gambler. I'd first learned to play blackjack, poker, and bridge while in college. What else are you supposed to do with your time except learn cards? But when I joined the army, I wasn't a gambler at all. It wasn't until Colonel Davis put up a memo at Selfridge Field that I started playing again. "Officers and gentlemen play poker and chess," read the memo. I certainly wanted to be both.

At sea, my luck grew by the hour. Before the first week was up, I had collected nearly 3,000 dollars. I had so many ones, fives, and tens in my possession that when I laid down in my bed, it seemed like my money was pressing me up to the bunk above. I couldn't have been happier. The money came at the perfect time, since my wife was expecting a child. I don't think I'd ever had so much cash at once before, and maybe, never since.

I managed to give the chaplain 1,000 dollars to send to my wife before my streak of luck started to end. My fate really changed for the worse when I played against Colonel Davis. He played both bridge and "Locksmith Poker"—he would have one ace up and one ace down. Since everything was "locked up" so to speak, he would win all the time.

The convoy began to split when we arrived at Gibraltar. Some of the ships went to Casablanca, while my group passed through the Straits, into the Mediterranean. As we sailed, P-47s and P-38s buzzed around above us. Our men would go up on deck to watch the planes making their vapor trails at 30,000 feet. It was somewhat agonizing for us to look at, since others were flying and we weren't.

We passed Algeria and Libya before arriving at the toe of the boot of Italy. Here, the convoy divided again. A number of ships went to Naples, but we made course towards the other side of Italy, landing in Bari. I think Bari was the site from which the Italians launched their assault on Ethiopia. I later thought it was ironic that Roosevelt would send a bunch of black troops here. Perhaps he was enacting some sort of racial revenge on Mussolini.

Our arrival was slowed when the propeller broke off of one of the ships in our convoy. The vessel had to be towed, causing the rest of us to lose speed. It was probably a good thing that this happened. If we had arrived any earlier, we would have been blown to smithereens. Hours before we pulled into Bari, a small, single-engine plane had flown over the fleet that was resting in the harbor. It located the ammunition ship and dropped a delayed reaction bomb down its smokestack. The ensuing explosion obliterated virtually everything afloat.

We could still see the masts of the destroyed ships protruding from the bottom of the sea when we pulled into the port at sundown. The smell of smoke and burning debris filled the air. Looking towards land, I even remember seeing the inside of a house with a bathtub hanging from its plumbing on the third or fourth floor. Green bathroom tile was spewed everywhere. I had never witnessed anything like this before, not even in England. As I would find out months later, there was much worse to come.

Some lighters (flat, barge-like boats) came out from the mainland to receive us as we sailed in. After disembarking, we walked to an area about five miles outside of the city, where we saw hungry, partially burned children running around, begging for candy and cigarettes. A lot of the guys wouldn't give them cigarettes, but they did pass out chocolates, since everyone had been issued a supply on the ship.

Just to show you how the army did things, we were forced to sleep outside in the February cold until we were picked up the next morning by trucks that drove us across the mountains. Our destination was the fishing village of Salerno, which was where the Allied forces had come ashore the previous year. This is also where Colonel Davis and the 99th had come in 1943. The other three black squadrons were stationed in Naples, but mine was stationed here, at an airbase under British command.

You might say that our war began the day that a German plane, which had been flying over Naples, turned and headed towards us at Salerno. At the time, one of the captains was teaching us how to use radar, how to plot the course of enemy planes, and how to perform the job of an aircraft controller. We desperately wanted to intercept the intruder, but he continued cruising, unmolested, at 22,000 feet. There was nothing we could do about it because we didn't have planes yet! Our feeling of frustration ran high. The last time any of us had flown had been in mid-December—perhaps. Standing by, watching the enemy maneuver at will and plotting his course, was definitely not our idea of war.

There were two planes on our airfield, however, two Spitfires. But they belonged to the British. Every day they went up on some mysterious mission—twice a day, in fact. Yet they never intercepted the Germans who flew over us. Eventually, we got used to the enemy sending a plane our way once a day. It was a part of our routine.

Interacting with the British was a tremendous learning experience for us. First, we discovered that since British airforce officers were members of the aristocracy, they didn't actually fly planes.[1] Their sergeants were the pilots; officers just went about dictating and giving orders. One day, a British officer named Captain Bertall approached me and asked, "Might you be interested in trading a box of cigarettes for a bottle of scotch?" In the military, Americans paid 50 cents for ten packages of cigarettes. They were relatively cheap. So I passed him the box and said, "Might *you* be interested in having another carton of cigarettes?" "Why, I'd be happy to!" he replied. And that's how we started chatting.

We built a nice rapport, quite different from what we had with many white American officers, and even with subordinate, enlisted personnel. I eventually got around to mentioning that I'd been in Bristol and he was elated! "Did you ever see a lady on a bicycle riding around the roads and downs (the equivalent of parks) like a crazy woman?" I actually did recall such a person during my outings as an MP. "Well now," he said, with a slight grin, "that would have been my mother!!" We had a great laugh and he invited me to visit the British Officer's Club. "I usually have a drink around 7:00," he said, "so if you chaps would like to come and have a drink, then pick me up on the road and I'll take you there."

I had three tent mates. Joe Louis was a classmate of mine from Tuskegee, Downs had been in an earlier class, and Purnell was a member of the original class of airmen. Downs didn't feel like going out that night, so Purnell, Joe Louis and I climbed into a jeep and headed out to meet Captain Bertall. When we got to the club we noticed that the entrance was draped with blackout curtains. To get to the bar you had to pass through a series of them. Inside the first set, groups of people were standing in a hallway. Inside the second set, we entered a spacious lighted area. What I saw could only be described as a very "British" Officer's Club—lots of formalities, plenty to drink, and plenty of fun. The hostess was a busty woman in her thirties, perhaps her late thirties. "Oh Sir! How nice to see you again," she said to the captain in a delighted, somewhat high-pitched tone. I remember these words vividly because they were the only ones being spoken; the rest of the room fell dead silent as we started to pass through.

We proceeded to approach the bar as if nothing had happened. We snuggled up to the counter and took a long look at the hostess' luscious busom. She asked what we wanted—of course, it was scotch. Getting our drinks, we turned around and surveyed the room. An American officer was there, perhaps a South African officer, and at least another British officer. I don't recall any female officers in the room. The American captain decided to get up, drink in hand, and confront us. With a look of disgust, he approached me close, then whispered in my ear, "You sure are a *picked* bunch!" He was mocking us, making fun of the fact that although we were supposed to be elite members of the armed forces—fighter pilots carried themselves with a certain swagger in military circles—we were still black. Half-drunk, the captain then started walking away, trying to be real cute, doing a swing dance step known as the "black bottom." To execute this step, you sort of pat your butt while hopping forward and backward to the music. At the same time, you twist yourself and make hand gestures in the air. He ended up making a real fool out of himself as he fell and busted his ass while dancing his little number. Embarrassed, he got up and went through the blackout curtains where, I guess, he enjoyed the rest of his evening. His spectacle broke the ice and we stayed in the club from about 7:00 until 10:00, talking, enjoying drinks, and listening to the jazz pianist.

It was at another club, where we usually went to drink something called Marsala, where we got to know some of the black South African troops who were in the war. These guys were predominantly engineers, responsible for building military camps. We had to talk to them in secrecy because they were explicitly forbidden from speaking to any black American officers at the base.

I began meeting Italians through my barber. After we'd started to develop a relationship, he invited me over to have dinner with his family. As was common with many Italian businesses, their house was located directly above his barbershop. It was here that I started learning about all the different varieties of pasta. I thought I had found culinary heaven! They fed me thin macaroni, thick spaghetti, thin spaghetti, cheese sauce, meat sauce, marinara—the works! But for all the good food I ending up eating with them, I came to realize that the Italians also wanted food from us. Italian women would regularly come to our camp and stand by the garbage can, waiting for our leftovers. Since we were flyers, our food was very nutritious, but we just couldn't eat it all. So we gradually started giving them anything extra that we had.

Colonel Davis found out about this and quickly put an end to it. He forced the mess sergeant to take all of our excess food and bury it in the ground, according to army regulations. However, one of the mess sergeant's cooks was Italian. He made secret arrangements to take our coffee grounds to use in the espresso machine of his private restaurant. He also managed to take a good portion of the food that was supposed to be buried. He was really living "high on the hog" for a while. In the meantime, our men had started contracting Italian women to do their laundry. When they stopped by the base, we would pay them with chocolate and cigarettes. Davis eventually discovered all of these schemes and brought them to an abrupt halt.

Just as we were starting to get used to our routine of military idleness, we heard the noise of planes overhead. This time it was not the sound of enemy aircraft, but the distinctive whistle of P-39s and their roaring engines. It sounded like hundreds were in the air. We rushed to the airfield from our tents to see what was going on, but Colonel Davis stopped us before we made it all the way. As the planes started landing, we could see that many were smoking badly. A group of trucks sped by us to pick up the pilots as they exited the aircraft. While one truck was driving back our way, one of our guys shouted, "Hey, how are those planes?" One of the incoming pilots responded, "Let's see . . . you got a match? 'cause 'bout the best thing to do with 'em is to burn' em!" At last, our planes had arrived.

The records showed that the airplane I was assigned had been used in the Battle of Britain in 1940. It was a real wreck! It had been shot in the tail and its motor had exceeded 2,000 hours, which meant that it needed replacing. We soon learned that most of these fighters had come to us from the aircraft graveyard in

North Africa. The army reckoned that if they could make the journey from North Africa to Salerno, then we should be able to put them to good use. So, these were the cards we'd been dealt—we were going to be flying planes that were not even as good as the trainers we had used at Selfridge Field! We had at least come to expect that much. What was perhaps more disheartening is that the first group of all-black fighters, the 99th, had brand new P-40s waiting for them when they first arrived to North Africa in 1943. Of course, they had been attached to a white P-40 fighter group, which made all the difference.

We believed that our planes were issued to make black pilots look bad. How could we be as good as the rest of the Air Corps if we were using substandard equipment? Rumors had been circulating throughout the military that blacks were incapable of flying in formation. Colonel Davis even had to testify in Washington, D.C. on this very issue. Lots of congressmen simply wanted to abolish the whole Tuskegee experiment, which they probably would have accomplished had not a member of the 99th, Lieutenant Charles "Buster" Hall, shot down one of the German army's fastest planes, a Focke-Wulf 190, in July 1943. This was the first time a black American pilot had scored a kill in World War II. At the same time, Hall managed to damage an even better aircraft, a Messerschmitt 109, which many continue to regard as the best single-seat fighter ever produced. I was in the United States when this happened, having just graduated from Tuskegee. But I still remember how the commandant of the cadet corps made a jubilant announcement in the mess hall after Hall's victory. The entire dining room erupted in celebration. Right then and there, we understood the gravity of the event. Hall was flying a P-40, which was a tactical aircraft used mainly for strafing ground targets and providing infantry support. It was not the type of plane you would expect to win a dogfight with some of Germany's finest war machines. Hall exhibited tremendous skill, determination, and competence in his success. Surrounded by nearly 50 German fighters, and nearly out of gas, he managed to escape alive. His accomplishment brought a lot of positive attention to the abilities of black pilots. Reflecting back on it now, maybe it was too much attention, since it probably caused some army officials to entrench themselves in their prejudices and seek ways to slow down our progress by giving us truly inferior equipment to fly in.

Honestly, though, just hearing the motors of the P-39s and knowing that they were *ours*, did give us some comfort. Many of us were just happy to soon be flying again. Smitty, my crew chief, got to work on fixing my plane. When I was finally allowed to look her over, she was still a wreck. There was no way, I thought, this thing will be flying over 22,000 feet.

We soon started doing something called "convoy patrol." Essentially, we would pick up convoys to the west and fly them safely to Naples. Two planes flew at 5,000 feet and two more at 8,000 feet. We had to be careful not to fly over the ships themselves because if we did, they would start shooting at us. Sailors from the merchant marine got paid an extra five dollars a day for firing their guns in a war zone. They were eager to collect this money whether they were shooting at friends or foe.

The first casualty from our group was a classmate of mine, a man named Williams. I guess you might say that the army killed him, since he died during a test flight. He and his mechanic had been working on his plane. Unsurprisingly, given the condition of our aircraft, we spent lots of time on maintenance. A plane needed to be tested, however, before it could be cleared for operation. Some pilots spent most of their flight time doing precisely this—executing "test hops." Anyway, Williams had climbed to about 1,000 feet when his motor cut out. You are almost assured a death sentence at that altitude. You need at least 1,500 or 2,000 feet to be able to use your parachute. We ran out of our tents when his engine failed and watched as he started to spin. He died instantly in the crash.

In the spring of 1944, thanks to the eruption of Mt. Vesuvius, which blew a coat of ash nearly a yard thick over our airfield, some of us at Salerno were rotated to harbor patrol at the airfield in Capodichino, near Naples. Capodichino was just a dirt field at the time, about a mile square. On the right hand side there were trees, and to the north there was a wall that stood about 15 feet high. Every kind of plane that you could imagine was there. We saw B-25 bombers, P-40s, P-47s, P-51s, and of course, P-39s. Many of us had heard about all of these types of aircraft, but few had actually seen them gathered together in one place at the same time. Of course, the communication between white American pilots and black pilots was kept to a minimum. It would have been great to benefit from their experience. But as usual, the Air Corps was keeping black and white pilots segregated—black pilots on one side of the airfield, whites on the other.

German light bombers harassed us at Capodichino. Every night around midnight, and again at two in the morning, they would fly over us, extremely low, right above the water. As they approached the hill where Naples was located, they would pull up and then fly straight over our airfield. That's when our guns would start going off. But by the time we started shooting, the Germans were gone! They were flying so low that there was no warning, no time for us to retaliate. Each time, a bomber would drop a single bomb that sailed over the airfield and fell into a space we called the "bomb dump." This happened so often that it didn't even seem like they were actually aiming at us. They were just trying to disrupt our sleep. I panicked the first night we were attacked and fled for cover in a slit trench, but afterwards, it got to a point where I didn't even bother getting up anymore.

One of the advantages of being in Naples was that the 99th was stationed there and they had their own officers' club. They ran it out of an apartment they had taken over in an upper-class area of the city, and it was here where they brought women and drank whiskey. A lot of the liquor they consumed had been issued by the army. Pilots were supposed to get a shot of whiskey after successfully returning from each mission, but black pilots didn't get anything to drink until much later. About every month or so, the army would provide us with a bottle of liquor, which we shared with our crew chiefs. Some of this stock made its way to the club. We also bought beer here. Unlike our fellow British aviators, though, we preferred drinking our beer cold. We cooled it down by pouring high-octane gas over it and letting the gas evaporate.

During its time in Capodochino, the 99th had also carried bombs to defend the beachhead at Anzio, north of Naples. The American army had landed there and had almost gone on to reach Rome, when the commander decided to draw back to the beachhead. The Germans brought up their artillery and pinned them down at Anzio. In the meantime, Lieutenant Hall, who became the first black American to shoot down an enemy plane, continued making history by shooting down more aircraft. He was on the brink of becoming an ace when he'd destroyed his fourth, but he was deprived of the glorious opportunity to become the first black air ace in U.S. history. I happened to be in Tresvel's office shortly after Hall had been grounded. Hall called Tresvel, the commanding officer of the 100th squadron, to plead for him to intervene and prevent his being sent home. I overheard Tresvel saying, "You know that I can't do anything about this because you're not a part of my squadron." According to rumor, Hall started crying. Afterwards, Tresvel told the rest of us, "Allright now, don't you boys go out and get yourselves killed trying to be air aces, because there are not going to be any black aces in this war." Even Colonel Davis agreed. There was nothing he could do about Hall's situation either. The 99th was no longer under his command, so the case fell out of his jurisdiction. Hall's fate gives you a taste of what it was like for us throughout the rest of the war. Every time a black pilot got four victories, he was rotated home.[2]

After some more time in Naples we were re-stationed in Salerno, where they'd managed to clean up much of the ash that had blown over the airfield from Mt. Vesuvius. I wasn't back long before I was sent on convoy patrol again, flying this time as the flight leader's wingman. This was a special position, since you were responsible for protecting the flight leader himself. As we took off, however, I noticed ash piled high on either side of the strip. They hadn't completely removed it from our camp. I didn't think much about this at the time, but soon, the remaining ash would cause problems.

I heard loud, strange noises as we returned to base and started our landing approach. Once I touched the ground I saw sheep, blackened by the ash, scurrying in front of my windshield. I'd completely missed them from the air because the ash had camouflaged their white coats, blending them in with the airfield itself. In retrospect, I couldn't figure out why the people in the tower didn't warn us with their flare guns. I later learned that they were aware an Italian shepherd was tending to his flock in the area.

I didn't have much time to react. My nose wheel broke and suddenly I saw parts of dead sheep flying about. Then the gas tank, located directly under my seat, caught fire. Let me tell you, there is nothing that can make you move faster than having a live fire under your ass! In a flash, I pulled the lever to open my door. To my surprise, the door fell completely off! I quickly unbuckled my seatbelt. Luckily, I was wearing a dinghy—a small rubber boat that we used in emergency situations to get across the Mediterranean. I also had a parachute on my back. When I stumbled out onto the wing to jump, the plane pivoted to the right. I ended up falling to the ground on my right side. Fortunately, the parachute and dinghy broke my fall and saved me from breaking my back. Meanwhile, the plane had turned such that it was starting to come toward me. I was lying down, helpless on the steel mat runway. I struggled to avoid getting hit by the guns under the wing. It is a wonder that I came out of the accident alive.

I must have lost consciousness because the next thing I remember was waking up in a bed, extremely sore. Then I realized I was paralyzed! I couldn't move my hands, my feet, or anything else. Oh, how lucky I was that my back wasn't broken! I laid there for nearly three weeks before I could get up and go to the mess hall, take a shower, or even use the restroom normally! In the meantime, the guys helped me urinate in my helmet.

The flight surgeon ended up sending me to rest camp in Naples. A former nightclub and shack-up motel, the rest camp had a nice view overlooking the Mediterranean. There was even a beach below. Eventually, I slowly started moving around by myself, but only with the assistance of a cane. I couldn't get upstairs or downstairs without it. If I accidentally stepped on anything, like a rock or a cord, I immediately fell down and broke my ass.

A few visitors came to see me every once and a while from Salerno. Geltzer came most often—he even taught me how to play chess. It was from him, I believe, that I also learned that the British officers in Salerno had picked up the dead sheep from my accident and used them for food! Their rations were horrible. Typically, they ate hunks of terrible bread, cheese, salt, pita, and scotch. Under these circumstances, lamb was definitely an exquisite delicacy, so in a morbid way, they benefited greatly from my accident.

On the other hand, we ate marvelously well at rest camp. In addition, the Italian-American woman who was in charge was able to get attractive, young local girls to come up and keep the men company. Since we had so much food, many of the G.I.'s would pay for the girls to eat, too. They took full advantage of our hospitality by bringing empty sugar bowls and napkins with them on their visits. They eagerly filled these up with butter and sugar. It didn't matter much to us since there was so much available.

One day, an alcoholic Red Cross nurse from Detroit named Mae Brooks arrived and spoiled the party. I was playing ping-pong when she arrived. The rest of the guys were lounging around with their girlfriends when suddenly, Mae stormed in shouting, "What are all these Italian whores doing around here?!!" Womack, the man in charge, stood up and bitched her out, saying, "Where the hell have you women been anyway?" This was the first day that the Red Cross women had even set foot in our rest camp. She, the other nurses, and their staff were black. We, the patients, were all black, too.

Rumor had it that a whole lot of hanky panky was going on in the upper ranks between white officers and Red Cross Women. A roll in the hay with a white nurse, for instance, cost anywhere from 20 to 50 dollars. Another rumor was circulating that even General Eisenhower was corrupted into having an erotic relationship with his driver. Honestly, I don't know what happened between the black Red Cross nurses and our guys, but at least black soldiers were able to have their Italian women, young and pretty, without paying the high fees that some white officers were supposedly paying. At least this was allowed in our camp until Mae and her staff showed up.

I was still in rest camp when somebody told me that the 332nd fighter group was joining the fifteenth strategic airforce. Up to that point, we had been in the twelfth tactical airforce, which mainly handled ground targets. Now we would be providing bomber escort services and flying P-47s, equipped with 2,000 horsepower engines, eight .50 caliber machine guns, broad landing gear, and a host of other advanced parts. I was in no shape to join them when they left, but I followed their progress closely in the army's newspaper *Stars and Stripes*. In their first mission, the 332nd fighter group shot down 18 German planes! I said to myself, "At last I have an airplane that is worthy of me." I stayed in rest camp through the month of May. In the meantime, the squadron commander sent word for me to rejoin when I was better. The 332nd had now relocated to Ramitelli airbase, near the Adriatic Sea. My tent mates had already packed my stuff and moved it there. All that was left was for me to heal.

Looking back on things, I should have just stayed and retired. But to tell the truth, I was seduced by the prospect of flying a P-47, and I was a little envious of everything I was hearing and reading about what our guys were accomplishing on the other side of Italy. I got better towards the end of June and finally made it over to Ramitelli. One of the first things the squadron commander instructed me to do was to take the P-47 up for 45 minutes. What a marvelous plane it turned out to be! It flew like a dream, like the AT6 advanced trainer. It had wide wings and landing gear, combined with considerable power. When I took off I heard a powerful humming, that of an air-cooled, radial engine, instead of an in-line engine that required liquid coolant. The manual warned that you should never fly the plane at speeds exceeding 400 or 500 miles an hour because it could cause a high-speed stall. But I executed some high-speed maneuvers in the P-47, the same ones that I did in other planes, without problem. I did some spins, turns, dives—and on the next day I flew her for another 45 minutes. On the third day I was flying a mission.

I was the wingman to a guy named Bill Williams. We took off in formation, that is, two planes at a time. At the end of the runway there was a grazing field. I was doing about 110 miles an hour. I pulled back on the stick and the plane sweeped up into the air. There were cows just a short distance underneath me. You can't imagine what that felt like. We *barely* cleared those cows as we took off. I got up to about 100 feet and tried to make a turn. But it wasn't turning, it was just "mushing"—just pushing the air. So I pulled back harder until at last, the wings began to bite the air. I reduced the throttle and tried to catch up to my leader, Williams. I was using a lot of fuel. The P-47 consumed about 2 gallons a minute, about twice as much as the P-39. My plane, as the others, was equipped with 330 gallons of internal fuel supply, another 330 in the tanks under the wings, and another 90 gallons reserve. I took off using the reserve, then I switched to one of the wing tanks. After making a circle around the airfield I followed the leader, climbing at 200 miles an hour. After half of my gas was used up I switched to the other wing tank. This kept the plane balanced.

Once everything was straightened out, I proceeded in formation to Yugoslavia. That day we were headed to Romania, where the Germans had taken over. The Nazis had been trying to take Russia, but they faltered in 1944 and were starting to be tossed back by the Allies into Europe. As we proceeded, little by little I found myself slipping behind formation. I used more gas trying to catch up. The plane was so heavy that I couldn't slow down when I needed to, and I was constantly overshooting. In the process, I wasted a lot of fuel unnecessarily. After about three hours I had used up all of my external gas.

I couldn't continue. I had to go back to base. I wasn't alone. We were at about 25,000 feet. I understood that members of the German airforce were sometimes called "Huns in the sun." This simply meant that they would hide in the sun and knock off early returns. That's what I was. To stay safe you had to keep swiveling your head around, keeping on guard—turning right, left, right, left. There was a rearview mirror that you could look into. I kept looking into the sun and sure enough, I saw a shadow. I called in and made a turn towards it. That's all that you could do is to make a turn towards the enemy and keep your eyes open. When we got out over the Adriatic I heard some radio chatter, but that was all. I was safe.

When I finally got back to base I was glad to learn that others were having the same problems I did. Everyone seemed to be running out of gas early and there was a mad scramble among the pilots to land before going empty. The next time up I made a much better showing, but it was a struggle to make slight adjustments so as not to overshoot. Fortunately, when the 99th joined us, we did not have to worry as much about losing planes due to early returns. On each of our missions, typically, four full squadrons went up. However, with the addition of the 99th, each squadron was further equipped with two spares that could take the place of planes that had to return to base.

Finally, I was flying the colonel's wing. He always flew with my squadron. Everybody thought that I was a big brownnoser because Colonel Davis and I played bridge together and he frequently called for me over the PA system. The truth is that I wasn't a brownnoser at all. I just liked playing bridge and Colonel Davis was a good player (although he regularly took advantage of the chaplain, who was constantly overbidding). In any case, we flew together and thankfully, my performance was acceptable to him. We had to keep a close eye on each other's tail.

In providing bomber escort service, we would fly around the ground target, meet the bombers as they circled out of the target area, and then escort them safely across the water. I'll never forget seeing one of our B-24s hit. The crew bailed out feverishly, some with their parachutes ablaze. There are times in your life when you see things to which you just have to say "hmmm . . ." and keep on going. That was truly an awful sight to witness that day because immediately, we all realized that those boys were going to die.

While Tuskegee pilots never lost a bomber, our own attrition rate was comparably high. The four squadrons in our fighter group needed about ten replacements a month, but the airfield at Tuskegee was only graduating a limited number of pilots. They took in just 60 cadets a month, which produced about 30 pilots per graduating class. Not all ended up in fighter groups. The Air Corps also needed navigators and bombardiers. Consequently, pilots who had once washed out, like my friend "Double E" Richardson, became assigned to B-25 bombers. Of the replacement pilots that did eventually join our fighter squadrons in Italy, we noticed that they came with far fewer hours in the air. I'd arrived, for instance, with over 200 hours before joining the war.

One day, one of these young replacements was taking off in formation, flying on the right of his leader. Because of his lack of experience, he didn't know how to respond to the "prop wash"—the air that came from the propeller of his leader's plane. He spun in from about 20 feet and burst into flames—over

600 gallons of gasoline! A geyser of fire and smoke shot up into the sky. Meanwhile, I was waiting to take off. I slowly got out of my plane, pulled out a pack of cigarettes, and had a smoke. I watched the intense blaze with the others, squinting my eyes, and waiting until the fire burned itself out. There was nothing anyone could do, and we knew it. His lack of experience killed him. You can't mourn. When somebody gets killed, they just get killed. It was horrendous, yes. But we were helpless to change anything. All one could do was stop, step out of the wing, shake your head, and then get back to war.

What really saved us was the day that we switched to flying P-51s, sometime in August of 1944. This plane weighed much less than the P-47, had a better fuel consumption rate, and could fly much longer—for almost seven hours if the weather was right. That was nearly twice as long as the P-47. Although it had the same wing tanks, the P-51's aerodynamics were superior, giving us greater maneuverability. We also could climb to 45,000 feet.[3] We painted the tails of our aircraft red so that friendly bombers could easily identify us. Throughout the corps, we became known as "Red Tails," and soon, we endeared ourselves to American bomber pilots. While there were many white officers and subordinates who continued to detest us, and would not bother to salute us throughout our years of service, I'll have to say that a number of white bombardiers were actually very glad to meet somebody who was a "Red Tail."

The contrast between white fighter pilots and us was great. White aviators callously used their own bombers as bait, getting German fighters to attack, while they waited to pursue the enemy and shoot them down. In their efforts to become daredevils, bomber crews were left exposed and at great risk. Colonel Davis, however, made it very clear to us that we were not going to be doing such things. Our primary mission was to escort and protect. He had us stay over the bombers at about 100 feet, making S-turns so that we wouldn't overrun them. That's why we never lost a bomber, whereas white fighter squadrons lost them all the time. When we received flak (barrages from ground-based, anti-aircraft guns), we didn't have to worry about enemy pursuit. Enemy fighters didn't venture into their own flak to get at our bombers, since it placed them at risk as well. The time we spent protecting and escorting bombers was far different from the boredom of convoy patrol. Now, we were into the thick of the action.

In the months between August 1944 and March 1945, I did undertake one mission that provided a unique diversion from the usual rhythms of war. I volunteered to go to Casablanca to ferry planes back to Italy. My group stayed in what had once been the Italian embassy. We were living in luxury—we had first-rate bedrooms, excellent cooks (the Italian chefs were still there), and we had bathrooms! We had grown accustomed to using makeshift showers out in the field. The water was hot enough, but we didn't enjoy much privacy. Now I had all the amenities that I remembered from home. Perhaps the most interesting thing about our experience was that we had the chance to meet men from the Moroccan army. These soldiers sure were a sight! Their black and brown faces contrasted with their yellow and blue silk uniforms. It was like taking a page out of a nineteenth-century novel. They rode beautiful Arab steeds and carried antique rifles. They possessed a certain civility about them. However, we soon realized that they thought that we black troops had come to liberate them. You see, these soldiers were also slaves.

Everything was so new to me here! This is a Muslim country and women walked the streets with a chaperone, wearing veils. All you could see was their rich eye shadow and those radiant, flashing eyes! They blinked at us like signals. We couldn't help but stare and wonder about the mysteries beneath the veil. As we looked at them, they looked back at us, seemingly with the same curiosity and wonder.

When we walked or sat in a restaurant, people would sometimes approach us trying to buy ammunition. Algeria was in the process of trying to liberate itself from French control, and the rebels were seeking supplies from friendly sources. I'm not sure what made them think to approach us.

One day, a French Muslim invited me to his house to celebrate a religious holiday. He lived close by, so I decided to take him up on his offer. Two women were there when I arrived, both without their veils. One was wearing a bolero-styled outfit, with her brassiere slightly exposed under her little jacket. We sat on hassocks while dinner was served. They brought grapes, wine, and a number of other fabulous dishes. We ate, talked, and drank. Afterwards, my host said, "On this occasion, it is always our custom to have one of our wives sleep with a stranger." I was startled. I looked over at my pistol in the corner and said, "Well, let's see what happens." The woman I was with didn't speak Italian. I certainly didn't speak Arabic and my French was awful, so we just sat together and laughed for a while. When I woke up the next morning I said, "Allright now! I'll be sure to tell my granddaughter about this someday." It was at this point when the woman said the only words I understood from her, "Oh, Grandaddy!" I put on my clothes and returned to the embassy.

Between December of 1944 and March of 1945 we saw more action. After having muscled into France, the Allies were preparing to make their final thrust at Hitler. I remember when we flew escort for over 1,000 bombers on their way to Germany. It was an awesome sight, seeing bombers in every direction for a

150-mile stretch. Looking down into the sea we saw still more activity, throngs and throngs of ships. During these months our planes bombarded German factories and troop positions that were preparing to repel the Allied invasion.[4] Thankfully, the Germans didn't have use of the French fleet, which had been scuttled. But the Germans did have friends amongst the French, which made the Allied job more difficult.[5]

Part of our responsibilities included strafing radar installations along the coast of France. On one sortie, I was part of a mission of four planes led by a man named Ballard. My wingman was Jefferson. His wingman was a pilot named Daniels. As we came in towards the ground from an altitude of almost 15,000 feet, I suddenly looked back to find Jefferson and noticed that Daniels, who was flying in front of me, was going up in smoke. I pulled up and started following Ballard, who didn't look back. That's when I noticed that Jefferson was being shot down as well. Ballard and I went in as close to the coast as we dared and fired furiously at our targets. One, two, three . . . fire! One, two, three . . . fire! That was the interval. I shot short bursts while flying above the ocean at nearly 500 miles an hour.

We lost a number of pilots that day. When I returned to base I learned that Faulkner, our squadron leader, who had been flying at 30,000 feet, turned over and went down. They radioed him, knowing that something must have gone wrong. He was probably unconscious because he didn't respond. A poor oxygen connection apparently caused him to pass out during flight. As for Daniels, I learned many years later that he had survived his ordeal and had become a POW. Ironically, once behind enemy lines, the Germans treated him with proper respect. He was an officer, not a *black* officer. It seemed interesting to me to see how black soldiers had to be in the clutches of the enemy before being bestowed some of the honor that they deserved.

After my accident in Salerno, I suffered immense pain during high-altitude missions. My right leg and shoulder bothered me terribly. At 35,000 feet they just went numb altogether. It's really cold up there, about 40 degrees below zero, which didn't help matters. To fight the cold I wore a pair of paratrooper boots and thick, wool socks. The plane's heater warmed my feet. It wasn't enough. I ended up flying using only my left hand and foot. It was absolutely reckless and I should have known better, but I was young and felt invincible! Imagine the discomfort of having to fly like this during a mission of six or seven hours! Moreover, you tend to urinate more under stress. With just one side of my body active, it was really difficult fumbling around, trying to get my relief tube in place and fly my plane.

My situation grew worse with time. Then, I went on a mission that really sealed my fate. I was flying over the Alps at about 35,000 feet. Walter Forman, a guy who played chess and bridge with me, was my wingman. Suddenly, he said, "Hey, my oxygen jut blew up in my face!" He started to turn and went straight down. I dropped my wing tanks and turned over and followed him. As I was diving, a thick black curtain draped over my windshield. In a rush, I turned my plane back over. The oil cap must have come loose because I realized that the black substance was oil. I couldn't see in front of me and I had lost 5,000 feet. I called Forman, but he was scrambling to get down below 20,000 feet. He had about fifteen seconds to do this. Without oxygen, that's all the time you had before passing out and dying. Fortunately, once you reach 20,000 feet, you can begin to breathe without an oxygen mask again.

Meanwhile, I had to throttle back because the oil was being pumped out of my engine. When there is no oil to cool the engine, it overheats and stops. At that point you have to bail out of the plane. I also reduced my RPMs and power. I needed time to think about my next move. I was rapidly approaching the Adriatic Sea. I realized that if started to bail out, I might actually make my situation worse. Few people had successfully bailed out over water. The shores of Italy were strewn with the dinghies and lifeless bodies of people who had attempted to do so. Looking at my instruments I saw that I had plenty of gas, and since my engine was still running and my oil pressure hadn't dropped too drastically, I decided to try to return to base.

Though I couldn't see in front of me, I could see on both sides and to the rear. I pushed the homer channel on the radio and said, "Mayday, Mayday . . . I'm over the Adriatic at 25,000 feet and I'm losing oil. It's covering my windshield and I can't see!" The homer said, "Begin counting from 1 to 10." I started counting. I stayed at cruising altitude and decreased power. The homer then asked, "What's your number?" "1651," I replied. "Fly one, eight, zero degrees," he responded. After about an hour, the homer said, "Look to your left and you should see the air strip."

"I have an oil leak and I cannot see forward. Would you please give me landing instructions?" No response. I changed over to the tower channel and explained my situation. "We see you!" they said. "You are at 5,000 feet." "Turn left ten degrees and descend at 200 feet per minute." I couldn't see anything, but I was losing altitude. "Allright! Allright!" "Turn a little to the left. Now turn right!" When I was down at 500 feet the tower officer said, "Oh! Pull up and go around! You have drifted off the runway!" I looked behind me and I could see across the runway. I cut the throttle and just dived towards it, putting the wheels down. When I landed, I got out and looked at my plane, which was black from its nose to the tail. The tower officer came out and said, "Never do that again."

Walter Foreman had made it back too and when I saw him he said, "You'll never get me in one of these things again!" You know what? I agreed. When

McDaniels came over to my tent, I explained the whole situation to him and asked to speak to the colonel. When I saw Colonel Davis I told him about my accident and the pain I was experiencing in the air. “Sir, ever since my accident in Salerno last April, I've had to fly with just one arm and leg. It's tough for me to be an effective pilot like this.” I had already flown nearly 63 missions.

When I saw McDaniels again a little later, he said, “You can't quit now Richardson. You have a son and you don't want your record to show that you quit flying because of an accident like that (the oil incident).” Charles had been born while I'd been stationed in Salerno.

“I'll tell you what we'll do. If you fly for me this week, I promise that you will be going home on Friday,” McDaniels offered. The proposal was extremely tempting. I went over and spoke with Foreman, who didn't have a wife and kids. Without hesitation, he thought I should accept. I decided to take McDaniels up on his deal.

I flew Monday, Wednesday, and Friday. When I returned from the last mission, I packed my bags, got into a truck, and headed to the Redeployment Depot in Rome. It was March 1945 and I had been in the army for more than four years. The war was nearly over. President Roosevelt died that April, and shortly thereafter, victory in Europe was declared. The Allies pushed through Germany from the west while the Russians ploughed in from the east. In May, it all came to an end.

Chapter 6

A Soldier's Homecoming

I went back to New York and visited Atlantic City with my wife. The army provided a month's leave upon returning from overseas, so I spent the next 30 days relaxing with my family before reporting to Tuskegee as a flight instructor. To tell the truth, from the moment I set foot back in Alabama, I was ready to leave. It was then when I really started regretting that I hadn't retired in July 1944. My knee and shoulder were still bothering me, I was becoming disinterested in what I was doing, and I didn't feel the same exhilaration that I'd experienced in previous years. I guess one side of me also realized that I'd joined the military to make money. In college, I labored hard to get things that my classmates seemed to acquire easily. They had the best of clothes and seemingly anything else they wanted. I thought the army might help me do the same. I thought it would give me the financial boost that I needed to make the next step in life. Especially when my first son was born, I found myself wanting to be in a position to be able to provide for him. I knew I had to save more. In my view, even being an officer, the army just wasn't allowing me to get where I wanted to be financially.

It wasn't long before someone made me realize that I had acquired enough points to get out of active duty. I submitted my paperwork and was released on July 5, 1945. I returned promptly to Fort Dix, the place where my war experiences had begun. Of course, I wasn't out of the service completely. I was placed on reserve duty for another five years. But I felt a new energy, a fresh perspective on my future.

My wife and I talked about having another child. We were living in an apartment on 163rd Street in the Bronx at the time. Aida had relatives who did not live too far away, which was convenient. She also had a teacher's certificate and was prepared to teach to gain extra income. I had other plans, however. Having retired from the army, the G.I. Bill was providing me with 95 dollars a month. But I was under no illusions about how far this would stretch for a family of four. I started looking for work immediately. It dawned on me one evening that rather than working for someone else, I'd probably be much better off if I were in business for myself. A classmate of mine from Tuskegee, a guy named Walter Palmer, had also retired from the army and was looking for something to do. Although he had lost his right eye in an automobile accident outside of Tuskegee, he was still able to work. Together, we decided that we'd purchase an old army truck and establish a delivery service in Greenwich Village. We split the startup costs evenly—the six-ton truck cost 700 dollars. My rank as an officer and my veteran's status allowed us to get a phone. Back in those days, telephones were hard to get. I'd applied for mine right after leaving the army. Being ex-military moved me up rapidly on the waiting list. Once we got the phone, we recruited my wife to be our secretary and we were in business!

We managed to get a contract with Dalma's furniture store. I became a sort of salesman who hustled business for the store from bohemian types that were interested in purchasing the lamps, tables, beds, couches, and other wares that Dalma's distributed. When an order came through, Palmer and I would deliver these products door-to-door. But believe it or not, although I was a certified and war-tested pilot, I didn't even have a driver's license! Palmer, one eye and all, drove the truck. We were making about 50 dollars a day.

Success breeds success, or so they say. It was definitely true for us for a while. Along with Dalma's, we started doing business with a man who sold expensive frosted mirrors. They were certainly elegant, but if you ask me, they were not practical. It was all about decoration, aesthetic appeal, presentation, and effect. Unfortunately, we had a costly accident delivering one of these. It happened on our way to a house in Brooklyn. We draped quilts, blankets, and everything else we could find to protect the mirror, but one of us got careless and cracked it. That was 300 dollars lost, right there. This was a major discouragement for the both of us. Fatigue was also starting to bother Palmer. His wife wasn't very enthusiastic about his being an entrepreneur in the first place, and he was starting to become sensitive about being handicapped. After nearly two months in business we decided to liquidate Palmer and Richardson Delivery Service. We sold the truck for what we paid for it. I lost touch with Palmer after a while, but later learned that he and his wife ended up moving to Guadalajara, Mexico. She had worked during the war and had managed to save a lot of money. Both of them decided to invest their savings in a Mexican bank, which was paying a ridiculously high interest rate, 40 percent a month, or something crazy like that.

It was a recipe for financial disaster since there is no way the bank could sustain this. Indeed, as I found out years later, the bottom collapsed on their deal. They ended up moving back to Houston where he found work as a security guard. This was in the late 1950s.

As for myself, I had a backup plan. Even as we were running our delivery service, I had applied to New York University (NYU) Law School. I had been a good student all through high school and college. I knew I could succeed at law, but what I didn't realize was that I should have gone to a different school, perhaps St. John's University or Brooklyn Law. NYU was a private school with strong racial prejudices. Unfortunately, I didn't come to understand this until later.

I was initially inspired to apply to NYU because of my relationship with the Dickens family. After leaving the army, I met David Dickens, a prosperous real estate agent and a politico. His family was from Canada. He once told me that during the days of slavery, his ancestors had fled from the United States northward, making it all the way to Canada by means of the Underground Railroad. In the 1920s and 1930s they returned to New York and established themselves as a prominent clan. It was David who introduced me to his brother, a young man not much older that I, who had graduated from NYU and become a lawyer. Together, the Dickens brothers persuaded me that applying to NYU was a good idea.

I got a real taste for what the law was all about when, shortly after being accepted to NYU, Dickens (the lawyer) asked me for a favor. He was trying a case in the Bronx County Courthouse of a black guy accused of rape. To help tip the scales in his favor, he asked me to come to the courtroom, dressed in full military uniform, and sit at his table. This posed no problem. What shocked me though, was what happened in the hallway during recess. The prosecution and defense attorneys stood around gossiping and laughing together, just as if nothing was the matter, just as if they were chummy old friends. I grew angry. I'll admit that before going into law school I was very idealistic about the merits of the legal system. I truly believed the law to be a "noble profession." But my quick glimpse of reality showed me that instead, the processes of justice were really little more than theater acting without the stage, and perhaps without some of the glamour.

To get through law school and to support a growing family I had to continue working. I persuaded the NYU Law Library staff to give me a job as an assistant librarian. In some ways, this was a perfect opportunity for me. I began learning where to find the books and pamphlets that I needed for my courses. The books I handled addressed topics that I had never even thought about as being important before. As I cataloged, stored, and retrieved materials, I looked them over to get a feel for the information contained within. I learned a lot as a librarian, but the work fed my mind more than my family. If it hadn't been for my connections with the American Negro Theater (ANT), we would have been living a very difficult lifestyle.

Since I had been an original, founding member of the ANT, I retained an important role in the organization after the war. For instance, soon after I got back, I participated regularly in the meetings of the board of trustees. In February 1946, I was elected to serve as chairman of the Constitutional Committee that looked into redesigning the ANT's ordinances. Even as late as 1949, I was still serving on the Administrative Committee, examining financial transactions, bookkeeping, legal matters, and membership.[1] Beginning in September 1945, the ANT started a weekly, half-hour radio program on WNEW called "A Voice is a Voice." Ted Cott, the director of the station, offered me a position as a radio actor for the Sunday show. Sometimes I also did narration, but I was principally an actor. "A Voice is a Voice" ran for about a year, allowing me to earn an additional 16 dollars a week.[2]

To make ends meet I also took a job as a chauffeur (I had finally gotten my license!). For about a dollar an hour, I drove a Manhattan-based doctor around in his Cadillac. I would get the car after school and pick him up at his office on Park Avenue. Unexpectedly, I got into an accident one day, and while the car was being repaired, I decided to abandon that line of work.

Fortunately, because of my show on WNEW, other stations began calling me. WOR or WMCA had a show called "New World A-Coming" based on the famous book by the black journalist Roi Ottley.[3] He had been a war correspondent (who had actually spent time with the Tuskegee Airmen) and did much to publicize the concerns of blacks during World War II.[4] In any case, the show, which was also somewhat political in its orientation, dealt with matters of race and aired a couple of times a month. As with "A Voice is a Voice," I was called upon to be a radio actor, playing the role of a Garveyite in *The Big White Fog*. With "New World A-Coming" I now had two radio programs. A while later, I was even called to do a network show, which paid very well.

What really gave me a financial breather was a call that I got from Fred O'Neal, my old friend and fellow cofounder of the ANT. He had gone on to become the head of the Actor's Equity Association, an influential union for stage actors. He rang one day and said, "Look, somebody wants a man to be John Mariot's understudy in the Eugene O'Neil play *The Iceman Cometh*. Why don't you go down to the Theater Guild and read for it?" I successfully auditioned for the part. By this time I was in my second year of law school. I'd already stopped working at the library. The income I earned from being an understudy was far better than what I made at NYU. Instead of scuffling around making 60 dollars a month, I was now earning 80 dollars a week.

My second son, Ray, was born on March 30, 1946. I became an understudy in October. My schedule was grueling. I would leave school at 2:00 P.M., dash home, eat, and play with my two sons. I only had a few hours, since I needed to be at the theater by seven o'clock. As I rushed out the door, I'd take my bag of books with me. Understudies had plenty of idle time. I used mine to read. Thankfully, *Iceman* was a long play. The last act would begin around 9:00 P.M. and I left the theater house at 10:00 P.M. Mariot generously offered me the opportunity to play the part, but I declined. I didn't need any additional distractions from my studies. Sometime in March the theater company moved to Chicago. They offered to increase my salary if I joined them, but this was never a real possibility. I was still immersed in my legal studies.

I learned much about the practice of law. I took an accelerated program, which meant that I had classes during the summer. For financial reasons, I was never able to get involved with things like moot court. This was unfortunate, since I believe that had I participated, I would have been much more encouraged to become a practicing lawyer.

As you might imagine, there were just a handful of blacks studying law at NYU. One guy in my class was from Panama. Another guy from Harlem, named Eastman, graduated the year before I matriculated. He was conducting research for the dean of the law school when I arrived. Sadly, with all of his advanced credentials, he was unable to land a prestigious job. We were all discouraged (at least the blacks) when Eastman accepted employment as a lawyer for a furniture store in Harlem. It was a sleazy position. Back in those days, stores coerced blacks to buy goods on credit. Storeowners found ingenious ways to stretch out payments for 15-to-20 years. Blacks could never really own anything; especially those who had trouble meeting the monthly payments. Eastman became the guy they sent out to deliver subpoenas and to scare customers who couldn't pay. Regrettably, his was a future that many black lawyers reluctantly had to look forward to.

After seeing Eastman, I decided that I wanted to work for the Legal Aid Society, providing free counseling. I knew that if you were black, poor, and needed legal services, you were in a situation of double jeopardy. There was no way I wanted to play the role of the oppressor. Unfortunately, my lofty goals were shattered by my slipping grades. After passing the difficult first year of law school, you might expect one's grades to improve. Mine got worse. What made the situation more disheartening was that I discovered my professors were grooming me to take a job teaching at a black law school in the South.[5] They were trying to steer me into something that I didn't want to do. I came to realize that NYU was a prejudiced place, which supported efforts to keep blacks from integrating southern law schools. My friends studying at Brooklyn Law agreed. Their faculty encouraged them in ways that I wasn't. In fact several students that I knew at Brooklyn Law had transferred from NYU because of racial prejudice. Others left NYU for St. John's.

In 1948, thanks to the help of one of my fellow Tuskegee airmen, I finally bought a car. I wanted a Volkswagen, but ended up getting a Crosley. It was small and economical, about the nearest thing to a Volkswagen that Americans had yet produced. It had four cylinders and got 35 miles to the gallon, but it didn't have a radio or heat. During the winter, even wearing my overcoat I'd be freezing inside. Still, I was able to drive this little car to Texas.

The truth is that around the time I bought the car, my wife and I were experiencing severe marital problems. We'd been drifting apart slowly since the end of the war; now we were reaching a critical point. To give you a small sense of what life was like for me, when I came home after a hard day at school I would want to talk to her about my legal studies and what I was experiencing. But as time went on she became less and less encouraging, less and less supportive. I was stricken by some of the things she'd say. Sometimes she'd snap at me, "I don't know what kind of lawyer you're going to make with *your* attitude!" It was mentally draining to be trying so hard to succeed while receiving so much negativity at home. I ultimately reached a point where I wanted to get a divorce and dissolve the marriage.

In November, I decided that I'd drive to Texarkana to visit my parents and to see my sister's son, Donald. I was also interested in reconnecting with a lady friend of mine whom I'd met as a student at Wiley College. She was now living in Houston working as a schoolteacher, and had actually come up to see me in New York. While driving down the New Jersey Turnpike, I pulled into a diner, or maybe it was café. I needed something to warm me up. My hands felt like icicles on the steering wheel. I thought it would be a good idea to take some hot tea with me to remain warm on my drive. I asked the white man who was serving me if he'd be so kind as to pour some in my thermos, which was still out in the car. He nodded and I walked outside to get it. On the way, I spotted some fruit in the store window across the street. "This would be good to have with me too," I thought, so I walked over to buy some, however, the store was closed. I returned to my car to get my thermos. No sooner had I opened the car door when a man rammed a pistol into my spine and said, "Put your hands up!" "Turn around . . . slowly." I was petrified. I didn't know if he was going to shoot me, torture me, or rob me. He did none of the three. We marched back to the diner where he called the state troopers to come pick me up. When they arrived, my captor began his story, "Officers, I had been told that there was a black man going around, peeping in people's homes." He started to gesticulate, then he spoke again, this time agitatedly, "Where did he go?" "People told me that he went thataway," he said, pointing in my direction. There was little I could do to protest. I was tossed in jail and brought before a judge the following morning.

The man in charge of the jailhouse revealed to me what was going on. "Listen mister," he started. "The man who turned you in is a night watchman working on a commission basis. He's trying to make money. I don't really believe that you were peeping into people's homes, and all that other stuff, but you'd better wait until they can call you into court to pay the fine. Then you'd best get the hell outta here!"

When I appeared before the judge the next day I told him that I hadn't committed a crime. In fact, I hadn't done any of the things that I was accused of. They had the wrong guy. But the man who apprehended me gave the same minstrel-like performance he'd delivered the previous night. The district attorney leaned over and asked me, "Can you make bail?" I sank my head. "No," I replied. I probably had 15 dollars in my pocket.

"Do you know anyone who can pay the 500 dollars?" he inquired. I thought for a minute. My brother Du Bois had recently moved into an apartment in the Bronx. I had lent him some money earlier, so he owed me. I figured that he could repay me by helping me out of this jam. The attorney advised that I plead guilty and pay the fine. I would also be held responsible for paying court costs and the fee for storing my car, which ran 2 dollars a day. In all, I spent ten nights in jail. When the check arrived from Du Bois, I was more than ready to leave for Texarkana. I decided, though, that I didn't want any more trouble. I left my car in a garage and boarded a bus. I picked up my car again in December, but instead of going back to New York, I returned to Texas to stay with my friend in Houston a little longer.

Something about that car brought me bad luck. On the drive to Houston I hit a lamppost and wrecked the car. I probably shouldn't have been speeding in the fog since I could barely see what was ahead of me. The car was uninsured and was a total loss. I had to cut my visit short and took a train back to New York.

In reality, I was still not ready to return. During the ride, I remembered that I had a friend in Pittsburgh, Carl Deck, a light-skinned roommate of mine from Wiley. When we pulled into town, I gave him a call. "My goodness, Virgil, how have you been?!" He was ecstatic to hear from me and suggested that I stop by to meet his wife. She'd also attended Wiley. We caught up on old times, talking late into the evening. I spent the night in their house before heading over to the YMCA the following morning. I hadn't planned on staying in Pittsburgh for long, just enough to catch up with Carl. After a night at the YMCA,

I packed up my belongings and started heading for the train station. Unfortunately, in the rush to leave, I realized that I'd forgotten my zipper bag. Returning to get it turned out to be a grave mistake.

I ran up to the desk attendant and asked for my key. Meanwhile, two police officers, one black and one white, came in behind me. "Turn around sir, nice and slow!" I was taken off guard, but carefully obeyed their orders. "Now, will you come with us please?" I was surprised. What was it *this* time? "What do I need to come with you for?" I fired back. About the only crime I had committed was being new in town. I was thrown in jail and spent much of the first night seething.

The loud shuffling of feet and the sound of people's voices woke me up the following morning. I opened my eyes and put on the hat that I still had with me. A couple of officers opened my cell door. A black police magistrate stepped in, bringing a portable pulpit along with him. He motioned his finger for me to approach, and in a booming voice he said, "Richardson!" I eased out of bed and walked towards him, but I didn't remove my hat. He scowled. I could tell he didn't appreciate this. "You're too damned smart! Sixty days!" I was then carted outside, shoved into a vehicle and driven to the county workhouse.

There were some real criminals in this place. Some were in for 20 years or more. The first thing the police did to me was to remove my clothes and issue my prison outfit. Then I lined up with the others to shave. They give you a razor for this. Stubble had been growing on me for a couple of days, but for the hell of it, I didn't want to shave. I certainly didn't want to lose my mustache. "Hey, I can't do this, it's against my religion!" I said, temporarily converting to the Muslim faith. For that little stunt I was thrown into solitary confinement for ten days. They gave me a supply of two slices of bread, three times a day, along with a metal cup full of water. I slept on a board and a blanket. They searched me, of course. Men going into solitary often wore belts under their prison clothes where they hid tobacco, paper, and cut-up matches. You see, one match can be made into two if you cut it right. The inmates were sometimes generous with their smokes. The blankets that we slept on could be tossed out of our cells, along with a lighted cigarette. Then it could be dragged down along the row of cells so that anyone who wanted could take a smoke. What ingenuity! It took me a while, but I too figured out the secrets of concealing my cigarettes.

After ten days in solitary the warden said to me, "Look Richardson, the state of Pennsylvania has got nothing against you." "It's the city of Pittsburgh that sent you here for vagrancy, and your fine is 25 dollars. Why don't you pay the fine and get out of here?" Of course, when I was arrested my money was taken from me. I didn't have 25 dollars. I started thinking hard about my predicament. "This was precisely the type of case that the NAACP should be involved in,"

I thought. Angry, I snapped back at the warden, "No way! I'm not going to pay the fine because you know that I'm not a vagrant!" That's when they sent me outside to do hard labor, breaking rocks.

There was a mean-looking man in charge who walked around with a cane that had a steel bolt at its base. He looked me over as I walked outside. I was then given a steel hammer and ordered to begin chipping away at a boulder. I protested. "Listen, I've been in the army and I was injured overseas. I can't do anything like that!" I said. Before I could finish getting the words out, they were sending me back to solitary confinement for another ten days.

Exactly half of my time at the county workhouse was spent in solitary. I don't remember the third reason they put me in there, but it was for another ten days. When I was out of solitary, I learned other things about prison life. For instance, what they say about homosexual activity is true. It got to the point where men were fixing themselves up to look like women to get a boyfriend. A group of guys whose job it was to make cloth, or something like that, were especially notorious. When all of us were assembled in the dining hall, these inmates paraded in, all rouged up, with their hair conked straight, looking very effeminate. A few of the prisoners who had been in jail for years were involved in deep love affairs with these men.

When I was finally released I unexpectedly had a fair amount of money. The Army issued a bonus check of 500 dollars to soldiers that had spent more than two years in the service. I had also invested some of my Air Corps pay in a real estate club in New York shortly after my return from the war. The investment had turned over a profit, and suddenly I found myself with nearly 1,000 dollars in cash and checks. In this condition, and with a neatly groomed goatee, I returned to New York to confront my wife and see my two children.

It was a Saturday when I arrived. My wife's mother opened the door and I walked in. I don't recall if I said hello or not. What was foremost on my mind was seeing my boys. I'd missed them dearly while I was away. Aida came into the room and I told her that I wanted to take the children outside. Next door was a concrete playground where kids played handball. I thought we could go over there and play. She gave me an icy stare and said, "No, Charles has to go and visit his teacher today." I paused. For Christ's sake, it was Saturday! What child visits a teacher on the weekend? I took matters into my own hands. I went upstairs and started dressing Charles. He started crying. I looked over at Ray, then I put his clothes on, too. He was smiling. He seemed happy to be going with his papa! Once they were dressed, I took them downstairs. When I got to the door I saw a police car pulling up. I stepped outside with the boys while two white officers jumped out of the car and approached me. I clenched the boys' hands tight. One of the officers pulled me aside and said, "Don't look angry, there's no use. You see, this guy, my friend, wants to beat you." I cooled down. My wife was in the front door crying. My older son started crying, too. I let go of my children's hands as the officers grabbed my arm and walked me to the squad car. I ended up spending the night in jail.

After I was locked away in my cell, another officer looked me in the eyes and said, "Look fella, I know how you feel. But if you want to visit your children, you have to go to family court and get an order because any time you go back there without one, your wife is going to call and we're going to have to bring you back to jail." I sunk my head into my hands. I missed my boys.

When I got out of jail this time, I started living with my brother on 135th Street in the housing project. My time with him was short lived since I really didn't want to get too involved with him and his family or intrude on their lifestyle. My brother was very busy, holding a job first as a Navy machinist, then as a diemaker for an aviation company. Thankfully, I had some friends in Greenwich Village who allowed me to stay for a while. I can't remember the guy's first name, but his last name was Stellar, or Stella. He was a talented black artist who drew portraits of Superman, among other things. His wife, who was Jewish, took samples of his work to the comic book company, and the next thing he knew, he was one of the artists involved in the Superman series.

I tried not to wear out my welcome with my friends either. I cashed my checks and used 200 dollars to buy my first cross-country plane ticket. I had an uncle, Eddie Clardy, who lived in Oakland that I was eager to see. My sister, her two daughters, and her husband were also living in California. I boarded the plane in New York and about 20 hours later, I arrived in Los Angeles. I had two connections, one in Chicago and the other in Denver. This, and the fact that the plane seemed to be traveling only about 140 miles an hour, made the trip a long one.

After a great steak dinner, I headed for Oakland. I'd decided to visit Uncle Eddie before seeing my sister. I had virtually nothing in my possession. Except for money and a few clothes, I left everything behind in New York. Yet, as I was to soon discover, the one thing that I couldn't seem to keep behind me was trouble. Perhaps it was my goatee. In those days, a tightly trimmed goatee was the unwritten sign used to identify black drug dealers. Whatever the culprit, my new round of trouble started not too long after I arrived in California.

One thing that I did do while in Oakland was to purchase another car, a 1929 Ford V8. The previous owner had really fixed her up so that the front seat fell back, creating sleeping space for two. I also bought a fishing pole and some cooking utensils, including an iron skillet. I especially liked my waffle iron, which I could put over any kind of fire. With these supplies I was virtually self-sufficient, able to go anywhere, prepare my own meals, and have a place to sleep at night.

I drove back to L.A. after spending time with Uncle Eddie. Here, I visited my sister's house and then arranged to meet one of my cousin's friends, a guy named Maurice. This is when trouble began again. It was around five o'clock in the afternoon. I'd parked my car and was waiting for Maurice to get off work. After sitting a while, I went to his apartment and knocked on the door to see if he had made it already. I didn't think I'd missed him, but I wanted to be sure. After a few more knocks, I checked with his neighbor who told me that she hadn't seen him return either. I walked back downstairs to wait in the car. All of a sudden, two cops jumped me from behind and said, "Put you hands up! Turn around … slowly!" I hesitated a minute, then obeyed. They walked me out to Central Avenue. I stood there with my hands raised while one cop called the station. The other kept his pistol fixed on me.

I couldn't help but listen to their radio conversation. They weren't talking about anything of importance. They weren't even mentioning why they had apprehended me. Instead they were gossiping about baseball, about the Brooklyn Dodgers! "What the hell was going on?!" I thought to myself. Once again, I had no idea what I'd done. People were walking along the street looking at me like as if I were a common criminal. I was starting to sweat. This is when I began thinking, "I've got to get out of this place, I've got to go anywhere but here!" After about 15 minutes of nothingness, the cop on the radio turned around and said to me, "You can go away now, you're wasting my time."

I was steaming. I almost yelled back, but calmed myself, and replied "Sir, this is a provocation of violence." He glared, started to make a move . . . then left. I got into my car and instead of heading back to my sister's house, or driving up to Oakland, I just followed the highway, heading aimlessly south. After cooling down some more, I decided that since I'd already driven about half the distance to Tijuana, I was going to cross the border into Mexico.

Chapter 7

Bienvenidos à México

"Is there a place I can get a room?" I was in a small store, a mom-and-pop operation that sold cigarettes, beer, snacks, and a few supplies. It was 1950. I didn't speak any Spanish, but my English seemed to be getting me by just fine. I knew next to nothing about Mexico except that Tijuana was supposed to have lots of places to drink, nice cabarets, and excellent whorehouses. When I was a kid growing up in Texarkana, Mexicans used to come and work on the railroad behind our house. My very first image of Mexicans came from these laborers, who would sit squatting around fires, warming up their tortillas on a piece of metal. We all thought that they were strange people, and that these tortillas were huge wafers, like those you eat in church during communion. I also associated Mexicans with the rich cigarette odor of *delicados*. Back in Texarkana, the railroad workers smoked these during their breaks and whenever else they had an opportunity. The smell was so distinctive because of the sour tobacco that was used to make them. Years later, even a mere whiff let me know that someone from south of the border was nearby.

"My sister rents rooms," the storeowner said to me with a thick accent. "You can go by there and tell her that I sent you." He was pointing towards a house along the street. I guess I didn't look that dangerous to him, since he trusted me with his sister, I thought. I made my way over to the building and went inside. After some effort, I managed to explain that her brother had sent me, and I was able to ask if she had any clean beds available. She showed me to my room. Once I settled in, I went outside, bought some cokes and a bottle of rum, and began to relax.

I was not too far away from the cabarets, bars, and brothels that had become the delight of American sailors stationed in San Diego. Once it grew dark, I went out to have a look around town. Just to show you how innocent I was, a man approached me and asked if was interested in buying any cigarettes. Although I mainly smoked a pipe, I told him that I only smoked Camels. His eyebrows furrowed. I continued my walk not realizing then that what he was offering me was marijuana!

My trip to Tijuana was not a long one. I spent just enough time there to familiarize myself with some of the local bars, especially the one that had a reputation for being the longest bar in the world, stretching for an entire "New York City block." After about two days, I grew tired and moved on. What really triggered my decision to leave was the domineering presence of rowdy, white American sailors. I had left the United States precisely to escape these types of people, not to be surrounded by them. So I decided to continue heading southward, towards Ensenada. I picked up a hitchhiker along the way, a young man who couldn't have been more than 22 years old.

Ensenada was close, about 60 miles away. The weather was cool despite the fact it was the month of July. This made our drive a pleasant one. As we rolled along he pulled out a cigarette and began puffing and sucking on it, trying to inhale the smoke. I had never smelled anything like it before—what a pungent odor! I coughed a little, but eventually adapted to the aroma. It was the first time I had seen anyone smoking marijuana!

I dropped him off at a cantina as we pulled into Ensenada. He'd been in town before so I asked him about a place to stay. He directed me to a small motel where I parked and went inside to get a room. On the way in, I noticed another cantina down the hill. I decided that I would I do a little investigating. I'd been in several bars in Tijuana, but I'd never entered a cantina before, which was a different experience. Perhaps the most distinguishing characteristic was that there was food available, and I mean full dinners! I also learned that a lot of business was conducted in cantinas, even in a small town like Ensenada. I drank my first tequila that night and began fraternizing with the local people.

The cantina became a regular spot for me. I was able to communicate both through English and Italian. The year and a half that I'd spent in Italy helped me to master many words and phrases that were close enough to Spanish that I was able to figure out some of the language. I'd also studied Latin in school, which again, served me well in understanding other Romance languages. Through my conversations and my walks about town, I was able to learn that many people earned their living by raising grapes. Others were involved in the fishing industry. Ensenada's main exports were wine and seafood, especially canned sardines.

During one of my cantina stops I met a Mexican farmer who lived ten miles outside of town. We struck up a good conversation and I agreed to give him a ride back to his farm and stay a while. I was excited. As a young boy, visiting my grandfather's farm in Arkansas was among some of my fondest childhood memories. Even as an adolescent I would spend time there. I thought that going out and staying on the farm in Ensenada would recall happier times for me. I saw the visit as therapeutic.

I don't think I was prepared for what I saw, in fact, I am sure that what I experienced there was nothing like my grandfather's farm. The region was undergoing a severe drought. Appreciable rainfall hadn't been measured in nearly five years. Apart from being parched, the farm was desolate. The man lived there almost alone, with his wife and small child. For breakfast they ate beans, tortillas, and strong Mexican coffee, without sugar. Tortillas and beans were also served again for lunch and dinner. The farmer's property was not too far from the ocean, near a cliff. Here, another man lived in a cave with his wife. They earned their living catching lobsters and selling traps. My host took me by for visit. We were greeted warmly and given some of their catch, as well as some dried turtle. We returned to the farm and feasted. But despite its reputed nourishment value, the turtle we ate reminded me of chewing a shoe.

Two or three days later I abandoned my romantic notion of farm life and returned to my motel. I eventually ran into the young man again that I had first picked up in Tijuana. We were both having drinks in my favorite cantina when I noticed that he had his rod and reel with him. Mine was in my car. I asked if he wanted to go fishing.

We walked out to the pier, which ran about 35 feet into the ocean. We pulled out our bait and threw our lines into the sea. He then slipped out one of his now familiar "cigarettes." After he started smoking, I persuaded myself to take a couple of puffs, too. Very soon, the pier began rising up and up! The sky rolled about like a merry-go-round and I was feeling loose and giddy. The waves looked larger than life, rushing up like an avalanche in slow motion, bathing over the pier. The mountains behind us walked closer to shore. Meanwhile, I heard roaring laughter echoing from ear to ear. When I turned around, I saw the spinning face of my young Mexican friend. None of this was funny to me. I staggered up, stumbled back towards my motel and into my room. I was in great distress because of the hallucinations, but now I'd finally done it. I had smoked and I'd inhaled! I also learned my lesson about marijuana.

I soon discovered that there was a boat running from Ensenada to Acapulco. I felt that I had little to return to in the States. In reality, I was still reeling from the harassment that I'd experienced there. I wanted to continue my adventure. But boarding the boat meant that I would have to part with my car. I decided to go back to Tijuana and sell it. Although I had money, I could use extra cash. I ended up getting 75 dollars for my Ford, waffle iron, and skillet. All that I had left were a few clothes and a sleeping bag. I bought a tin suitcase and a zipper bag to carry my polo shirts, pants, socks, and underwear. Then I took a bus back to Ensenada where I boarded the *Maria Dolores* on August 6, 1950.

She was a landing craft of the type used to land our troops in the South Pacific; however, she'd been converted into a passenger boat. The transformation made her resemble a small yacht—steel, with gray paint. As the rowboat approached, taking me to her, I caught a glimpse of a man on board. He had a deep vertical cleavage in the middle of his forehead. It gave him a permanent frown. His cranial groove didn't move up or down as he talked. I studied him in more detail as we got closer. "You could stick a fountain pen on that head!" I thought. When I climbed on board, he introduced himself in fractured English, "Hel-lo, my na-me is Jésus." He was from one of the islands near Ensenada and was traveling with his wife, who was almost nine months pregnant. I tried not to stare as we talked, but I couldn't stop fixating on the unforced intensity of his expression. "Jesus Christ," I said to myself, "with that forehead this man looks like he's about ready to be crucified!"

Another passenger on board was a man named Raúl. Everyone meets a Raúl when they visit a Spanish-speaking country. This one was a young Latin lover, maybe 23 or 24 years old. He was a handsome stud with a superb body, which he flexed vigorously on deck during his daily workouts. He was broke, though, so he was paying his 30-dollar fare by scraping rust off the deck. Raúl spoke excellent English and it was through him that I first learned that people named Jesús are also called "Chucho" in Spanish. This gave me some consolation, since it seemed a little strange that I'd just met Jesus!

We were on board for an eight-day trip, inching towards Acapulco at 10 to 15 knots per hour. The *Maria Dolores* had two diesel engines, which the crew used alternately. While one was running, they would set to repairing the other, keeping the ride seamless and smooth. As for our sleeping arrangements, Chucho, his wife, and two children slept on one side of the cabin, while Raúl and I had bunks on the other. A sheet separated both sleeping quarters, providing at least a hint of privacy. There were bathrooms on board with salt water showers. A dining room featured a cook who served three meals a day. I'd brought a bottle of rum on board, and in the evenings, after Raúl had finished scraping the deck, we'd sit facing east, lounging in the shadows, talking and drinking. Our conversations were both in Spanish and English. He was my first real "teacher," teaching me simple things about basic communication. I had only intended on staying in Mexico for another couple of months, so I didn't think I needed to know too much.

Raúl and I had both gone through some bad experiences with women. We drowned these in evening rum. He told me that some bitch had turned him in to the INS. That's why he had been deported. He'd been living with her for some time when one day, she came home early and found him in bed with her best friend. She snapped. It didn't seem like anything for her to get that angry with, Raúl said, since she was well over 30, but she was furious nonetheless. Raúl was certain that she would return to Acapulco soon, and when she did, he was going to track her down and beat the hell out of her. He was going to take back his clothes, watch, and records. He was angry as only a macho, a Mexican macho man could be. I sat back and listened.

I shared with Raúl some of my experiences in the war. You should have seen the admiration in his eyes. He'd thought that I'd been some sort of hero by serving in the Air Corps. He mentioned that there was a Mexican squadron, called the "Doscientos Uno" (the 201st) which flew P-47s in the Philippines.[1] I was intrigued. But since he hadn't served himself, he couldn't provide more details.

We passed the tip of Baja California and headed southeast towards the Costa Grande, a stretch of coastline running just north of Acapulco. Along the way, we picked up a few more passengers, including a woman and her husband. The new woman on board did not get along with Chucho's wife, and the rest of the voyage was fraught with tension and arguments between the two. Finally, the *Maria Dolores* slowed as we approached the mainland. On August 14, we landed in Acapulco. It must have been a sizzling 114 degrees outside. Raúl didn't disembark, since he still had to finish working on deck, but he gave me the name of a hotel where I could stay. Chucho and I started talking as well, and I found out that he was continuing on towards Mexico City. Before saying our goodbyes, he provided me with contact information, too—giving me his street address, along with the name and address of a woman who rented rooms to young male students. If I was ever interested in visiting the capital, I could surely stay with her. I looked at the information he scribbled. I was definitely interested in seeing the city.

I got a tourist card from Immigration before heading to the hotel. It was located downtown, not far from where we had docked, maybe a couple of blocks. After checking in, I went outside to have a cold beer. What I liked about it was the way they prepared the glass. They placed the beer mug in a freezer so that when it was removed, it would look completely frozen. Then they took the beer out and poured it in the mug. Let me tell you, this is a *very* good way to have a beer on a hot day! After a couple of beers I went back upstairs, took a shower and drifted off to sleep.

I woke up in the dark to the sounds of music outside my window. I stood up and walked over to have a look. There were beautiful dark bodies, women in white skirts and sandals, young men in white pants with guitars, walking toward the beach, singing. Taking my cue from the rhythm, I swayed from side to side, enraptured in the melody. The moment was special. The serenity of the scene and the beauty of the people made a deep impression on me. I would say that this was the first time that I felt a connection with the population and the land itself. Perhaps it was being in the state of Guerrero that brought this on. I later learned that Acapulco was located in Guerrero state, named after Mexico's second president. Guerrero himself was of mixed-race ancestry, and probably had some African ancestors in his bloodline.[2] In the United States, we would have considered him black, but in Mexico, he was a *pardo*, which essentially meant that he was a black and Indian *mestizo*.[3] I also learned, again much later, that the state of Guerrero was one of Mexico's blackest regions. Along with the state of Veracruz on the Gulf Coast, much of the modern black population lives here.[4] Reflecting back on my stay in Acapulco, what I may have unconsciously been experiencing was a sense of homecoming in a foreign land, a return to the curiously familiar; a bond with a population that was racially like, and unlike myself.

From my room I could also see a huge cliff from which young men dove into the ocean from heights of 150 feet. They held a torch in their hands on their way down, which they would throw away just before hitting the water. You could faintly see the splash in the late evening sky. Sometimes a single diver would jump; at other times two or three men would take the plunge simultaneously. Theirs was a real precision event since they could kill themselves if the tide was too low.

I watched Acapulco from my window for a while more before returning back to bed. I eagerly wanted to join the group dancing on the beach, but I didn't feel like I had anything appropriate to wear. Raúl stopped by later that night. He was broke again and wanted some money. I lent him 20 pesos and fell back asleep.

About eleven o'clock I heard loud banging at my door. "Virgil, Virgil, open please." Raúl had returned. He had taken the 20 pesos and won a lot of money playing *cubilete*, at least ten times more than what he'd started with. *Cubilete* is a popular cantina dice game, using a leather cup and five dice. It is truly a game for *machos* and the players demonstrate their manliness through cursing—"*cabrón*" (fucker), "*puta madre*" (whore, bitch), and things like that. That's the *macho* way of talking. Raúl paid me back my pesos and then asked if I wanted to go with him to "Boys Town," the popular red-light district.

We stepped into a cabaret that was playing loud mambo music. Mambo was all the rage then, with Tito Puente's group topping the charts. All these shapely women were there in tight dresses, shaking their hips. Some had a nice caramel complexion, others were lovely Indian women, a few were even chocolate colored. I saw a woman that I liked and danced with her. We squeezed each other and moved around the dance floor. She began grinding her body against mine and things got exciting. I motioned for her to join me in having a seat at my table. Then I invited her to a drink.

While we were enjoying each other's company, a white American merchant sailor who had been sitting at another table, sent a drink my way. The waiter pointed him out to me and I gave the sailor a nod of approval, thanking him for the gesture. Some time later, he came over and struck up a conversation. I don't remember the details, but I do recall him saying in a very apologetic tone, "One day we will discover that the U.S. is a country for both whites *and* blacks." He took a long sip of his drink while I remained silent. I didn't have anything to say in response. Two Americans, one white and one black, had to be all the way in Mexico for us to come to this realization. Something about the situation seemed a little absurd. Back in the States, he might never have had a drink with me, much less sit with me at my table.

I continued living the moment. I offered to buy him a drink, but the woman I was with said "No, don't buy a drink, buy a bottle, because the drink *es muy chico* (is very small) and is more expensive." Drinks were running 5 pesos apiece, while a bottle of rum, coke, and a bucket of ice cost just 15 pesos, or roughly 2 dollars. So I ordered the bottle, poured the American a glass, and went back on the dance floor. He returned to his table.

We danced late into the night and I was becoming ever more enchanted by my woman's company. She let me know that she wanted to sleep with me. I was happy with the idea of spending the night with someone. I took her hand, left a tip, and grabbed our bottle of rum. Instead of going back to the hotel, she led me into a banana grove behind the cabaret. I had never seen a banana plant before. The air was filled with fruit fragrances. Mixed in with the banana plants were lemon and orange trees, whose aromas blended well with the bananas. I followed her to her place, a thatched hut with woven palm fronds for privacy. Opening her door was like entering a scene from *Arabian Nights*. She had candles inside, a bed, and a table. She lit the candles all around the room and we drank some more. In the background we could still hear the music from the cabaret. I had never been in a situation quite like this before. I lit a cigarette, a Mexican brand that I can't recall. Finally, she blew out the candles. There was just enough light from outside for her to undress and get into bed. She was lushly endowed, and young. Her name was Carla.

The next morning she got up and went outside to bathe. She fetched me a basin of water and brought a washcloth. When she came back she told me that she needed to go up into the hills to take her family some money. Every week or so, she brought them goods from Acapulco, like cooking oil, food, and money. Then she returned and continued her work at the cabaret, where she was a dancer and a prostitute. I think I gave her five dollars and a kiss. I returned to my hotel.

My time in Acapulco was brief. It must have been the following day when I decided on going to Mexico City. Raúl told me that if I traveled by bus, it would take nearly 10 to 12 hours to cover the roughly 250-mile distance between Acapulco and the capital. I decided that I would take a plane instead, which cost only about 20 dollars and arrived within an hour or two.

Mexico City was not nearly the bustling urban sprawl that it has become, but it was still a busy place, even then. I gave my cab driver the address that Chucho had left with me and he made a dash for it. It seemed to me that there were no street rules. If someone stepped out in front of us the driver blared his horn furiously and shouted some obscenities, but he didn't alter speed. Remarkably, many pedestrians simply ignored him and kept walking. I surely thought that someone was going to get killed that day, either them or us.

The city I caught glimpses of along the way was beautiful. There were no skyscrapers at the time, and much of the drive took me snaking in and out of streets with decorative, stone colonial buildings, with baroque-looking façades. I saw some new constructions too, but most were only three stories high. The largest building I recall seeing was a hotel that stood maybe six stories tall.

We arrived at Chucho's address on Pedro Romero Street, but no one was home. Apparently, I had beaten him to Mexico City. I asked my driver about the second address on my list, which was the boarding house. It turned out that it was within walking distance, so I paid my fare and went over to 19 Zarco Street on foot.

An old hag answered the door. Her name was Señora Jiménez. By this time I was speaking enough Spanish to ask for a room intelligently. Fortunately, she still had space and took me to one of the empty rooms upstairs. It was huge, about the size of a studio apartment in Manhattan. However, it was only lightly furnished. There was a bed in the middle of the room, a chair, and a dresser in one of the corners. For the bathroom, I had to go to the second floor, where I shared space with two other young men. All of this, including three meals a day and full laundry service, cost me only about a dollar a day. I didn't realize it yet, but I would be calling this place home for the rest of the month of August and part of September. In fact, I would be calling Mexico City my home for the next 47 years.

Chapter 8

From Tourist to Resident—Being Black in Mexico City during the 1950s

In the early 1950s, the black author Ralph Ellison published his highly acclaimed masterpiece *Invisible Man*, about a nameless black character searching for his place in America. While a lot of what Ellison wrote concerning the experience of blacks in America was true, I cannot say that I felt the same in Mexico. Here, I was *always* visible. People always looked at me with admiration, envy, affection, and friendship. I was and became "*un negro.*"

Mexicans are accustomed to giving nicknames to people according to physical characteristics. Virtually everybody has one. A fat man is called "*el gordo.*" A fat woman—"*gordita.*" A blond person is known as "*guero,*" while a black person is "*moreno*" or "*negro.*" Mexicans also use diminutives, so that a "*negra*" (black woman) can also be "*una negrita muy bonita*" (a pretty little black woman). A short person (*chaparro*) becomes "*chaparrito*" (shorty). And using the diminutive with the word mother, "*mama,*" becomes "*mamacita,*" or a very "hot" woman. For me, my blackness made me very visible, but not in a bad way. I can recall walking down the street alone sometimes. On many occasions, young, working-class girls who worked in shops along the street would pass me on their lunch breaks. As they went by, they would make contact with my hands. Actually, they would lightly caress my hands. I would look back, and they would be looking back, too. Working-class Mexicans often thought of blacks as being some kind of "superpeople." According to custom, any man who was especially brave or daring was called "*el negro.*" An especially hard worker was rumored to work like "*un negro.*"

Near Mexico City is a place called Teotihuacan, an ancient city that must have been magnificent during the height of its power.[1] I hadn't been in Mexico a year yet, when my younger brother Morris came down to visit with his new bride.[2] Since they had a car, we decided to take a drive to the archaeological site. What we saw was stunning—two massive pyramids dominated the landscape, the Pyramid of the Sun, which is one of the world's largest pyramids,[3] and the Pyramid of the Moon, equally as impressive sitting atop a hill. I'd never seen anything like this in my life. As we strolled up the Avenue of the Dead (the main thoroughfare of the ancient city), a tremendous sensation of calm overcame me. The only other pyramids that I knew about were those in Egypt, and suddenly, at that moment, being in Teotihuacan made me think about Africa. I looked over at Morris. He was still walking. I gazed back up at the Pyramid of the Sun. Taking a deep breath, I sighed to myself, saying, "Ahhhh . . . at last, I'm home!"

In Mexico I felt liberated for the first time in my life. I felt free! Liberation is a hard feeling to explain and is experienced in so many different ways. Let me start explaining to you what it meant for me by giving you an example. My mother was educated by English pacifists, which deeply affected how my siblings and I were raised. The greatest effect was probably on my sister and me. Growing up, we had access to the radio. But we did not have a single jazz record in our house because mama did not think jazz or blues (which her younger sister loved) was appropriate for us to listen to. It was during my first few months in Mexico when I stumbled upon a public market along the street of the "Niño Perdido" (Lost Child). I discovered a section full of second-hand stores selling records at one peso apiece! I bought my very first jazz record ever in Mexico City. It was a Billie Holliday recording, a 78 with one song on each side. I also bought a record of the jazz All-Stars, including Bill Norris, Charlie "Bird" Parker, and Nat King Cole. I ended up building an impressive collection over the years, which I listened to over and over again with friends or by myself. While I didn't discover jazz in Mexico, you could say that I was now free enough to enjoy, acquire, and appreciate it like never before.

For a number of years Afro-Cuban music had been sweeping through and conquering all of Latin America. People in Mexico City were wild about the mambo, and it wasn't long before I became intoxicated with the rhythm, too. What's more is that I found Afro-Cuban music as relaxing as jazz. In my early years living in Mexico City, there was a young orchestra leader and composer named Pérez Prado who was topping the charts. The *Voodoo Suite*, which came out in the mid-1950s, was perhaps his greatest masterpiece. The man was simply a genius, a real musical innovator! After being forced to leave Cuba in the late 1940s, he had even spent time in Mexico on an extended tour. He wasn't a big man, yet he towered over the music industry. On stage he had an orchestra with a horn section. The percussion instruments included bongo drums, cowbells, and sticks with ridges cut in them. Pérez Prado was so creative that he would sometimes even direct the band with his feet!

Music became my metaphor for liberation. It wasn't just sound, melody, and rhythm that I heard with fresh ears, but it was what I could *do* to music and where I could perform to music that made a difference in my life. The sensation of dancing became powerfully new. In the cabarets, I was intrigued watching different couples gliding on the dance floor to the mambo. I learned this, too. Of course, I had danced in the United States. I had danced in college. We'd even done some "dirty dancing" in the dining hall (which was also Wiley's gymnasium). The girls would spike the punch of the matrons, and when they nodded off the real dirty stuff would begin! But had I truly *danced* before? In the Mexican cabarets, the difference was the total sense of being free. I was free from American racial segregation. I chose my own partners without worrying about the interference of social rules and racial rules. I was free from police harassment. I indulged in the pleasure of dancing, carefree, in the arms of a beautiful woman, embraced together in lovely melody.

It is a little ironic that Afro-Cuban music produced such a sense of liberation for me. Something that I later learned from a friend of mine, José Burmudez, was that all the basic Latin dances had their roots in the slave experience. I don't know to what extent this is true or not, but José would tell me that when the Spanish conquistadors marched through Central America to Venezuela and Colombia, they brought African slaves with them. Each slave had iron rings around their legs. A chain stretched from one leg to the other, connecting both rings. Then another, longer chain stretched from one slave to the next, linking them together. Because slaves were joined this way as a group, in order to move, they had to take steps together—one, two, three—then they would all have to "kick" in unison to move the big, long chain. The mambo, salsa, rhumba, merengue—all of the core Latin dances involve some variation of this basic step—one, two, three, kick![4] Imagine. My musical freedom was attached to the chains of slavery.

What I'd started to learn in Acapulco, but realized even more during my years in Mexico City, was that the deeper I traveled into Mexico and the deeper I plunged into Mexican culture, the more I encountered whites and white Americans who were not like those I'd met in the United States. Whites felt liberated here, too, or at least they were free from being brainwashed by other Anglos to despise blacks. I'd never had a white American friend before, but in September of 1950, I met a man named Roger Denny. He was a World War II veteran and a journalist for a California-based newspaper. In Mexico, he was studying creative writing at Mexico City College. This was a school that offered classes in English and catered mainly to American expatriates, especially G.I.s who enrolled under the G.I. Bill. Denny and I became very good friends.

We met shortly after I'd enrolled at the college. I too had done some writing and had even written a few plays in my spare time after the war. By chance, some time earlier, I'd seen an advertisement for Mexico City College's Writing Center in the English-language newspaper. Eager to improve my education, hone my writing skills, and meet new people, I enrolled.

Denny and I hit it off immediately, soon becoming roommates. In November of 1950 we moved into an exotic, three-bedroom house, situated on a cliff with a magnificent terrace overlooking the city. The home was located in an exclusive and beautiful residential neighborhood called the "Turf Club," about nine miles outside of Mexico City. Inside the gated community lived some of Mexico's most renowned artists and architects, including Orozco.[5] Originally, the Turf Club had been conceived of as being an off-track betting club. Fortunately for us, the plan was never realized.

Denny and I stayed there until January. We eventually had to leave because of the climate. The Turf Club was located about 1,000 feet above Mexico City, and the evening temperatures could get very cold. Although we had a fireplace, it wasn't enough to keep Denny from catching influenza, which nearly developed into full-blown pneumonia. We moved into a nice, new, three-bedroom apartment on Thiers Street, complete with maid service, shortly after leaving the Turf Club. I stayed with Denny for at least another nine months before moving out on my own. About a year later, I finally got the apartment that I lived in for most of my life in Mexico City, on 32 Rio Balsas Street, in the summer of 1952.

Falling in love was another reason why Mexico was so liberating for me. Love was exactly the therapy I needed at this point of my life, with my marriage in question. I had a relationship with a white, Jewish American woman from Los Angeles named Mary Eastman while I was still living with Denny at the Turf Club. Several months later, I had another relationship with a stunningly attractive Mexican woman. Although she looked white, she said her ancestors were black Mexicans and that she had cousins who looked just like me. Her name was Maria Luisa.

They became the two Mary's of my life—quite fitting for me, living in a Catholic country that honored the Virgin of Guadalupe[6] and the Virgin Mary. Let me point out, however, that neither of my Marys were virgins. Eastman remained my girlfriend until the Christmas season of 1950. She didn't live too far from Mexico City College, where she shared an apartment with a German woman who had been an Allied interpreter during the war. One of the good things about Mary Eastman was that she always had plenty of money. After I'd decided to stay in Mexico for the long-term, I arranged for my G.I. checks to be sent to me in Mexico City. But it wasn't until December that I saw my first one come in. I was living rather precariously until then. Mary Eastman helped me with my expenses. Thankfully, our rent at the Turf Club was just 20 dollars a month, cheaper than anything I'd previously paid, so rent didn't present a major hardship. Denny also had a car, so we went back and forth easily between the city and our house. Unfortunately, soon after my first check arrived, Mary Eastman had to return to the States. Our wonderful "tryst" was over just when I was in a position to spend more on taking her about town.

My relationship with Maria Luisa began taking off much later, when I moved into my apartment on Rio Balsas Street. We met through mutual acquaintances—Alicia Mejia and her husband Hector Monjerés, who had been in the diplomatic corps in Chicago. Because of the time they'd spent living in the United States, Alicia spoke perfect English. She also loved jazz. Alicia became one of my dearest and most trusted friends over the years.

It was Alicia, in fact, who first introduced me to Maria. I could tell that Maria liked me from the moment we met. After that, she made it a point for me to see her whenever she crossed the hall of Alicia's building. I was always treated to a *real* good look. Her eyes glowed with excitement when we saw each other. Soon into our courtship she'd made big plans for us. We were going to get married and have a fairytale life together. She would study the piano (which she played) and I would dedicate myself to writing. We'd be a fantastic, artistic couple on the Mexican "bohemian" scene. Our idyllic times together lasted for two years. We actually considered getting married, but our togetherness was just too beautiful to last. Late into our relationship she'd become immersed with family problems and suddenly, she just vanished! I continued keeping in touch with Alicia, but neither of us was ever able to track Maria down.

The first social contact that I made with another black American was on a sightseeing trip that I took to Guadalajara during Christmas 1950. I'd probably been in the city for about a day when I saw two Americans, one black and the other white, driving around in one of those Nash cars that had become popular in the United States. When they spied me looking at them, they stopped. "Come on, get in," they said. The black guy was immaculately dressed, wearing wing-tipped shoes, argyle socks, a Brooks Brothers suit, a button-down shirt, and a fancy tie. He looked the part of an aristocrat. His name was Cole. I later found out that Amos was the son of a West Indian man and had learned to cook in the military, where he had attended the army cook and baker school. He was also a communist, but of the variety that liked to joke that it was not Stalin's policy to make it possible for Russians to drink more vodka, but to sip more Western champagne! The white guy was a Jewish man named Abner. Both had come to Guadalajara with big dreams and big hopes, but with little money.

Fortunately, I had enough to give them a few dollars for their pockets and a bit more to get some food and gas. I also put them up in my hotel for the night, one of the best hotels in the city.

I went down to pay the bill the next morning. Amos and Abner were out loading the car. As I left the hotel to join them, the bellhop rushed out yelling and shaking his fist, "*Ladrones! Ladrones!* (thieves)." "Hey, give me that bag back there, quick," Abner shouted. As I reached over to get it, I caught glimpse of a collection of beautiful, broad towels stuffed inside, laced with intricate embroidered designs. These rascals had taken all the towels they could get from our hotel rooms! Since they were virtually broke, they were probably hoping that they could take these and sell them somewhere. Some security guards started chasing us. By now, we were on the road, bumping along a rugged highway full of potholes. Looking back, I could see that they were gaining ground, but having difficulty maneuvering. Abner floored the accelerator. There must have been something else in the bag, or otherwise they would have stopped their pursuit. In a frenzy, Amos started throwing the towels onto the road, and finally, the bags themselves. We eventually got onto a stretch of highway where we could speed up enough to get away. "I'll be damned," I thought to myself. I was at a loss for words. We headed south towards Mexico City.

Amos and Abner ended up getting an apartment located on Avenida Veracruz, about two blocks from the Paseo de la Reforma, one of Mexico City's primary boulevards. It was a nice two-bedroom place with a splendid view. My good friend Alicia lived right across the hall, so I continued to see these guys frequently. Some years later, however, Amos eventually left and went to San Francisco.

It was in 1952, or at least in the early 1950s, that I also met Everette Somersille, another black American of West Indian ancestry. Everette's father, who was from St. Thomas, had died suddenly, leaving his son to take charge as household head. Using the G.I. Bill, Everette came to Mexico to attend the School of Dentistry at the National Autonomous University (UNAM). Through the Bill, many G.I.s found themselves in a unique position to continue their education after the war. But they virtually overwhelmed the American higher educational system, especially in fields like dentistry and medicine. Like so many others, Everette took the option of attending a foreign university and ended up in Mexico City.

Everette and I became good fishing buddies, catching trout and carp in the waters surrounding Mexico City. Like myself, Everette experienced a tremendous sense of freedom in Mexico, which is probably why he has never left. He once wrote me a letter saying that the day he crossed the border a man told him, prophetically, "You're free in Mexico." That couldn't have been truer, given the circumstances of the time. Everette's highly successful dentistry practice situated in the heart of Mexico City probably could not have been achieved in the United States during the 1950s and 1960s. His home, a Frank Lloyd Wright-inspired mansion located in the mountainous suburbs of the capital, was certainly out of reach for most blacks living north of the Rio Grande during his day.

Black Americans were not the only blacks living in Mexico City. I ran into three black Panamanians, José Bermúdez, Prince Clemenceau, and Bill Ford, all in the early 1950s. José claimed to be pursuing a humanities degree at the UNAM when I first met him. The university was based in downtown Mexico City[7] at the time, and he was living in a room the size of a broom closet in the vicinity of the school. Since I had three bedrooms in my apartment, I offered him my extra bed. All he had to do was buy blankets, sheets, and a pillow. Later on, when we got to know each other better, I started asking him to contribute 30 dollars a month towards the rent.

José had what you would call "classic" African features. He was tall and skinny with high cheekbones that showed through his skin so boldly you could literally see much of the bone structure of his face. He had been a cook on a Panamanian ship before coming to Mexico. It wasn't long before I also discovered that José was a great liar. He was so convincing and artistic with his tales that I considered him a tremendous actor. Sometimes when we went out he claimed to everyone that he was an American major league baseball player—Marvin Williams. He manipulated his blackness and his foreignness to get some undeserved attention. Another act that he had mastered was pretending to be Jewish. He was determined to use his "Jewishness" to land a rich, Jewish wife. He had his eyes set on the daughters of the Cohen family, who owned a supermarket chain in the city. One of their stores was located in front of my apartment. José got to know the Cohens, even endearing himself to them, until he wrote a phony check that made him lose all credibility.

José ended up dating a fat, Spanish woman who must have weighed at least 200 pounds. She'd been a .50-caliber machine-gunner during the Spanish Civil War, which is a tremendously heavy piece of equipment![8] Hearing her talk, the gun weighed nothing; she would fling it over her shoulders and tote it like a loaf of bread. It was easy to imagine this seeing how she greeted José with her big bear hugs. She would squeeze him like a dishrag until he would almost disappear into her chest!

Among other things, José was a teacher. He spoke fine English and started giving classes for extra income. But he lost a great deal of his money betting at the racetrack. Things got so bad that he started failing to make the rent. He tried to make up for it with me at the cabarets. We frequented a spot called "The Swing Club," where we'd order rum and coke and make passes at the *señoritas*. We also danced. Thanks to José, I was able to learn the basic Latin dances. José sang too. He would occasionally get up and sing "Babalu," an old hit made famous by mambo king Desi Arnaz, Jr., about a deceased man who loved women and was loved by them in return. José's wonderful voice had the women in Mexico City swooning.

I don't recall the first time I met Bill Ford, but we became good friends over time too. He was a dentist with a German-Mexican wife. Her mother was a German *mestiza*, and her father was Mexican. She was big and very attractive. In fact, Angelita was much taller than her husband. They had two sons together, one who was dark and nicknamed "*el negrito* [the little blackie]," and the other who was younger and light-skinned. The more talented of the two boys was the younger son, who became a ventriloquist and eventually moved to Canada.

Bill and his family moved to the small town of Tenancingo located about 60 miles west of Mexico City. Today the town probably has about 100,000 people. It was far smaller back then. The family became well respected and Bill went on to become one of the primary dentists in town. People would line up for appointments at his office (which was his house) but oftentimes they wouldn't have money to pay. They gave him chickens, eggs, milk, and meat instead. Needless to say, Bill never lacked for basic necessities.

Prince Clemenceau (named after the famous French statesman) was another character altogether. The first time I saw him he was walking the streets of downtown Mexico City, near the Bellas Artes building.[9] Like Everette and Bill, he too was involved in medicine, and had recently graduated from medical school at the UNAM. After graduation, students are supposed to give six months of service to the government. This is known as the *servicio social*. Clemenceau was involved with fulfilling his when we first met. In any case, he certainly was an eyeful! He strutted down the boulevard wearing one of those big brimmed hats they used to wear back in the forties in New York City. He also had on a pair of shined-up shoes that also looked like throwbacks to the forties. He was suited up and had on a long overcoat. Hanging out of his pocket, painstakingly misplaced, was his stethoscope. Make no mistake about it, he was advertising himself flamboyantly! Behind him trailed his wife, a Mexican *mestiza*. Another guy, a black who I later learned was American, pulled up next to Clemenceau in a Cadillac convertible. He and his wife, who had been a nurse, had recently moved to Mexico City from Detroit, where he'd been selling drugs. Between the two of them, they had stolen enough cocaine from her hospital to buy a fancy car and reestablish themselves in Mexico. They didn't speak Spanish. Clemenceau, like all the Panamanians that I'd met, spoke excellent English as well as flawless Spanish. When the Cadillac pulled up,

Clemenceau hopped into the back with his wife and started riding around town. When they stopped in traffic, Clemenceau yelled out in Spanish to passersby, "Look, this is my chauffeur, and the other woman, she is my maid." The owners of the car didn't know what the hell Prince was saying. I was deeply amused.

Somehow, Clemenceau convinced the guy from Detroit to give him 3,500 dollars in order to buy a house for him. Clemenceau knew a woman who was selling a place in Colonia Churubusco and proceeded to purchase the property. With another 500 dollars, he bought a Frigidaire. Mexican kitchens were made so small back then that refrigerators couldn't fit in them easily. Clemenceau ended up putting it in the living room, of all places. Regardless, the house was quite nice, with a private stairway to a separate bedroom, a living room, an open area, and a second bedroom beyond the kitchen.

Clemenceau was clever. He knew that a person had to become an *inmigrante* (immigrant status) to own property in Mexico, and so the man from Detroit, who would eventually have to go back to the United States, would end up losing his house. When the guy finally realized what was happening to him, he got in touch with me and asked me if I would move into the home and stay there for six months. I wouldn't have to pay a dime. He just wanted me to take possession of the property so that Clemenceau wouldn't be able to move in. I wasn't living on Balsas Street yet. It looked like a pretty good deal.

I took my things with me. By that time I had acquired a run-down typewriter, a record player, and five tailored suits. I'd never had so many tailored suits before in my life, but it was easy and cheap to buy material on the black market. I also had a coat, a nice sport coat tailored from fine tweed woven in Tlaxcala.

I lived better in Churubusco than I had ever lived before, but it wasn't long before I got into a conflict with Clemenceau. I'll never forget the astonishment I felt one day, as I was walking along the street trying to catch the bus. A car suddenly pulled up beside me and stopped. The driver turned and asked, "Are you Mr. Virgil Richardson?" He spoke perfect English. "Yes sir, I am," I replied. "I am with the Mexican Secret Service, will you get in please?" My heart skipped a beat. I looked around. There was a man walking towards me holding up a newspaper. Quickly, he put it down. Meanwhile, another man was coming up behind me. I was being followed but I hadn't realized it. Reluctantly, I got into the car. The other two men climbed in, too. That's when the secret service agent informed me that he had a warrant for my arrest.

"Are you armed?" he asked. I wasn't. "Dr. Clemenceau informed us that you were armed and dangerous. He told us that you sell drugs and are a homosexual." I couldn't believe my ears! That liar! That's when I started to explain the whole ordeal about the house and how he had tried to finagle it for himself. "I understand," the agent stated, "but we still have to act because of this warrant."

I was taken to the police station and turned over to the local authorities. The agent told me that he would take care of Clemenceau, whatever that meant. In the meantime, I was sent to jail, albeit for a very brief visit. Thanks to Clemenceau I opened my arrest record in Mexico.

Some of the other blacks that I met in Mexico during the fifties were Americans. In 1952, I remember running into a guy from Chicago, Richard Evans, who had a sidekick that seemed to always wear a cap pulled down over his eyes. Evans was tall, about six-foot-six, and had come to Mexico to learn the art of bullfighting. He had big plans of being a *matador*. The pair had driven down in an old convertible and spent a good deal of time practicing their fighting on farms outside of Mexico City. Oftentimes, they would sneak onto property illegally. When there was no bull, they would use cows. Cows are much smarter than bulls and don't fall for the tricks of a *matador*. I recall one incident where Evans went up and slapped a cow in its face in order to make it angry enough to go at his cape. I don't know if these guys ever realized their dreams, since becoming a bullfighter requires a long apprenticeship. You also have to save up enough money to buy what they call a *traje de luz*—a bullfighter's suit, cap, and sword. Still, these two made an interesting pair.[10]

A man named Milton Redi came down with plans of striking it rich in Mexico. He and his wife owned a house in Fort Huachuka, Arizona, not far from the Mexican border. After visiting Mexico, they sold their home in order to purchase a farm outside of Mexico City. Milton, who had never lived or worked on a farm before, was planning on growing radishes! It was a foolish plan and it wasn't long before he was swindled again. His Mexican business partner persuaded him to buy nearly 2,000 acres of farmland in the state of Veracruz, where the topsoil was supposedly a meter deep and extremely fertile. Milton was going to grow three crops a year, or so he thought. Milton was crazy. He bought the land, sight unseen!

The more successful black entrepreneurs in Mexico included men like the Jones brothers, George and Edward, who came to Mexico City during the 1940s. They had been in the numbers business in Chicago before it was taken over by Arthur Flegenheimer, also known as Dutch Schultz, the notorious Chicago gangster. Taking their money with them, the Jones's fled to Paris before resettling in Mexico during World War II. According to rumor, they had millions of dollars to invest when they arrived. They started several businesses in downtown Mexico City, one of which was located in the historic district, directly across from the famous "House of Tiles," Sanborn's Restaurant.[11] They owned a second store near the intersection of Insurgentes and Reforma avenues, which specialized in painted cloth and traditional folkloric Mexican dress.

Carter was another successful, enterprising black American. An ex-Marine, Carter came after the war and helped establish the Mexican American Institute, a school specializing in English language instruction for Spanish-speakers. He had also written an influential textbook used by the institute. Unfortunately, Carter got caught up in institute politics and became a casualty. During the 1950s, or maybe it was in the 1960s, a vocal Jewish American faction pressed for control over the institute's administration. Carter was pushed out of his position and relocated to Veracruz, where he was forced to teach at a reduced salary, with less prestige.

John Williams, a dentist who was originally from Trinidad, made a name for himself through his professional practice. Mexicans, particularly the working class, were crazy about having gold in their mouths, whether they needed it to repair their teeth or not. John gave them what they wanted and stayed busy all of the time. He also speculated in the commodities market, where he made a fortune. Perhaps his most lasting influence was as an inventor. Holding a degree in chemistry from McGill University, Williams used his scientific talents to successfully create a number of popular household cleaning agents that were sold in a variety of Mexican supermarkets. John was one of the few blacks I knew that was able to purchase his own plane, which he kept parked at Mexico City Airport. He took me up a couple of times. He was fond of performing dangerous stunts—low altitude acrobatics. He used his plane to fly back and forth to Trinidad. Through his trips, he managed to continually keep in touch with his mother country.

A singing trio, two black guys and a white man from the States, hit it big in Mexico City in the early fifties. I can't recall the white man's name, but one of the blacks was named Eddie and was from New York. I believe that he had some shady connections. However, this didn't diminish his superb talent as a guitarist and a singer. The other black, Jim Weaver, was married to a white American nurse and lived in the suburbs. We became more intimately connected later, but in the early fifties, I knew these guys mainly through their performances and through casual conversations, although Eddie and I sometimes got together for drinks. Eddie wasn't married and always had plenty of money from performing. He was also a local celebrity. This made him great company. In any case, his group performed regularly at a piano bar called the Cadillac Restaurant and were in great demand elsewhere in the city.

One night after being out with Eddie, I returned to the place that I'd been house-sitting in Churubusco. It couldn't have been later than 10 o'clock. I opened the door, as usual. All the lights were out. I walked into the living room and immediately noticed that the Frigidaire was gone. My radio was gone. I ran upstairs and my typewriter was gone. My five suits were gone. Everything of value that I owned was gone. I didn't have a telephone, so the next day, I paid a visit to a lawyer that I'd met sometime earlier, when I was trying to help my friend find a way to outsmart Clemenceau. Together, we went to the police station to report the robbery. I didn't dare go to the U.S. embassy. They wanted to stay clear of such matters in Mexico. If Americans had a problem, their best bet was to go straight to the police or to the British Embassy, which had plenty of experience in getting people out of jams and provided all kinds of help to Americans, sort of as a favor for helping England during the war.

It was pretty well known at the time that the police were involved in robbing people's homes. They were rumored to steal things like radios and typewriters, so I suspected it might have been a police job. Still, I wanted to officially report the crime. As we were filling out the paperwork, an officer asked me if I would come with him to his office. I starting following, when, unexpectedly, another officer wheeled around and grabbed me by the arm. Holding on real tight, he marched me out the backdoor and down the steps. The next thing I knew, I was being locked up in a cell. My intuitions were probably right. The cops had committed the crime and were trying to cover up for it. I was jailed because I had a prior arrest, they said, and they needed to detain me. But truth be told, I was being warmed over for reporting the robbery.

They confiscated my wallet, which had about 1,000 pesos in it. Then the warden looked at me, as I lay helpless in the cell. "Hey, *señor*, if you want to sleep on something besides the cold concrete floor you can buy some newspaper from us," he taunted, with a chuckle. They had just taken all of my cash. I started having a helpless feeling in this strange and different country that I now thought I barely knew.

My lawyer finally decided to place a call to the American Embassy, trying to explain what had happened. It was probably both a good and bad move. Sometime later, a man showed up from the FBI, asking me questions about people I knew in Mexico City. Maybe you've heard about the Hollywood Ten? They consisted of a group of ten Hollywood screenwriters who refused to testify before the Dies Committee in 1947 [also known as the House Un-American Activities Committee], to face questions about possible communist ties and affiliations. You have to remember that all of this was happening during the heyday of the McCarthy era. In trying to get out of testifying, the Ten pleaded the First Amendment, instead of the Fifth. This was their mistake. They thought they could gain judicial immunity by using the First Amendment's freedom of speech clause, but instead they were issued prison sentences and were blacklisted from working in Hollywood. Probably the most famous of the group was Dalton Trumbo, who wrote *Spartacus*, and was among the wealthiest screenwriters in Hollywood.[12]

In any case, the FBI agent started asking me about some of them. While not officially a member of the "Ten," I knew John Bright, who had moved to Mexico after being blacklisted in 1951, and who had gained notoriety for his work depicting gangsters, especially in the film *The Public Enemy* (1931). Like many of us, he had gone to Mexico City College on the G.I. Bill, and became a rather good friend of mine. Bright had a wife and two children with him, so he got 105 dollars a month from the army. I had spent quite a bit of time at their house. Reluctantly, I answered the agent's questions and was released shortly afterwards.

"Here's your wallet and here's your money," an officer said as I was ready to leave. I opened the billfold and counted the pesos. At the same time, I began to fume. Funny. I wasn't so angry with the police as I was at Clemenceau. I can't confirm it, but I have always believed, in fact I am almost certain that he was responsible for having me robbed. He had the connections and he definitely had the motive. A few days after my arrest I appeared in court on some other allegations that Clemenceau had raised against me. He'd told the judge that I had once threatened him physically, and that I had called his wife a "goddamned son of a bitch!" The whole ordeal was a fiasco, and the judge, a woman herself, dismissed the charges. For the six months that I was in Churubusco, Clemenceau found ways to make my life a living nightmare!

I finally moved into my apartment on Rio Balsas Street, several months after leaving Churubusco. At this time, another black American entered my life, a man named Ralph Scott. He lived near me, behind an expensive apartment/hotel complex on the corner of Rio Balsas. He'd come to Mexico with a man named Alfred Stern; he'd worked as a chauffeur and a timekeeper at Stern's factory in Connecticut. Stern was well-to-do, owning a shop in addition to several factories in the States. But the Dies Committee had gotten after him and his wife for illegally helping to bring a group of Hungarian refugees to the United States Fleeing the country, they stuffed Alfred in a wardrobe trunk, drove him to Texas, and then put him into the back of a private plane that they flew from San Antonio. All of this was done in utmost secrecy.

Mrs. Stern, the daughter of the ex-American ambassador to Germany, had a lover who was a painter. Ironically, it was her lover who helped the Sterns to escape the country. Shortly after their arrival in Mexico, he even provided them with temporary shelter. Finally, Ralph, Alfred, and his wife moved into a place near my new apartment. Theirs was a wild but successful effort to avoid the clutches of anticommunism back home.

Ralph was leaving a lot back in the States. He had made good money there, not just in the factory, but working on the side as a chauffeur and butler during the war. This money was paid to him "under the table," tax-free. After the war, he bought himself a Cadillac convertible, which he used to cruise around Harlem. He used to describe to me how he had a "chick" on his right side, a bottle of Scotch in the glove compartment, and he'd be "Cadillac-ing" down Seventh Avenue in Harlem, with the top down. Few blacks had the cash to do this at the time, so he was truly living "in style."

Ralph didn't fully understand the scope of the Sterns' political problems until well after arriving in Mexico. Because of Ralph's relationship to Alfred (and because Alfred had managed to keep Ralph out of the war), he walked around Mexico City calling Stern "The Boss." I couldn't help but to laugh sometimes at this silliness. It wasn't long before Ralph picked up a girlfriend, a German woman who was actually seeing my other friend, Amos, at the same time. None of this was too serious, though, and I think they both knew they were sharing the same woman.

I had a spare room and decided to rent it out to Ralph. I threw an extravagant party at my place one evening, one of countless memorable soirees over the years. A stunning Mexican woman named Conchita was there. She was a nurse at the army hospital, married to a soldier. Throughout the evening, I could tell that Ralph was entranced by her. He kept a fixated stare on all of her movements. He kept talking, fidgeting, and rustling up close to her, doing everything possible to be as near as he could. Looking like a puppy, Ralph fell madly in love that night.

Ralph wasn't the only one. In fact, I had starting inviting Conchita regularly to my parties because Bill Ford was very interested in her. But Ralph was insistent with me; he simply *had* to have her. With my arm half-twisted, I decided to pay a visit to her house, a shack in a poor section of the city.

Her small son was playing when I arrived. I looked around at the makeshift walls and the sagging roof. It looked to me like she could have a much better life. When we finally sat down and started to have a conversation, I explained how crazy Ralph was about her. "I hope you can make Ralph happier here," I said to her, thinking about all that he had recently been through. Ralph wasn't at all pleased with his life as fugitive. He wanted a fresh start, distanced from the Sterns. Somehow, I managed to convey this to Conchita.

Her marriage was not the best, and eventually, Ralph ended up convincing Conchita's husband to get a divorce so that he could marry her himself. The man agreed, under the condition that Ralph pay him off. I don't know exactly how much was exchanged, but Ralph "bought" himself a beautiful bride, whom he loved dearly. They had a daughter together and then a son. Ralph was deliriously happy, despite Conchita treating him like a dog.

With Ralph married, I had the apartment to myself, but not for long. Between parties, guests, and renters, there was near-constant activity at 32 Rio

Balsas. Getting this apartment forever changed my life. It was an address I kept for the next 45 years. In no uncertain terms, Rio Balsas became my home. Because I had a fixed address for so long, expatriates and foreigners coming into the city would always stop by. I became an integral part of the American expatriate social scene, for blacks and whites alike. Reflecting on it, it seems a little ironic. The apartment was located not far from the U. S. embassy. I'd come so far from the United States to be so intertwined with the social network of American citizens, even if it was in Mexico City. Of course, the big difference was that when they came by my house they were brought into my world of friends, contacts, and relationships. Newcomers were introduced to Mexico on my terms.

Photograph of Virgil Richardson in army uniform, Oakland, California, 1941.
From Mr. Richardson's personal collection.

Movie poster from **Su Excelencia** (1966) depicting Virgil Richardson as the Ambassador of Zambombia and Mario Moreno Reyes (Cantinflas) as an embassy worker from the Republic of Los Cocos. Photo reproduced courtesy of the Mr. Mario Moreno Ivanova and Posa Films International, S.A.

Movie still from **Su Excelencia** (1966) depicting Virgil Richardson as the Ambassador of Zambombia and Mario Moreno Reyes (Cantinflas) as an embassy worker from the Republic of Los Cocos. Photo reproduced courtesy of the Mr. Mario Moreno Ivanova and Posa Films International, S.A.

Mr. Virgil Richardson in his apartment in West Columbia, Texas, 1999. Photo taken by author.

Virgil Richardson, his wife, Aida Harrison Richardson, and their two sons, Ray and Charles, New York City, 1948. From Mr. Richardson's personal collection.

Mr. Richardson and his son Charles, taken in the Bronx shortly after his return from WWII, April, 1945. From Mr. Richardson's personal collection.

Aviation Cadets at Tusekgee Army Flying School, Class 43-E. From Mr. Richardson's personal collection, Yearbook of the Tuskegee Army Flying School and AAF 66th FTD, 1942.

Training planes of the type used to instruct the Tuskegee Airmen. From Mr. Richardson's personal collection, Yearbook of the Tuskegee Army Flying School and AAF 66th FTD, 1942.

Mr. Richardson and his son Ray in front of Virgil's apartment in Mexico City, 1969. From Mr. Richardson's personal collection.

Virgil Richardson after graduation at Tuskegee, 1943. He is shown wearing his wings, officer's cap and summer uniform. From Mr. Richardson's personal collection.

Virgil Richardson's 1938, Wiley College yearbook picture. From Mr. Richardson's personal collection.

The Wiley College Biology Club, 1938. Virgil Richardson is located on the top row, fifth from the left. The attire gives a good indication of what it was like to attend a "silk stocking" school. From Mr. Richardson's personal collection.

Areceli, a flamenco dancer in Mexico City, was one of Virgil Richardson's girlfriends in the mid 1950s. This picture was taken by Virgil shortly after they met at a party in May, 1956.

Virgil Richardson reading a script for an American Negro Theater production on WNEW, New York City, 1945. From Mr. Richardson's personal collection.

Troops being reviewed at Tuskegee Army Airfield, 1942. Not only were airmen trained at the base, but all types of colored soldiers, including military policemen, supplymen, etc. From Mr. Richardson's personal collection, Yearbook of the Tuskegee Army Flying School and AAF 66th FTD, 1942.

Chapter 9

Livin' and Workin' the Mexico City Scene

My experiences at Mexico City College put me into contact with a whole group of Americans, many of whom were progressive thinkers and liberal-minded when it came to race, like my old roommate Denny, but a few still couldn't shake off their old, constrained way of seeing the world. Using the G.I. Bill, I started classes at the Writing Center in September of 1950.[1] The woman in charge was Margaret Shed, a short-story writer who had come down from U.C. Berkeley with two of her teaching assistants.[2] I wrote a piece for her class entitled *Delilah, Delilah*, which was intended to be a parody on the biblical Sampson and Delilah story. The protagonist was a woman with beautiful hair, but with snagged teeth who worked in a Japanese restaurant. There was another main character, a street vendor who sold curlers from a wig on a wooden mannequin. Once he met Delilah, however, he imagined how successful he would be if he could somehow use her as his mannequin instead. He approached her with his proposition, but she adamantly refused. Distraught, the man went on a drinking binge. In a stupor, he cut her hair off. This was the basic plot.

One of Margaret's assistants read the piece and thought it was very good. Afterwards, Margaret invited me to join her small group of "outstanding" students. She wanted us to explore all kinds of phenomena, social issues, and sensory experiences. We were preparing to become master craftsmen and I was excited about this special opportunity to learn some of the intricacies of the art of writing. One day, however, Margaret walked in class and said, "For this session, we're going to explore the menace of the black man in society. We are very fortunate to have Virgil Richardson here with us. Virgil, can you please tell us something about this?"

I was startled. My fellow students were probably startled, too. It was like someone had thrown a glass of cold water in my face. The class got real quiet. I didn't look at anybody. I just started mumbling something. When I got back to my apartment, I thought of all the things I could have said and of all the anger I could have displayed. It was too late to do anything now. Thankfully, it was still early in the winter quarter. I quickly withdrew from all my classes at the Writing Center and took up painting and photography.

In the spring quarter, mainly because the college administration informed me that I needed one more course at the Writing Center to receive my G.I. check, I enrolled in "Manuscript Analysis." Much to my surprise, some very interesting developments had taken place since I'd left. Margaret's husband, who was an advertising executive in the States, had been indicted for helping the Taiwanese ambassador to Washington smuggle five million dollars into Mexico. The U.S. authorities had persuaded the Mexican police to cooperate in their investigation and stage the arrest. He was taken into custody at the end of the quarter. Everyone was shocked, particularly Margaret's teaching assistants, who were very close to her. How could this have happened to a Berkeley professor, they thought? In the back of my mind, I was laughing. "Who's the *real* menace to society?" I wondered.

I studied under the G.I. Bill until 1952. That's when the funds ran out. Because of my bad knee, I qualified for 30 percent disability—I was bringing in something like 50 to 75 dollars a month, but I needed more to survive. A couple of strokes of good luck saved me. My friend John Bright had written a screenplay for a motion picture based upon a novel by the enigmatic, anarchist German writer B. Traven. The novel was called *Rebellion of the Hanged* and detailed the plight of Indian mahogany workers in southern Mexico who had led a rebellion during the Mexican Revolution. The Indians were forced to cut down a certain number of trees, or face the punishment of being hanged by their thumbs!

John wrote the screenplay. It had a Spanish soundtrack and Pedro Armendáriz, one of the best screen actors in Mexico, played the lead. It was released as *La Rebelión de los Colgados* sometime in 1953–1954.[3] Of course, they wanted an English soundtrack for the film. Through friends, I had gotten to know some of the directors at Churubusco Studios and they liked my voice. I was offered the job of dubbing *La Rebelión* into English. I did my work well and got paid handsomely.

In fact, dubbing was probably far more lucrative than acting because you get paid by the number of "loops" that you do. A loop is a part of film that they clip off for you to voice over. The loop has the picture of the character, and you perform the dialogue so that it is more or less timed to fit the movement of the actor's mouth. This has to be done repeatedly until you get it right. It is difficult work. You have to improvise all kinds of sounds to fill up empty space. A lot of things make it highly technical. But after doing several loops, they pay you according to the number you've completed.

My success with *La Rebelión* immediately led to other dubbing projects. I was being called for all kinds of Mexican films that were being remade for American television. They were particularly fond for having me do the "macho" roles. I have no idea how many films I dubbed over the years, since I rarely saw the finished products. I didn't stop dubbing until a cataract developed in my right eye which prevented me from reading as well as I would have liked. This was after 1989.

Between 1955 and 1957, the series *Sheena, Queen of the Jungle* began shooting in Mexico City. Thanks to my connections from doing dubbing work, I got involved with the series as an actor. Each episode's plot featured a six-foot-tall white girl, played by Irish McCalla, running around Africa with a chimpanzee. She would jump into the bushes and break up tribal fights. All of us on the set had a good laugh about this. You can just *imagine* what we thought went on in the bushes!

It was a successful series for me because I played so many roles, but they all basically amounted to the same thing. I was the "bad African" who played tricks on my tribal members to get the white man's gold.[4] There was another featured white actor in the cast, a man who played a hunter. Then there were two chimps. It was amazing to me how well they got paid—the chimps, that is. They made more money than the whole cast put together, about 1,500 dollars a week! The trainer got another 500 dollars. He would have to smack the chimpanzees to make them do things, like type on a typewriter or shave. But the trainer cried when he was forced to hit them.

Around 1955, I also developed a close acquaintance with a white American named Scott who was a cartoonist. He called me to join him on a project he was working on with the Mexican newspaper *Excelsior*. Scott was sent cartoons from a company in New York called *Laughs Inc.*, which he reworked for a Mexican audience. Since my Spanish was pretty good at this time, he would pass them along for me to translate. Although I spoke well, translating English jokes into idiomatic Spanish was a whole different affair. I started learning Spanish all over again through this project. I came to really perfect my knowledge of the language. Sometimes the humor of the jokes had to be changed significantly. I recall one cartoon in which a football coach instructed his team on how to run a special play, "You take out the guard, and you take out the center." "*I'll* take out the cheerleader." When we did it in Spanish I made the football team into a soccer team. Since there were no cheerleaders in Mexico, I changed the cheerleader to "Mrs. Gómez." Mexico City had a good laugh!

When we were finished reworking the cartoons we took a stack of them over to *Excelsior's* comic magazine, a publication called *Ja-Ja*. We sold them for a dollar apiece to Licenciado Colmenares, who was an assistant editor.[5] Each week they were published and sold on the streets of Mexico for a peso. I would get a copy for myself. On each cartoon my initials appeared, V.R. Unfortunately, Scott didn't live long. He'd suffered a back injury during the war and underwent surgery in Mexico City. He passed away shortly after the operation. I still managed to keep up with the cartoons, taking them to Colmenares myself. Licenciado Colmenares eventually started a publication of his own called *Parisian*, which continued to buy my cartoons.

As I started finding more work, my social life became as active as ever. In 1955, I frequented a jazz spot close to my house (actually a store) called the Bob Morales Record Shop. The jazz scene wasn't great in Mexico City, but enough talent came through to keep it interesting. That year a black quartet toured the city from Houston. I met them one day as they were playing at the shop. The pianist was a guy called "Candy Green," who also sang the blues. "Shake, rattle and roll!" was one of his favorite expressions. He caused great commotion with his animated performances. Candy couldn't read music, but boy, could he could play! He eventually became famous. The group's bass player was from Michigan. There was also a drummer and a lead singer in the group, a big man with a stout stomach.

In the audience one afternoon was an attractive redhead who struck up a conversation with me. Somehow, she immediately knew that I was American and started speaking English. Her name was Heidi Mahler, of Swiss-German descent, but born in Mexico. After attending the German High School in Mexico City, she'd done undergraduate work at Reed College and had gotten a Master's degree from Berkeley. I guess this is where she had gotten acquainted with jazz.

We started talking at the jam session but ended up taking things back to my apartment. We continued our conversation about jazz, but also explored other topics. I learned some things about Mexico that I didn't know. During World War II the United States had asked the Mexican government to intern all its German citizens in the country. Mexico agreed under the condition that Roosevelt build a steel mill and a glass factory in Mexico. Glass was expensive and was in great demand. Heidi knew these things because her father owned a retail store in Mexico City that specialized in selling glass. Being German, he was among the citizens forced to remain in the country during the war. So in a way, he both felt the pressure and reaped the benefits of World War II policies.

I noticed Heidi's features more clearly when we were at home. She was delightfully voluptuous. Her skin was radiant and smooth—a nice contrast to her burning red hair. She was about ten years younger than I. She was both corruptible and corrupting! I couldn't resist. As we lounged in conversation, I knew I was falling for her. Our relationship developed quickly from there. Thanks to Heidi, I learned about horse racing and won frequently at the racetrack. We would bet a little, love a little, and then bet some more. Heidi had a tremendous heart and a deep social conscience. She worked with the handicapped, teaching them important life skills and showing them how to defend themselves. Unfortunately for us, Heidi was on her way back to the United States to study, so our relationship was short-lived. But it was great while it lasted.

I met Cora Van Millenger in 1956, not too long after Heidi had left for the States. British by birth, she had been a showgirl in the Folies-Bergère in Paris. Because French women tended to be short and dumpy, the Folies preferred using women who were British or Swedish for the show. Cora was tall and had a beautiful body. Although she was eight years older than I, she was in magnificent shape when I met her.

Cora had been in France before World War II broke out. She'd married a Frenchman and had a daughter by him; however, when the hostilities erupted, she found out that he was pro-Nazi. She wanted to return to England, taking their daughter with her, but he wouldn't let her leave with their only child. She crossed the English Channel alone in 1939.

Once back, she learned how to drive a tractor and began working on a farm to help feed those who were devastated by the war. After World War II was over, Cora unexpectedly discovered that she was an heiress to a fortune. Cora had what they called "an expectancy." She didn't actually have money in her hands, but she would inherit riches in the future.

Cora met her second husband after the war, a Swedish count. Although a member of the titled nobility, he didn't have a dime either. Regardless, Cora fell deeply in love and was able to borrow against her inheritance to get cash. The couple used this money to reestablish themselves in New York. She arrived to the States using the title, "Countess Van Millenger."

The pair didn't remain in the United States for long. Relocating to Mexico, Cora became a painter and got involved in the business of raising chickens. Through contacts with Purina Animal Food Company, she was taught the proper way to feed and care for them. Just as the business was getting started, though, Cora's husband left her for a wealthy Mexican. Meanwhile, Cora settled into her role as an "earth mother" type, raising chickens and making chutney. When I first met her, she had moved to Mexico City and was living with Jackson Burke, a journalist from New York who had come down with his girlfriend, Kathy. They were all staying in an apartment building that had been converted from a sixteenth-century convent.

Cora and I dated briefly. One of our main pastimes was attending parties throughout the city. Cora didn't have an extensive wardrobe, but everyone knew that she possessed a talent for making the most of what she had, always wearing it with great elegance. Besides her charming personality, Cora and I had fantastic chemistry together. But our relationship formally ended when Heidi came back from the States. I told Cora that my "girlfriend" had returned, then I introduced them both to each other. They ended up becoming good friends.

It was in December of 1960 when I started seeing Jackson Burke's old girlfriend, Katherine. After leaving Mexico with Burke in 1956, she came back with her mother, who had recently divorced her father and married a wealthy German, of all things. Kathy had been born in Germany and was Jewish. In any case, circumstances brought Kathy back to Mexico and it wasn't long before she found her way into my bed.

Through Kathy, I became acquainted with some of the Ghanaians who were living in Mexico City. Ghana had gained independence from British rule in 1957. Shortly thereafter they established embassies both in New York and Mexico City. Kathy had spent some time with the Ghanaian diplomatic corps in New York and had grown fond of their company. She arranged for us to attend one of their receptions at the luxurious Chapultepec Castle in Mexico City.[6]

It became clear at the party that most of these guys had attended missionary schools, and that the experience definitely affected their personalities. Although they'd brought their wives with them to Mexico, I watched as their eyes wandered the room like stray cats. All of the top Mexican emissaries were there, but neither rank nor social status seemed to matter for the Ghanaians. A few dared to take quick pinches at the Mexican women—ambassador's wives! When she could, Kathy held onto their arms tightly. I'm sure she saved a few from getting shot that night.

The Ghanaians were truly outrageous and I started inviting them to my parties. They'd arrive with their wives, of course. But around 10 o'clock they'd take their women home. They'd return later, stag, to enjoy the party, right around the time when it was getting good! To tell the truth, though, I think a few of them abused their privileges while in Mexico. At one party, the Ghanaian ambassador himself showed up at my house. As we were talking, he started to complain that the Mexican people seemed prejudiced. The Ghanaian embassy was located in a wealthy, upper-class neighborhood called Las Lomas, and he swore to me that there had been endless petty, unfounded complaints about the behavior of his staff.

In between getting drinks the ambassador stopped. "Wait a minute," he said. "Let me check on my car." He walked over to my terrace and looked down. I followed a few steps behind. As I peered over I saw his bright red, Chevrolet convertible parked directly on the median! I didn't bother to tell him he was breaking the law (he must have known that). It was clear that having diplomatic plates probably enticed him to break all the normal rules of decorum. I started wondering to myself just how much of the supposed Mexican "prejudice" he was speaking about was actually related to episodes like this, where the Ghanaians were simply caught abusing their privileges and doing something wrong.

By this time during my stay in Mexico I had made many Mexican friends and had developed a sort of party circuit. This meant that an invitation from one person would lead to an invitation from another, and so forth, until the whole network had thrown a party. Entire families would come by my apartment during a typical *fiesta*. Babies would be taken back into the bedrooms where their mothers would periodically nurse them. Young kids between the ages of four and six would be serving the drinks to the adults and having their own fun. I had a nice ceramic tile floor that people loved to dance on. My hi-fi always played the best music. People enjoyed strolling onto my terrace to talk and observe the activity on the street. I never spent too much money throwing any of my parties because my guests generally brought their own liquor. Since my maid came on Mondays, even though I had to clean up by myself after a Friday or Saturday night party, I could count on her to take care of the rest at the beginning of the week.

Kathy was eventually compelled to return to the States. She had an apartment in Greenwich Village that she was illegally subletting. Actually, it was the same apartment that Washington Irving used to write some of his classic works, such as "The Legend of Sleepy Hollow." When her landlord discovered what was happening, she kicked out the tenant and Kathy had to go back. This occurred in the early spring of 1961.

Kathy and I missed each other, and she began calling me to come up and stay with her. Except for a bus trip that I had taken to see my parents in 1960, I hadn't been to the States for any real length of time in over ten years, much less to New York, of all places.[7] I wasn't sure about returning.

I still had family there. My two sons were teenagers now. I'd been sending them gifts as they'd been growing up. I sent guitars, inscribed watches, and money. On one occasion, I even told Aida to use some of the money I was sending to buy them both bicycles. We were on such bad terms, though, that it took my mother's intervention for her to finally start giving them the things that I sent. Other people had tried to deliver gifts for me, but Aida stubbornly refused to let them in the door when she found out that they were friends of mine. I later learned that she wouldn't even let the boys have the keys to the mailbox, just in case something might be there from me. It was like she was trying to punish me from afar for not staying with her. Aida and I were no longer together. But there was still leftover bitterness, anger, and pain. Her temperament had made her a difficult person to live with in the final months of our marriage. Her aggressiveness and mean streaks were simply too much for me to handle. Now, here I was seriously considering returning . . . home.

Chapter 10

New York Interlude

"Can I speak to Ray," I asked slowly, with a pause. I had sold my hi-fi and some of my record collection for the plane ticket to New York. I had also sold a lovely painting that Cora had done called "Ying Yang." It was almost April 1961 and I was talking to my ex-wife from Kathy's apartment in the Village.

"Virgil . . ." Ray was on the line. He was my youngest son, but spoke with a deep, rumbling voice, just like mine. I had already talked to Charles, who was graduating from Horace Mann High School at the end of the year. I made the boys call me "Virgil," instead of "Dad" or "Daddy" because I thought this might be the best way to bond with them.

I invited them down to the Village and to my surprise, their mother let them come. We went out to a Mexican restaurant. Walking around the city, I realized that so much had changed. The whole social and political situation was virtually unrecognizable to me. Sure, things were far from perfect, but blacks seemed to be acting with a new attitude, a confidence that I hadn't seen when I left. It was on the streets, in the restaurants, in the stores. Maybe I'd changed a lot, too.

The day I took my sons to dinner I recall seeing a group of black and Puerto Rican boys playing bongo drums on the subway. The Puerto Ricans occasionally spoke Spanish among themselves. I turned around and took a long look. At other times on the train, I'd hear people speaking Spanish non-stop. I'd find myself easing up to them. I wanted to be near *that* group. The language sounded so beautiful, and listening to Spanish sounded so . . . natural for me. Sure, English is a practical language, but Spanish is a Romance language in every sense of the word.

Several days after I had dinner with my boys, Charles called me at Kathy's asking for 20 dollars. He needed the money to rent a tuxedo for his prom, but his mother wouldn't give it to him. I was short on funds, but I promised that I'd help him out. I wasn't sure how long I was going to be staying in New York, so I knew that I needed to find some work soon to continue making ends meet.

My situation with Kathy wasn't going too well, either. We had a great time attending parties, but some rifts were developing between us. Being back in the States we both came to realize that we didn't view matters of race the same. In Mexico, we didn't think so much about these issues. Even though the Civil Rights movement was taking place, we were following it on the radio from a distance. We were reading about it in the newspapers in silence. That's different from living the Civil Rights movement. Coming back across the border, it was hard not to become involved in discussing, experiencing, and reflecting on the struggle. The Freedom Ride campaign of 1961 created the split between us.

In May, an effort staged principally by CORE (Congress on Racial Equality), but including SNCC (Student Non-Violent Coordinating Committee), the NAACP, and others, set out to test the Supreme Court's 1946 ruling for desegregating interstate bus and train travel. Groups of blacks and white civil rights sympathizers began boarding and riding buses throughout the South. They became known as the Freedom Riders. Although the courts had ruled dramatically against segregation 15 years earlier, the reality was that blacks still had trouble riding Greyhound, or using the newly "integrated" facilities at bus and train stations. It seemed that the laws of Jim Crow continued to outweigh the laws of the land. I had experienced some of this myself. On a brief bus trip that I took to Texas to see my parents in 1960, I was asked, after crossing the Mexican border into Brownsville, to move to the back of the bus. I was enraged. I had become accustomed in Mexico to sitting wherever I wanted. But once I got back stateside, my status suddenly changed. Taking a swig of my bottle of vodka, I reluctantly moved to the *middle* of the bus.

What really ignited the feud between Kathy and me was a difference in opinion over the treatment of the Freedom Riders. James Peck, a journalist and a member of the original group of Freedom Riders, had been injured by shattered glass on a bus trip to Alabama on Mother's Day, 1961.[1] Bricks and a bomb had been thrown through the bus's windows by a mob of angry whites in the town of Anniston. The bus was completely destroyed, but thankfully the passengers survived. Kathy thought the episode was horrible. I certainly couldn't disagree, but my take on the situation was far more measured. The Freedom Riders had been schooled in the methods of non-violence and were fully aware of the hostilities they might encounter. In my view, civil rights had to come at a cost. There was too much ingrained racist tradition to overcome for civil rights to be simply handed out to blacks. Maybe my opinion reflected the difference in thinking between a soldier and a civilian. But Kathy was no ordinary civilian.

Being Jewish and of German descent, her parents had fled Germany when she was a child. They could have easily perished in the concentration camps in Auschwitz had they not managed to escape Hitler's terror. Kathy's Jewish background and her impressions of the Holocaust made her perceive the Freedom Riders' exposure to violence as heroic. I saw that same exposure as a routine part of the broader civil rights war.

Another problem that I had with the Freedom Riders' incident was that in my view, white sympathizers enjoyed the luxury of being able to float in and out of the civil rights struggle at their own choosing. They could participate in protest, but they could also return to the comfort of their homes, the comfort of their secure, white-picketed worlds. Blacks could not do the same. For them, there was no escaping the weight of the civil rights war, at least not within America's borders.

My arguments with Kathy were magnified by our living conditions. There were so many constraints for me in her apartment—"Don't go upstairs until my building superintendent leaves." "If you see the super standing outside, go someplace so that he doesn't know you're entering my apartment." I found myself sneaking in and out. Rules, rules, rules! I'd been a free man for ten years! Although I knew she was being cautious because her lease allowed for only one person to stay in her apartment, the whole situation provided an uncomfortable reminder that I was back in the States.

Well, Charles took my 20 dollars, went to his prom, and enjoyed it. Imagine my surprise when he called and said, "Guess who I met? There was a girl there who I danced with that I kind of liked. She ended up being my first cousin!"[2]

It turned out that my brother, DuBois, was still living in the city. He had two daughters, Judy (who had been Charles's dancing partner) and Jackie. Once my ex-wife found out about what went on at the prom she tried to sever all connections between my relatives and my children. Despite her best efforts, DuBois made it a point to come by and take my boys over to his house. His daughters, Charles, and Ray had a lot of interaction that summer, regardless of my ex-wife's intentions.

I had another brother in the New York area. Like my son (whom I named after him), his name was Charles, and he had become a captain in the army. Charles had a home in Long Beach, New Jersey, where he lived with his wife and children. The couple met and had gotten married shortly before he'd completed a tour in Germany.

Because of my deteriorating living situation with Kathy, I decided to move in with Charles and his family. They had just had a baby, Charles, Jr., who was their second child. Unfortunately, Charles' wife had contracted multiple sclerosis and was unable to care for the kids as she would have liked. Charles was visibly bothered by all of this—one problem seemed to lead to another. Thankfully, my mother came up to help out with the newborn. But the house was pretty crowded. I slept in the basement.

A couple of job opportunities opened up for me while I was living with Charles. Ironically, Jackson Burke, whose ex-girlfriend I was dating, phoned one day to let me know about a writing position. When I'd first met him, he was an investigative journalist on assignment in Mexico City; now he'd become an editor for West Park Publications. The company had recently released a men's magazine called *Dude*, patterned after *Playboy*. "Look, I've got some great pictures from the Mexican cabaret scene," Burke said. I remember how he used to walk around taking pictures in the cabarets—a camera in one hand, and a bag of marijuana in the other. "If you write an article, I'll buy it and we can split the fee," Burke offered.

At about the same time a man named Moon, whom I'd met at the Ghanaian reception in Chapultepec Castle, had gotten in touch with me. It turned out that he was with the NAACP and they were screening folks to become social workers downtown. He was trying to persuade me to come and take the examination.

I seriously pondered both offers, but decided to take the position writing for *Dude*. As I started preparing the essay I found myself unable to do the piece that they originally wanted. They were hoping for an exposé that uncovered the grit, grime, and decadence of Mexican cabarets. My take was quite different. Having lived in both the United States and Mexico for long periods, I was inclined towards writing a piece that made subtle comparisons between the two. From my perspective, Mexico's more liberal attitudes towards sex and alcohol made for a better society. Incredibly, after over a decade in Mexico, I couldn't ever recall seeing a Mexican stagger down the street in a drunken stupor. I couldn't say the same for the States. I also observed that Mexican men generally drank in cantinas. They might pass the entire day there, drinking, talking, and playing dominoes or cup dice. When they finally went home, if it was late, they typically took their wives a *torta* (sandwich) to calm them down. It was points like these that I wanted to cover in the article. I assembled Burke's photos and wrote a classy essay.

With the pressures of a newborn and a sick wife, the tensions in my brother Charles' household made me think twice about staying there for much longer. I eventually moved in with DuBois's family on Long Island, where I stayed until I returned to Mexico in August.

I finally left the States because I was growing uncomfortable. It wasn't so much with my family. I enjoyed catching up with Charles, DuBois, and my mother. I enjoyed being with my sons. I had two other brothers, Woten and Eugene, who also lived in the New York area. Part of what was bothering me was that despite all of the changes that were taking place in the country, there were some deep social problems that needed to be resolved and that would take time to reconcile. People were being tossed in jail for ridiculous things. Kathy had a friend who had been arrested because he wouldn't get into the subway during an atomic raid drill.

I also vividly remember the day Kathy and I went to visit Odessa, one of my children's godmothers. When we were ready to go back downtown, her husband offered to drive us to the subway. Along the way, we were pulled over by the cops, presumably for running a red light. The last time I looked, the light had been green. Everybody in the car except for Kathy was black. It didn't help matters that the driver didn't have his wallet with him. He was hassled and issued a ticket. I remembered, and momentarily relived, my own experiences of 1949 and 1950.

Chapter 11

Transitions—Back in Mexico during the 1960s

Some might want to believe that the opening of civil rights in the sixties slowed the movement of blacks crossing the U.S. border into Mexico, making them less inclined to come because racial discrimination was easing at home. In my opinion, the Civil Rights movement had little effect. Mexico continued to represent a place of opportunity for blacks from all stations in life. Retired ball players came and used their pensions to live like kings. Higher education was cheaper. Blacks continued getting medical training easily and more economically than at home. The cost of living was lower. The Civil Rights movement did nothing to change any of these positive features of life across the border, and blacks kept coming.

On the other hand, many blacks that came to Mexico eventually returned to live permanently in the United States. I was one of the few who truly made Mexico a new home. I'm sure there were many who would have liked to have stayed, but it wasn't easy finding employment that would allow for permanent residency. I was fortunate in being able to stitch together an existence. I would still be in Mexico City now if it were not for my age and health problems. I no longer have the agility I once had. Since my apartment on Rio Balsas does not have an elevator, and I walk with a cane, it became increasingly difficult for me to get around, even within my own building. My brother Morris convinced me in 1997 that I would be better off moving near him in West Columbia, Texas. Now I'm close to Houston, with its excellent V.A. (Veteran's Administration) hospital. I also have the support of family. It was a tough decision for me to make, but in the end, health concerns won out.

Spending the summer of 1961 in New York assured me that my decision to stay in Mexico was the right one. When I returned, though, I was not ready to plunge immediately back into big-city life. New York had simply been overwhelming. I made arrangements to stay with my black Panamanian friend, Bill Ford, in the small town of Tenancingo. This was just the transition I needed.

I soon got to know many of the townspeople. There were even some other black Americans around—an amateur poet named Vivian Allen, who had come with her two young girls, Debbie and Phylicia. Debbie Allen went on to become a famous dancer and actress, as did Phylicia, who starred opposite Bill Cosby in the 1980s and 1990s hit sitcom, *The Cosby Show.* I saw the Allens somewhat frequently, since they would stop by the house. However, to become better acquainted with the local culture, I ended up leaving Bill's place and renting a room of my own. I could tell how popular I was on the days that I went shopping in the public market. On my way back, a bunch of guys who I knew would stop me to have a little "social drink." "*Oye, Virgilio, ven acá*" ("Hey, Virgil, come over here"), they would say. Naturally I would stop, talk, have a quick drink, and move on. About two hours later, after several of these little "stops," I would make it into my room, usually way too drunk to cook.

I would have stayed in Tenancingo longer had my brother DuBois not contacted me. He wanted to send his daughter Judy to study at the National Autonomous University of Mexico (UNAM), in Mexico City. The real truth of the matter, though, was that Judy had started dating someone that DuBois didn't like, and he wanted to separate them from each other. DuBois also knew that school was cheap in Mexico, about 120 dollars a year. So sending her to live with me seemed like an excellent good idea.

I talked with Licenciado Colmenares to see if he could get her enrolled. When everything was arranged, Judy came down. She spent a little time with me in Tenancingo before moving to Mexico City in November 1961. Since Everette Somersille was staying in my apartment at this time, I thought it would be best to send Judy to live elsewhere. She ended up moving in with an American girl in her early twenties from Los Angeles who was renting space from a Mexican woman. The pair got along well together.

Although my niece ended up staying in Mexico until 1964 or 1965, she was enrolled at the UNAM for only about one year. The problem was that she didn't want to get up and go to class. Her first course began around 7 A.M.—I think it was French or anthropology. Eventually, her parents got her enrolled in Mexico City College, where she didn't have to be there until 8 A.M. or 9 A.M., but DuBois ended up paying much more money for this.

Judy met her husband while at Mexico City College, a young black American named Jim Houston. He'd been a postal worker in San Francisco and was now studying dance. Sometime in 1964, arrangements were made for the couple to go to Nigeria where he became a teacher. I tried to convince Judy to stay in Mexico a while longer. I wanted her to take some more formal courses in Spanish so that she could be able to teach language classes herself, but I couldn't stop them. They ended up living in Nigeria for three years.

While Judy was studying, I began a new phase of life in Mexico City. For years, I vowed that if I were ever forced to start teaching English in order to make a living in Mexico, I would prepare to leave. However, in 1961, an opportunity came about that proved so inviting and I had to reconsider my initial plan.

A wealthy meatpacker named Urebe asked me to teach English to his family. They didn't live far from me, in a splendid house along Ejercito Nacional Avenue. Urebe had a beautiful wife named Jane whom he'd met in Holland. She had been raised in an orphanage and must have been barely 18 years old when they got married; he was nearly 40. The couple had three children and I was offered a handsome sum for teaching them, between 50 to 75 pesos an hour (10 dollars). This rapidly expanded my economic base. To my surprise, I also found the work fun and didn't have to work too strenuously to earn a good living.

There were some unanticipated benefits thrown in as well. Jane occasionally picked me up at my house and took me to the cabaret. We would cruise around town in her convertible with the wind blowing through our hair. Once, she took me to an apartment where we spent the night. Along the way, I noticed someone trailing us. She parked the car in a narrow street to avoid being spotted, but as I was leaving, I saw someone still spying on her. I was nervous, yet I realized that Jane had more serious problems to worry about than being with me. She had fallen in love with one of her son's friends, a young man no more than 17 years old. I was just a pleasurable distraction from a much deeper affair.

As my teaching reputation increased, I was referred to other families. Most of my classes were concentrated in the south of the city, in the new, exclusive residential neighborhood of "El Pedregal." Here, I taught a Cuban dancer's daughter, as well as the family of my friend Licenciado Colmenares. One of Colmenares's sisters had a young son whom I instructed, too. Dr. La Rollo was my next pupil. He'd studied philosophy in Heidelberg and was the chair of UNAM's philosophy department. He'd written several books on pedagogy and aesthetics and wanted to improve his English in order to speak more effectively in delivering his presentations. Looking back on it, I actually learned more from him than he did from me. We would talk about everything—religion, politics, art. He was an intellectual tour de force. To my credit, though, I did help him improve his cadence, breathing, and speech patterns.

This is the way it was for me throughout the sixties. I taught others, including the daughters and sons of the Richau family. In 1964, I gave classes to the family of President Díaz Ordaz's chief of staff. In the process, I ended up meeting Mexican engineers, professors, businessmen, politicians, actors, directors, and the like. I was teaching all age groups, from kids to young men and women, and even to my elders. One of the secrets to successful teaching, I discovered, was being able to laugh. I used humor to win over many of my younger pupils, and in the case of the Richau daughters, I allowed them to play and joke with me. Some of the children that I taught went on to become prominent individuals themselves, taking university and business positions in the United States, or becoming influential players on the Mexican social scene. Dr. La Rollo used to joke with me, especially after I'd started teaching politicians, that I was turning into a veritable "fat cat" since I'd found the way to move up within the ranks of the PRI![1]

My financial situation steadily improved. Everyone was paying me the going rate of 10 dollars an hour. Thanks to Urebe's wife, I also got my first car in Mexico City, a fine little Dampf Kraft Wagen (DKW), which I bought from her for less than 1,000 dollars. Then, around 1966, Evangelina Elizondo, the Cuban dancer who's daughter I'd been teaching, tipped me off about a movie role that was opening up at Churubusco Studios.

"*Oye*, Virgilio," she said, "Mr. Cantiflas is going to do a picture called *Su Excelencia* (His Excellency). They need someone to play the part of an African diplomat, the Ambassador of Zambombia. You should go over and talk to Cantinflas and audition." Evangelina thought I'd be perfect for the part.

Cantinflas, whose real name was Mario Moreno, was one of Mexico's most prominent movie stars. He filmed scores of hits between the late 1930s and 1970s.[2] Prior to filming *Su Excelencia*, he had recently received acclaim for his performances in *Pepe* (1960) and *Around the World in Eighty Days* (1955). He was a comic actor, and his antics were frequently compared to Charlie Chaplin. Cantinflas had a unique way of playing with words and dialogue so that he could be speaking the Spanish language without speaking it at all. Combined with his gestures, he was making sense to his audience, without really making any sense. All of this double meaning and language play fittingly acquired its own verb. A person could be said to be "*cantinfleando*" if they babbled and gesticulated in his particular, nonsensical way.

Talking with Mr. Moreno, I learned more about the screenplay's plot. Cantinflas was playing the role of a fictitious Central American diplomat from the obscure Republic of Los Cocos. Set during the Cold War, Los Cocos suddenly acquired global significance in the midst of a peace conference held in Pepeslavia. Holding the deciding vote between East and West, Cantinflas found himself in the middle of elaborate schemes to win his vote. My character, the Ambassador of Zambombia, was also caught between the two global factions.

I got the part and filmed for three or four days, earning 500 dollars. I was a stereotypical African diplomat, wearing a reddish robe and some sort of fez-styled hat made out of leopard skin. The woman playing my wife was a Cuban lady. Cantinflas went about the floor, performing his famous pranks. Part of the plot involved him being courted by a beautiful, scantily clad spy, whom he passed over to me in one scene. When the movie was released, the studio used one of my clips to design the promotional posters. Soon, my face was plastered all over the streets of Mexico.

Cantinflas had an adopted son who was about five years old. After filming, he asked me if I wanted to teach him English. I thought seriously about his offer. However, it appeared to me that the job would actually involve more than just teaching. Cantinflas's wife had recently passed away, and I got the impression that I would have been more like a guardian to the young boy. I didn't want to get this involved. One thing I was starting to learn in life is that if you get too absorbed in the affairs and politics of the rich, especially people in the movie industry, you are likely to get into some trouble. A lot of that crowd was involved with cocaine and I didn't want to be a part of it, so I passed on the opportunity.

I did continue my acting career. Shortly after *Su Excelencia* was released, my friend Evangelina told me that a series of Tarzan movies was going to be filmed at Churubusco Studios. The production company, Banner Inc., was American. Evangelina was able to talk with one of the assistant directors, telling him about my talents. They scheduled an appointment to see me. When I got to the studio, the director asked me to pull off my shirt so that he could have a good look at my chest. Size mattered.

I got the job. Soon I was in the studio, preparing to film 20 episodes out of 40 or so installments for the Tarzan television series.[3] I had some very good parts. After just one week's worth of work I was paid 500 dollars. The next thing I knew, I had 1,000 dollars. I hadn't had that much money in a long time. Before the end of my work with the series in 1968, I was earning 200 dollars a day. It was taking about a week to shoot an entire episode.

I was shocked when I ran into an old acquaintance of mine on the set, a guy named William Marshall. We'd met through the American Negro Theater in 1950. He'd put on some weight since then and had added impressively to his résumé. The first movie that I saw of his was *Lydia Bailey* (1952), in which he played a Muslim trying to protect a white woman (Bailey) from harm during the Haitian Revolution. Marshall gave a compelling performance. In fact, I thought he was the star of the movie. Eventually, he'd gone on and gotten married to a white woman who helped him to get his doctorate. Afterwards, he started teaching black history in the University of California system. He told me that he had a special contract with the university, allowing him to leave each spring to perform *An Evening with Frederick Douglass* at select Negro colleges throughout the country.

Not everything was rosy. Despite the success of *Lydia Bailey*, Marshall's acting career had been rocky. He had found it increasingly difficult to land movie and television roles between the 1950s and the middle of the sixties. To some degree, he was responsible. Prior to getting married, he and Billy Eckstein, the great jazz icon, had been seen running around openly with a couple of blonde French actresses. Even in a place like Hollywood, interracial dating was not acceptable and Marshall was quickly blacklisted. On our set in Mexico City, Marshall used to joke with me that the Tarzan series was his "Mr. Abraham Lincoln." Just as Lincoln had freed blacks from slavery, Tarzan had liberated him from being blacklisted.

The star of the series, Ron Ely, was not much of an actor. He did have a tremendous body, and had boasted (whether it was true or not) that he had sparred several rounds with Muhammad Ali. It was probably his physique that landed him the role.

Ron thought that the most important thing was for him to get face time. At every opportunity he would stick his head out in front of everyone and hold the position to be on camera longer. He committed artistic suicide in the process. Ely's megalomania even made him try to take over the directing of each episode. He drove the producers crazy, and we ended up changing directors frequently.[4]

Throughout the series, we shot scenes involving whole African villages, complete with chickens, kids, and women. Truckloads of blacks from the States couldn't be brought across the border just for this, so many of these other "Africans" were actually Cubans who'd migrated to Mexico with their families. When they weren't enough, Mexicans would sometimes fill in, too—darkening their skin, putting on headdresses, and wearing grass skirts.

Most speaking roles, however, were filled by Americans and American blacks. *Tarzan* featured some of the best black American talent around. A noted black Shakespearean actor whom I'd once seen do *Hamlet* was contracted for one episode. James Earl Jones and the Supremes came down to do another. The Supremes played nuns and Diana Ross was trembling like a bee. As a musical performer, she was used to dancing and having rhythm in the background. She felt a little out of place on the set. Needless to say, I didn't mind having to hold her hand to keep her still. James flanked her on one side while I was on the other.

The series was a hit for me in other ways. I became a celebrity among the families for whom I taught English in El Pedregal. During the shooting of my very first episode, I invited some of their children down to the studio. Tarzan was trying to reinstate an African queen back on her throne and I was playing the role of an African chief. The kids were thrilled! They watched me parade around in my feathers and beard. They *loved* Tarzan's chimpanzee. I talked with the director about letting them meet Ron Ely and the chimp. From then on I was the toast of the town in the eyes of my students and their families.

During the sixties, I was fortunate enough to be able to combine acting with a radio career. A Jewish guy named Churchill Murray had a show called the *Anglo-American Hour* to which I lent my voice. He knew that I had prior radio experience in New York and wanted me to spice up his show. The original format was boring. They basically read news and stock reports sent over from the British embassy. I immediately started improving things by airing a broadcast of the World Series that I'd been able to tape from my short-wave radio. I also recorded and aired Art Linkletter; he was the famous game show host who created *Kids Say the Darndest Things*. We developed about an hour of general interest material that aired regularly. Churchill soon appointed me to be program director. I was getting paid nearly 1,000 dollars a month. Unfortunately, Churchill was senile and took away my position. When he gave it to a white kid from the States, I quit the station altogether.

In the meantime, another opportunity opened for me. One of my niece's friends, a tall and attractive black American language teacher named Angela, decided to start a program called *This is Jazz*, targeted for a Spanish-speaking audience. Listeners were invited to the studio to play jazz records from their personal collections and to talk about the music. Angela did the interviews. We quickly learned that these folks oftentimes knew a great deal more about jazz than either of us. The show aired from 10 P.M. to 11 P.M. on Radio Femenina and was sponsored by Nescáfe, a coffee company. My main contribution to the show was to announce it in a deep, thundering voice . . . "THIS is JAAAZZ!" Nescáfe eventually withdrew their sponsorship, killing the show after only a month on the air.

Towards the end of the sixties I became more deeply involved with my friend, Licenciado Colmenares, who had started a publishing company called Editores Associados. He'd published some very controversial works; among them was one about a teacher who started a revolution in the state of Guerrero. I approached him to publish a book that I was working on, a grammar text called *Basic Spanish*. He accepted my proposal and the book was printed in 1971. It appeared in a number of bookstores, hotel shops, and in the Sanborns restaurant chain. I made 10 percent from each sale.

Some time later, my work as a teacher inspired me to develop a device called a "Grammar Clock." I was discovering that that Spanish and English were not really parallel languages. For instance, Spanish word order and syntax is more fluid than English. I captured some of the differences in the clock. I made my prototype out of cardboard, with a wheel stapled to its base. Using it, you could go from the simple future to the idiomatic future: "I'm going to eat," "I will eat," "I shall eat," etc. Other tenses were included so that a Spanish speaker could quickly master a range of English verbs, verb forms, and conjugations. It was difficult trying to include the subjunctive tense. I had to work hard to make the proper verb conjugations fit logically.

Sometime in the early 1980s, I approached Sanborns to see if they were interested in selling the clock and *Basic Spanish* as a package. To my surprise, they agreed, and sales were made at about 15 different locations throughout Mexico City. Through the book and the clock I felt that I was making some small contribution to the lives of people who were trying to learn about Mexico. In some small way, I was mediating Mexican and American culture, helping both peoples learn about the other through the art of language. My initial reluctance towards being a language instruction teacher now seemed strange in retrospect, given the impact it had on my life and the lives of others.

The years 1968 to 1970 turned out to be historically momentous times. The Olympics were held in Mexico City, the first time they had been hosted in a Latin American country. The Mexican government massacred scores of innocent citizens and students at Tlateloco, claiming that they were suppressing communists.[5] Carlos Madrazo, the former president of the PRI, died mysteriously in a plane crash that many believed was caused by the PRI itself. Stateside, Dr. Martin Luther King and Robert Kennedy were assassinated, dealing heavy blows to the Civil Rights movement and American liberal politics. On the international front, the bloodshed of the Tet Offensive changed the complexion of the Vietnam War. Meanwhile, in my life, personal tragedy struck when my father died in the autumn of 1970.

Papa had gone virtually blind. All of his brothers died blind, but he didn't want to acknowledge that it was happening to him, even after he'd developed glaucoma. When friends and family brought up the subject, he scoffed and simply started drinking more. Morris's wife told me how dad would get in their car and drive into the telephone pole in the corner of their yard because he couldn't see where he was going. My other brother, Charles, told me how when they would go fishing together, papa's eyesight was so poor that he had trouble figuring out what he was catching. Still, he denied that he was losing his sight until the very end.

When Morris called me in Mexico with the bad news I started weeping. I couldn't seem to stop. Dad had done so much for the family, for all of us, especially when I was going through college. He was a selfless man who put his wife and family first. I was still crying when I got to Texarkana. I walked the town numb and nursed a bottle for days. It took me a while to get right.

My son Ray came down after he received the news. He'd been working in Boston as a television producer for a program called *Say Brother*, before being released from the show. Now he was teaching. He and his girlfriend Vashti rode down in Ray's Volvo. Meanwhile, my brother Charles flew in from Germany, where he'd been stationed. Morris was already in Texas.

After the ceremony, I asked mama if she wanted to get out of Texarkana and move on with her life. She couldn't leave. "I'm the director of the Day Care Center," she said. She'd recently started working away from home for the first time in many years. I didn't want to interfere with that. When it was time for me to go back, Ray and Vashti offered to drive. I was elated. Ray had already come down to Mexico City once for a quick visit in 1969. I was glad to be with him again, building our relationship, especially during such a tough time in my life.

Honestly, though, I thought it was time for Ray to move to Mexico permanently. I'd been thinking about this for a while. He had gotten into trouble with the Federal Communications Commission for accusing the mayor of Boston of corruption. In retaliation, the FCC threatened to remove his show from the air. Fortunately, Ray didn't protest, but he soon lost his job as a television producer.

Ray was also a member of the Black Panther Party. He told me that he'd joined because he was infuriated at the way blacks and Puerto Ricans were being treated in the States and was determined to do something about it. However, I suspected that the FBI had infiltrated the organization. When Ray started talking seriously about smuggling weapons to party members, I figured it was time to get him across the border for his own protection and safety.

Ray and Vashti stayed with me throughout the month of December, spending most of their time in Mexico City. I suggested one day that they take a tour of the country, see the coasts, and take a stroll around Veracruz. Ray was a savvy young man who had mastered the complexity of getting around Mexico City in a short time. With some maps, he could easily find his way around the country.

"Look, now don't you two take any marijuana with you," I warned. A while ago, a female friend of mine had given me two sacks of marijuana that someone had pushed off on her. She suggested that I sell it, but I decided to keep it. It was quite a stash. By now, though, all that were left were some seeds. Still, Ray and I had sifted out enough to roll a couple of joints the night before he and Vashti left. I didn't want them to get into any trouble while wandering the country. If the cops caught them with drugs, even a small amount, who knows what the consequences would have been.

My son and his girlfriend didn't leave alone. About a week prior to their departure they randomly picked up a married couple in the park. They were Americans, claiming to be affiliated with the University of Buffalo. They also said they had been sent by a government agency to become investigators in Mexico. It sounded like a whole lot of crap to me, but Ray and Vashti seemed intrigued. Ray decided to take them with him to Acapulco, the first stop on his grand tour. He asked me if I wanted to come too, along with Elena, my girlfriend at the time. I really didn't feel like being bothered with that obnoxious couple he was traveling with, so I said no.

Their plan was to stay just for the weekend. Acapulco was not too far—they could drive the distance in a few hours. On Sunday morning, I came home and there was a note under my door from the American embassy. I immediately called the number that was on the card.

"Mr. Richardson, we have very bad news for you," the man on the line said.

"Ray crashed his car?" My head was spinning. "No, Mr. Richardson. Your son and two women drowned in Acapulco yesterday." I panicked. I strained to breathe air. I slammed down the phone. Tears streamed from my eyes. Ray was just 24 years old! His entire future lay ahead of him. Here was a young man who had taken care of himself in Boston, a place where blacks didn't get along well with whites, who had attended Boston University and excelled there, a school that challenged the brightest students. As I looked around the empty room, guilt set in. It wouldn't have happened if I had gone with them. "I wouldn't have let Ray drown," I moaned.

Some time later, I managed to call Ray's mother. "Is there a place I can stay?" she asked. She was thinking about coming down. "Of course," I said, coolly. But Aida never did make it. Charles, my other son, did arrive to pay final respects to Ray.

I took the first bus I could to Acapulco. When I got there, I ran into Givens, the husband of the couple from Buffalo. He was clearly distraught. Through his grief, he told me that the four of them had checked out of the hotel and were on their way back when they decided to have one last swim. They weren't out in the water long before his wife started screaming. Then Vashti started screaming. Givens called out for Ray, but Ray was gone. Soon he looked around and his wife was missing. Vashti was missing. None of them had realized that the place where they were swimming had a strong undertow. It was maliciously called *El Revocadero* ("the place that revokes").

Three days passed before the first of the bodies was recovered in the open sea. A friend and neighbor of mine, Ray Sinatra (a cousin of Frank Sinatra), went with me to the morgue. He read the report, then looked at my son's corpse. I hadn't seen either yet. "You don't want to read this . . . you don't want to see the body," he said, lowering his head and shaking it, sadly. Ray had been decomposing in the salt water and baking in the sun. A shark had savagely bitten one of his legs. I couldn't bear to look for long.

Vashti's body was found some time later, but they never did recover the last corpse. In my anger and sorrow I couldn't help but reflect on all the possible reasons as to why Ray had died. When I first arrived to Acapulco in 1950, it was certainly a tourist destination, but it had become considerably more commercialized since. It was now extremely noisy and had lots of tourist hotels catering to foreigners, even more than before. I am sure that it was the flood of white people, the pressure of white foreign tourists, that made my son go out to this forbidden place where they could be by themselves to swim. If only I had been there. . . .

Chapter 12

Border Crossings

Mexico never could be the same for me after Ray's death. It is sadly ironic that in 1950, I left the United States and eventually made a conscious decision to stay in Mexico. Ray, a tourist, never intended to be there for very long. In a curious twist of fate, Ray was the one who stayed there permanently; I am the one returning to the States, alive.

I became closer and more distant from Mexico during the 1970s and 1980s. I remained an active writer, completing a play called *After Hours* that was performed by The Los Angeles Society of the Performing Arts in 1975, and a movie script entitled *The Spookwaffe Diaries*, about my experiences in World War II.[1] The "Spookwaffe" was what the Primary Training instructors called us at Tuskegee, and it was a term we used ourselves at Selfridge Field up until when Colonel Davis took charge. My script concentrated on the experiences of 15 airmen, exploring some of the double meanings of war that we endured. Not only were we fighting against the Germans abroad, but we were also fighting against white racism at home. I had to be careful with this script. All the Tuskegee Airmen knew that nothing definitive could actually be written about their experience until Colonel Davis had his say. My characters rendered a semi-fictional account of the war.

Diaries still hasn't been released, either on screen or in print. Sometime after 1975, though, my son Charles passed along the script to some friends who were lawyers and movie producers. I went to meet them in L.A. at a fancy office on Rodeo Drive. They took an option on my work, paid me a nice sum of money, and handed me a contract.

This altered my relationship with Mexico. Up until 1973, I'd been living on a tourist card. I would have to come to the border twice a year to renew it. I normally went to Brownsville by car or plane. In 1973, I started the process of acquiring *immigrante* (immigrant) status, which takes about five years. Back then you needed to show income of at least 350 dollars a month. The movie contract put me into the stratosphere as far as income was concerned, even though the movie was never produced. I used some of the contacts I'd developed both through my teaching and acting careers to smooth the process for me. I suppose I could have arranged to marry a Mexican woman to acquire citizenship—you could do this under the table by paying lawyers a fee. But I didn't want to exercise this option. The only woman I would have ever considered marrying was Maria Luisa. After her, I reconciled the fact that I had grown children in the States. I didn't need to complicate matters more.

Thanks in no small part to my Hollywood movie contract, I got my Mexican passport and finally became a *migrado* after having spent over 20 years in Mexico.

I started returning to the States more and more during the 1980s. Much of this travel was not by choice. My mother's youngest sister passed away in 1984, and I attended her funeral in San Francisco. Shortly after that, I returned to spend a month with mama in Texarkana. She'd fallen and broken her hip while supervising some repair work to the greenhouse. During our time together I taught her how to get around by herself using her walker. She was on her way to becoming an invalid—or at least that's what she wanted me to believe. I helped her learn how to use the stairs again, go outside, weed her flowers, and move around the sides of the house. Our month together was the last time I saw her alive. I attended her funeral later in the year.

In 1985, I went to Houston for a hernia operation. My son, Charles, and his wife, Charlotte, came down from New York to be with me. Instead of going straight back to Mexico, I decided to spend a couple of weeks with them back East. That's when I learned Charlotte was pregnant. I was going to have a grandchild!

Because of vision problems, I found myself traveling back and forth from hospitals in Mexico City, New York, and Houston, especially during 1989. I was in New York on two different occasions that year. I took advantage of the time to see two of my brothers, DuBois and Eugene, who were living on Long Island. The need for an operation brought me back to the Houston in 1990. I did not return to the United States again until 1997. I have not been back to Mexico since.

Am I Mexican? Am I American? Am I both? I never felt homesick when I was living across the border. From Latin America I could see clearly what the United States was doing abroad. The Americans dethroned the Marxist government in Guatemala and plunged the country into a 30-year bloodbath. They tried to do the same thing with Fidel Castro. When he returned to Cuba and took power after being exiled in the United States and Mexico, the Americans sent Cuban refugees back to attack him at the Bay of Pigs. In the Dominican Republic, Lyndon Johnson sent the army to keep an elected president, who was a socialist, from taking office. In Central America, the United States interfered constantly in politics. They kidnapped Noriega from Panama. They were deeply involved in supporting the Contras against the leftist Sandinistas in Nicaragua. Even in South America, the United States participated in overthrowing President Salvador Allende of Chile after he became the first Marxist president to be elected in a Latin American Country. Allende was eventually killed, and in 1973, the United States helped put the cruel dictator Pinochet in power. Pinochet ended up murdering countless of his fellow countrymen. In Argentina, too, the Argentine army took over the government in the 1970s and began slaughtering everybody from the left. Unsurprisingly, the United States had its hands in this. Some aspects were disgusting. Corrupt Argentine army officers who did not have children of their own were involved in kidnapping babies. When they captured a pregnant woman from the left, they waited to kill her until after she gave birth so that they could take the child for themselves.

I grew up in the States and lived there until I was 33 or 34 years of age. I was black. So I had accumulated enough experiences to know that this was not the land of the free and the home of the brave. Spending time in Mexico gave me a different perspective, a view from south of the U.S. border. I could understand Latin American sentiments better.

You ask if I feel American? Well, I fought for my country. I wouldn't change that. Yet, I was conflicted. I did seriously think about becoming a conscientious objector before the war. But I ultimately decided that if I took that course, I would have had a hard time both during the war and afterwards. I also ended up developing a real love for flying, especially the P-47. In some senses, I fought because I loved to fly.

Did this make me feel closer to my country? Lord, no! I was well aware that the army didn't want to see any black aces. When a Tuskegee pilot shot down four planes, the army found a way to get them grounded immediately. On the other hand, we were also forced to fly more missions than white pilots, provided we hadn't shot down too many of the enemy. White pilots flew about 50 missions before being rotated home. Black pilots flew about 70. I flew 63. None of this seemed fair.

In the air, I was just trying to survive. The reason why I may have run the extra mile and performed my best while in uniform was for my son, Charles. I wanted him to have some respect for me and for himself. One of the first things I did when I returned home was to give him my wings and medals. He was so small then that he didn't know what the medals were. He barely knew who I was. But as he grew up, he kept the medals and I think they are a source of pride.

In Europe, I was an American soldier, a supporter of the Allies, and a pro-German sympathizer all at the same time. Let me explain. It's not that I favored Nazi rule or fascism for that matter. It's just that in my mind, the Germans had never been involved in the slave trade like England or France. England and France had devastated Africa and India.[2] They ruled the world! There's an old saying: "The sun never sets on the British Empire." In prewar maps and geography books, when you look at the world, it is virtually covered in pink (representing the British Empire) all the way to China! But I knew about the Boxer Rebellion.[3] I knew about the Opium Wars, and how the British tried to foist drugs upon the Chinese population against their will, causing a whole nation to become addicted.[4] I knew how the French had taken over Indochina and had been clobbered in the battle of Dien Bien Phu.[5] What these two nations stood for and the misery they'd caused in the world was, and is, hard to defend.

I'm not the only soldier in my family. My youngest brother, Lieutenant Colonel Charles Richardson, went on to be in charge of communications in Southeast Asia and was stationed in Thailand during the Vietnam War. The Richardsons have fought bravely for our country. This doesn't mean that America or its allies are always doing the right thing. Do I feel American? Well, I was glad when the United States got its butt kicked in Vietnam. I remember that I was visiting my son Charles in New York when I saw television coverage of the fall of Saigon. There were all these people on the roof of the American Embassy, trying to clamber onto helicopters. I saw many more scrambling to get on a passenger jet, which was getting ready to take off. They were holding onto the door. A part of me was overjoyed that the American bully finally got whooped! Those were valiant people in my mind, the Vietnamese. That defeat demoralized the U.S. armed forces until President Bush, Sr. launched his war against Iraq and Saddam Hussein.

I suppose I see the good and the bad in America based on the life I've lived. After 47 years of living in Mexico, it would be a mistake to say "Yes, I feel more Mexican than American." I have enjoyed the freedom of being in Mexico. I did whatever I wanted to do with whomever I wanted to do it. Mexico offered me the opportunity to relive my adolescence—actually, to live the adolescence I never could have in this country. If you can imagine it, in a way, I was a teenager again in my thirties. Without a doubt, Mexico has helped me learn to see things clearly, especially politics. I have and always will have a deep affection for the country.

Epilogue Black American Yankees on Montezuma's Soil

There's an old story about a Revolutionary general who was seated in a famous American-owned restaurant [in Mexico] when a negro was refused service. Drawing his revolver and laying it carefully on the table in front of him, the general said, "The gentleman will be served." He was.[1]

As the life of Virgil Richardson poignantly reveals, the story of black Americans in Mexico is one about self-determination, the yearning for humanity, and the quest for simple freedoms. But stepping back and looking at the African American legacy from a broader, historical perspective, we also discover that the story is deeply intertwined in international politics, cross-border intrigue, and class struggle. Especially during the nineteenth and early twentieth centuries, blacks found themselves thrust into the role of cultural mediators, helping to define and articulate the boundaries of the relationship between white North Americans and Mexicans.

The episode cited in the quotation above, actually based on true events in the life of the legendary black heavyweight boxer Jack Johnson, captures the spirit of this role. The revolutionary general, who had spent years fighting against the dictatorship of Porfirio Díaz (1876–1910), found himself unexpectedly confronted with the intolerant attitudes of an American entrepreneur, Walter Sanborn, the owner of what was to become one of Mexico's most famous restaurant chains. In the general's mind, Sanborn was just one of many in a long list of foreigners who had been allowed to profit in Mexico at the people's expense. The new quest for national sovereignty sought to not just eliminate their presence, but to eradicate the cultural baggage they brought with them, including their repressive, discriminatory behavior. Other versions of the story recount that Sanborn was explicitly reprimanded by being told: "This is Mexico, not Texas."[2] The mayor of Mexico City, who also happened to be dining in the restaurant, then personally intervened to make sure that Johnson and his white wife were well accommodated. Effectively, this momentary flash of history contrasted two different treatments of the black man, that of Sanborn and that of the Mexican revolutionaries.

All of this proved illuminating for Johnson, who had been living in exile from the United States, spending time in England, Spain, and Cuba.[3] For the next two years (1917–1919) Johnson gladly called Mexico his home, becoming close to leading politicians such as President Venustiano Carranza, as well as key intellectuals and businessmen. He also befriended radical members of the American expatriate community—mainly communist sympathizers who had dodged draft service in World War I. Already well known for his vocal anti-American sentiments during the war, Johnson grew no less vocal in Mexico. Combined with his passionate antiracist platform, he became emblematic of what the United States feared most about linkages between black Americans and Mexicans. Together, they represented a strong, united front against the prejudicial belief system that underwrote the expansionary activities of American capitalism. Properly allied, they might be enticed to engage in seditious pursuits that could threaten to destabilize America itself.[4]

Mexico's warm reception of Jack Johnson was just onc instancc of contact with blacks in a long history of complicated and sometimes hostile interactions stretching back to colonial times. While debate continues over whether Africans arrived to the New World before Columbus, we can assert confidently that a number of servants, slaves, and possibly soldiers participated in the Spanish conquest of Mexico in 1519. Throughout the 1520s and into the 1560s, blacks participated in exploring large portions of Mexico, stretching from the Yucatan in the southern frontier to Baja California, and eventually into what is today the American Southwest. The sixteenth and seventeenth centuries were also intense periods of slave trade activity. Because the conquest era brought a host of new diseases to Mexico, the indigenous population began dying rapidly. By the early 1600s, Mexico's native population had fallen from between 12 to 25 million to just over 1 million individuals. To help replace these losses and to exploit booming colonial industries such as silver mining, cotton production, and sugar cultivation, African slaves were introduced. Nearly 110,000 arrived between 1521 and 1646, making Mexico one of the world's leading importers during this period. The numbers had a profound demographic and social effect. By 1553, colonial authorities in Mexico City complained to the Spanish king that the number of blacks was growing out of control. The city had narrowly avoided being overthrown by them in 1537. At the time, blacks numbered over 20,000 residents, far outnumbering whites. More reliable statistics from 1646 demonstrate that blacks and mulattos had reached 150,000 throughout the colony, well above the 14,000 whites. By the late eighteenth century, thanks to decreases in slave shipments, greater demographic balance was achieved. But blacks and mulattos still comprised 10 percent of the overall population, standing at 370,000 in 1793.[5]

The first arrival of North American blacks into Mexico came much later than the sixteenth century. Keep in mind that colonial Mexico was enormous, stretching deep into the modern states of California, Arizona, and New Mexico. The North American British colonies, by contrast, were huddled along the Atlantic coast, far removed from Spain's Mexican holdings. Prior to 1763, British colonists and their slaves had far more contact with Spanish territorial holdings in Florida than with Spain's Mexican territories in the West.[6]

The independence struggles of Mexico (1810–1821) and the United States (1776–1783) marked the beginning of new and more intense relations between both countries. The issue of blacks, their movement, and their status rose prominently in the correspondence of politicians and diplomats as never before, particularly in the mid-1820s and 1830s. There were several reasons for the change, but at its core, the debate over blacks centered on the different ways in which each country came to view their presence. Comparatively speaking, blacks were more integrated into Mexican society and its independence movement than they were in the United States, sparking differences of opinion when the subject of blacks arose in political circles.

The higher degree of integration had a history. In no uncertain terms, throughout the eighteenth century, Mexico was a far more liberally minded region for blacks, despite the existence of a caste system that attempted to regulate the behavior of colonists and limit the socioeconomic ascension of nonwhites. The system proved difficult to implement in practice, which allowed Mexico's black population to exercise greater liberties than in the United States. While the United States did possess a few great black entrepreneurs, like Philadelphia's James Forten, who became the city's leading sailmaker by the beginning of the nineteenth century, Mexico arguably had a larger black middle and professional class. Major urban centers, such as Mexico City and Puebla, routinely recorded at least a tenth of its blacks involved in the middle- and high-status artisan trades. Additionally, there were a number of black and mulatto lawyers, doctors, merchants, educators, and clergymen. Some families, such as the Santanders who lived in Puebla, had enough wealth to qualify them to be virtually full-fledged members of the colonial elite, complete with all of the material trappings.[7]

The decline in Mexican slavery that began in the middle of the seventeenth century and continued throughout the eighteenth century also meant that by the early 1800s, the vast majority of blacks were already freedmen.[8] Furthermore, there was a tremendous amount of racial mixture, which had the impact of bringing together, in a single household, whites, Indians, blacks, and *mestizos*.[9] Quite simply, while repressive restrictions undeniably existed for

Mexico's black population, in comparison to the United States, these individuals were much further along toward becoming a part of the new nation's citizenry upon the eve of independence.

The independence movement itself offered Mexican blacks a tangible means to express their citizenship. Although the influence of blacks, mobs, and the masses definitely impacted the revolutionary movement in the United States,[10] Mexico's independence probably began more decidedly as a multi-ethnic grassroots effort. While there were several early stages in which a white elite attempted to orchestrate the insurgency, the years 1810 and 1811 saw the lower-class Indian and mixed-race masses push independence in directions that sought to address their demands. Disaffected blacks, who were part of the rebel masses, came to enjoy a greater profile in the revolutionary effort, especially under the command of José María Morelos, a parish priest from Michoacán who himself was rumored to be a mulatto.[11] By 1813, except for a few pockets of resistance, Morelos exercised virtual control over the Pacific lowlands, a region that had held large concentrations of blacks for at least a century.[12] Success on the battlefield eventually helped him rise up to become the key figure of the insurgency, a position he assumed in 1811. Before his death in 1815, he issued a number of decrees that were to become important after independence was secured. Perhaps most memorable was a document called *Sentimientos de la Nación* (Sentiments of the Nation) which was delivered to the Revolutionary Congress at Chilpancingo on September 14, 1813. It included the following remarks:

> Slavery is forbidden forever, as well as the distinction of caste, leaving everyone equal; Americans will only be distinguished from one another by virtue and vice.[13]

Morelos had hoped to integrate these points into a new constitution and in doing so, he followed the tradition of his predecessors. On December 6, 1810, just months after inciting the uprising that launched the revolution, Miguel Hidalgo called for all masters to free their slaves within ten days. In his 1811 document, *Elementos Constitucionales* (Constitutional Elements), the insurgent leader Ignacio Rayón upheld Hidalgo's decree.[14]

The United States simply had no parallel for the levels of black military leadership and advocacy found in Mexico. Blacks certainly participated in the revolutionary cause. Although just 1 percent of the total black population of 500,000 served under George Washington (less than .5 percent served under the British), by 1779, the Continental Army was remarkably integrated, being almost 15 percent black. It would not be until the Vietnam War that the United States would see this level of integration in its armed forces again.[15] Regardless, no blacks rose to the stature of Mexico's Morelos. Similarly, the only hints of legislation aimed at abolishing slavery were quickly overridden. The first version of the Declaration of Independence did contain antislavery language, but the words were removed at the request of South Carolina, New England, and Georgia's slave-trading interests.[16] By contrast, Mexico's independence movement, while far from being driven by black demands, had a greater racial agenda and edge.[17]

This argument should not be overstated. Within the very advantages that Mexican blacks enjoyed over their American counterparts were a series of limitations. The emerging Mexican nation did not support the concerns of blacks unconditionally. Despite the efforts of Morelos, Hidalgo, Rayón and others, slavery was never truly abolished during the years of the independence struggle. Blacks living in bondage were pressed to take up these matters on their own. Between 1811 and 1817, on the coastal haciendas and plantations in the region of Veracruz, a series of slave rebellions were launched that burned their masters' estates into the ground. As for the plight of free blacks, the independence movement still threw barriers in their way. The liberal constitution of 1812 extended formal citizenship to Spaniards and Indians, but did not enfranchise blacks and the racially mixed *castas* (castes).[18] Even in 1821, when peace was finally achieved under the Plan of Iguala, the document spoke primarily to individuals of Spanish ancestry, excluding Indians, blacks, and the *castas*.

In July 1822 deeper change started to occur. The recently crowned Mexican emperor, Agustín Iturbide, issued a statement declaring that except for Indians, everyone, regardless of race, was to be considered a full citizen of the empire. In October, Church officials were ordered to abandon using caste labels to identify and record their parishioners. The only exceptions allowed were for classifications taken during the ceremony of matrimony.[19] In 1824, the newly drafted Mexican constitution upheld these positions and formalized them by decreeing civil equality regardless of race and origin. Gradually, slavery was abolished. In July 1824 the slave trade was outlawed, although slave owners were permitted to keep slaves already in their possession. In 1825, in order to speed up the process of emancipation, the Mexican government began purchasing slaves from landholders. The slaves were issued their freedom amid much fanfare in a public ceremony commemorating the anniversary of independence. Finally, on September 15, 1829, President Vicente Guerrero, most likely of *pardo* origin himself, banned slavery completely in Mexico.

It is easy to interpret the elimination of slavery and caste distinctions in Mexico as more radical acts than they really were. Keep in mind that by the 1800s, Mexico had ceased being a major slaveholder. During any given year between 1800 and 1829, there were just 6,000 to 10,000 slaves in the country, as opposed to nearly 700,000 in the United States at the beginning of the nineteenth century. In short, Mexico could comfortably afford to abolish slavery because banning the institution did not fundamentally alter the economic and social structure of the nation. To be sure, there were certain sectors of the economy that might experience dislocations. Estate owners in Acapulco and Veracruz, where the largest concentrations of slaves were held, protested that economic crisis would sweep their regions if slavery were removed too quickly.[20] But on the whole, the violence and destruction produced by the wars of independence was far more damaging for Mexico. From this perspective, the eight-year gap between independence and the abolition of slavery demonstrates the conservatism of the young Mexican nation-state, despite the fact that emancipation came far sooner than in the United States (and even several other Latin American nations).

Because of the masses of freedmen that were already living in Mexico in the early 1820s, the nation's new stance towards caste categorizations proved a potentially more radical proposition and, in principle, the elimination of caste distinctions demonstrated a more substantive commitment to racial amelioration. But here, too, there were important shortfalls. As with slavery, to an extent, Mexico could afford to be liberal with its caste policy. Preexisting weaknesses in the caste system meant that its sudden abolition would not immediately introduce ripples into the social order. Newly enfranchised racial groups would not be climbing and pressing eagerly, en masse, for privileges they had not had before. More significant, the elimination of caste categories was not accompanied by legislation that punished transgressors of the new law, or that attempted to repair the social damage produced by years of discriminatory legislation and custom. This is to say that the eradication of the Mexican caste system did not come with a plan designed to rectify a history of caste inequality. Nor were there any efforts made to define what caste inequality actually meant. It should not come as a surprise, therefore, that by the 1830s and 1840s, church records in several Mexican states reverted to using colonial racial classifications to describe parishioners. Additionally, despite some modest gains in the political arena, where blacks began appearing as officeholders in the town councils and assemblies of Veracruz, by and large, politics remained infused with racism. There were vigorous efforts to prevent people of color from acquiring power.[21]

Much more important than true racial change in the mind of Mexican legislators was the symbolism behind their actions. It was enough for them simply to issue decrees, since these acts alone were sufficient to differentiate the ideology of the nation-state from the old, repressive colonial regime. Yet Mexico's new cohort of politicians realized that without sharpening the teeth of their legislation, many colonial privilege structures would remain in place. In part, this was the plan. There were many who wanted to retain access to the power they had enjoyed in the colonial period, without having to deal with the cumbersome apparatus of the colonial regime.

However, since the independence movement had shown itself to be remarkably multi-class and multi-ethnic in scope, with up to three-quarters of the rebel army being drawn from the peasant masses, the magnates had to be careful how they translated their power into the new nation-state. To some degree, they had to appear sensitive to the needs of the lower social strata, whose grievances varied regionally in character. Compressing their concerns, and articulating their grievances as being caused by the concept of "caste" offered politicians a convenient means of assigning their troubles a false cohesion, while not necessarily committing themselves to dealing directly with rectifying the material conditions of peasant lives. It was easy for a government to announce the abolition of a caste system, but it was difficult to engineer the substantive changes needed to alter livelihoods, if indeed they truly wanted to.

Collapsing peasant concerns into the framework of "caste" was also a nice rhetorical tool with which to build a cohesive citizenry. It coaxed the racially mixed poor into believing that their disparate problems were embedded in the past colonial order. It enticed them to recall the early, heady days of independence, when Hidalgo and Morelos offered messages of unity to the downtrodden and oppressed. Apart from bridging internal tensions and regional differences, the act of eliminating caste designations provided the additional illusion of inviting the poor to enter the civic world of the rich, but of course without the necessary cash to exert any real influence.

Whether we ultimately judge Mexico's policies as conservative or progressive, the difficult dance of politics that was performed to forge a national citizenry had a resounding international effect. The abolition of slavery immediately curried favor with England. Having abolished its own slave trade in 1807, the British were committed to dismantling the slave trade in other parts of the world. To the delight of the Mexican government, abolition was interpreted as a gesture of good will and served to attract further British investment in the young nation. The money was sorely needed to help rebuild an economy that was mismanaged and still ravished by the effects of war.

The abolition of slavery placed Mexico in a more difficult position with the United States, which, although having abolished its own international trade in 1808, continued to preserve the institution of slavery and had a thriving illegal trade. Matters came to a head when the emancipation decree angered U.S. colonists living in Mexico.

In order to stimulate growth in their economy, Mexican government officials had not only sought foreign loans and investments, but also foreign settlers to work the country's land and develop huge tracts of open territory in its northern regions. Beyond its immediate financial rewards, immigration was considered a positive, transformative tool. Mexico lacked a vigorous, self-sustaining middle class. Some legislators were optimistic that the Mexican peasantry would be quick to imitate the work habits of imported foreign workers, thereby becoming a vibrant and productive class of its own. European immigrants were preferred for this project, but it was Americans who answered the call in surprising numbers, especially in Texas. Stephen F. Austin's colony brought nearly 20,000 colonists to Mexico in the 1820s. Much to the chagrin of the Mexican government, a notable concentration of these immigrants comprised wealthy landowners rather than the hardy agriculturalists originally envisioned. Of course, many brought slaves with them. They had been preconditioned in the United States towards seeing slaves as indispensable for economic success, especially in the cotton enterprises that were being established in east Texas. By 1825, one out of every five people in Austin's colony was a black slave.[22]

Americans living in Mexico acquired some allies in their protests against Mexican abolition. Bureaucrats from the northern states and territories who profited from American revenues were inspired to support slavery, despite the growing national consensus against it. During the heated Mexican congressional debates of the late 1820s and early 1830s, American diplomats turned to more coercive tactics against those who could not be persuaded to support slavery. Sending a hail of threats and reminding Mexico that the matter of slavery could irrevocably dissolve the friendship between their nations, they literally bullied Mexican functionaries into granting some concessions on Texas slavery.

Mexican congressmen wavered under the pressure, but they never completely capitulated on the issue of emancipation. As American protests mounted, Mexican resolve against slavery solidified, particularly when Mexico's territorial integrity started being challenged by the steady influx of Americans. American colonists were found squaring off against Mexican landholders over property rights as early as 1826. In what was to become known as the Fredonian Rebellion, colonists took up arms and declared their land an independent republic—the free state of Fredonia. The rebellion was a precursor of greater things to come.

In the context of such belligerence, a number of emancipation-minded Mexican officials came to view their position on the question of slavery as a weapon in their difficult struggle to preserve their national borders. Although Texas had been exempted from the effects of the 1829 abolition decree, by 1830 tides started shifting. Stiff alterations were made to Mexico's immigration policy so that no new slaves could be brought into Texas. Indirectly, this would limit the influx of unwanted whites. In 1831, during the midst of a series of impassioned speeches presented on the floor of the Mexican Senate, Francisco Manuel Sánchez de Tagle argued eloquently what was probably on the minds of others at the time. Not only should Mexico take steps to restrict slavery in Texas in order to slow American immigration, but it should also adopt a proactive policy towards receiving fugitive slaves from the United States. He urged his compatriots to welcome black slaves into Mexico so that they might serve as a "barrier" against a potential invasion by American whites. Their loyalty to their new home would be unquestioned since, if they ever had to face Americans in combat, they would fight to the end to avoid returning to bondage.[23]

Nothing prevented the loss of Texas, but the words of Senator Sanchez de Tagle resonated in the minds of Mexican policymakers for years to come, precipitating a strategy whereby Mexico extended an open border policy to blacks attempting to flee American control. We do not know exactly how many black slaves crossed into Mexico, although there were several thousand in residence by 1851. What is clearer is that beginning in the 1830s, Mexico came to be imagined by American blacks as a place of refuge, peace, and opportunity. Especially after the loss of Texas, Mexico was willing to uphold and even promote this image in its game of geopolitics with its powerful northern neighbor. Consequently, the proverbial "negro problem" acquired new meaning in the American Southwest, since a porous border with Mexico fanned the flame of black restlessness and insubordination.

These problems did not cease when Texas was annexed to the Union. In fact, the problems were magnified as white settlers dramatically increased the new state's slave presence. In 1830, there were between 2,000 and 4,000 black slaves living in Texas. By 1850 there were over 58,000, and by 1860 their number had grown to over 182,000.[24] Their yearning for freedom intensified upon realizing just how close they were to Mexico. More episodes of flight, border conflict, and loss of slave control ensued. By 1855, Texas officials noted that since the war for Texas Independence had begun, at least 4,000 slaves, valued at 3,200,000 dollars, had crossed into Mexico. At least 10 percent were women. Generally, the strongest and healthiest ran away. They were the best conditioned for making the dangerous trek across the border, which involved long exposure to semi-desert conditions, attacks from Indian groups, lack of food and shelter, and possible capture by slave-hunting parties.[25]

Just as black Americans started viewing Mexico as a beacon of freedom, some whites began sharing this vision, too. Abolitionists such as Benjamin Lundy, who had attempted to settle blacks in Canada and Haiti, saw the country as ideal for establishing a black colony, especially in the state of Tamaulipas. Lundy reached an agreement with Colonel Juan N. Almonte in 1834 to settle ex-slaves in the region. Less sympathetically, even a few racist American legislators came to perceive Mexico as a republic that was a natural home for "negroes," mainly because of the population's diverse ethnic and racial composition. In 1844, as arguments surrounding the annexation of Texas heated up, Sen. Robert J. Walker of Mississippi declared that it would be fine for Texas to be brought into the Union as a slave state (thereby upsetting the traditional balance of slave states verses free states) since blacks would eventually evaporate into Mexico, leaving the country free of a race problem:

> The sparse population occupying the land would welcome the Negroes and treat them as equals. The people of Latin America are overwhelmingly persons of color. . . . These people cherish no race prejudice against Negroes. The barriers of color, which in the United States would exclude Negroes forever from the privileges of equality, would not operate there. The Negroes would be integrated as equals in a society of equals and not always sullen inferiors in a despised caste.[26]

Even during the later stages of the Civil War, such opinions continued to be held. On January 11, 1864, James Lane of Kansas introduced a bill in Congress that sought to create a colony of four million blacks stretching from the Rio Grande to Colorado, and westward to New Mexico. He justified his resolution on the grounds that Mexicans would not object to the colony, given their racial tolerances, and even their proclivity for intermarriage.

After Slavery's Footprints

The termination of U.S. slavery after the Civil War may have ended Mexico's role as a land of liberty for slaves, but it did not diminish Mexico's position as a land of opportunity for blacks. The United States during the Reconstruction era left much to be desired, and blacks quickly discovered that being released from slavery did not mean sudden enfranchisement and material success. As early as the 1830s and 1840s, free blacks had begun exploring their options by settling in Mexico. Those living along the U.S.–Mexican border were among the earliest to travel there, as were individuals from port cities, such as New Orleans, who could travel great distances with more ease.[27] During the 1830s, Matamoros, in particular, attracted a noticeable black expatriate population. Discussions were held between Mexican officials and the city's black community to open up a formal colony there, but it is unclear if these plans ever materialized.[28]

Several black colonization projects were successfully launched in the 1850s. Under the direction of Chief "Wild Cat," hundreds of Seminoles made the journey from what is now Oklahoma to La Navaja, in the northern Mexican state of Coahuila. Traveling with them was John Horse, a tribal leader of former slaves, who brought a large Afro-Seminole contingent with him. Together, John Horse and Wild Cat established a military colony along the border, not far from Eagle Pass, Texas. Another was founded in Nacimiento. The settlements proved valuable to the Mexican government, who praised the colonists' "industriousness," "faithfulness," and their fighting abilities. Throughout the decade, Afro-Seminoles fought in no less than 40 armed conflicts for Mexico without losing a single battle, many against other Indians who inhabited the northern frontier.[29]

Meanwhile, in 1857, the Mexican government proceeded to issue a land grant in the coastal region of Tampico to the free-black Floridian, Luis N. Fouché. His colony, which became known as Eureka, was home to nearly 100 black families, each of whom was granted full Mexican citizenship. As an added incentive for settlement, the colonists were released from all but their municipal taxes, and were freed from providing compulsory military service, except during emergency situations. Around the same time Fouché's settlement was approved, another 40 American blacks arrived from New Orleans to the state of Veracruz, where they proceeded to found a smaller colony in the town of Tlacotlalpan. As with the Afro-Seminoles, their character and work ethic were praised in certain circles.

When the French emperor Maximilian briefly took control of Mexico (1864–1867), black immigration came to an abrupt halt. Maximilian openly courted relationships with members of the U.S. Confederacy and flirted with the idea of reinstating slavery. But by the 1880s and 1890s, the ambitious, export-oriented economic policies of Porfírio Díaz spawned the flourishing of new colonization schemes.[30] In 1886, F. E. Roesler, an immigration agent in Dallas, wrote a letter to President Díaz, requesting permission to settle blacks on empty land.[31] This was followed in 1888 by an announcement from the Mexican Land and Development Company (reputedly the owner of seven million acres in Tamaulipas) that it was going to sell stock to black investors and colonists at five cents a share. In 1893, the Colored Colonization Company of San Diego, founded by the black entrepreneur James Fowler, revealed that it would be selling shares at one cent apiece. Fowler aggressively tried to lure blacks by praising the fertility of Mexico's soil, the abundance of fishing opportunities, and the country's vast mineral resources. Blacks in San Diego were excited by the possibilities for acquiring quick wealth in an environment deemed free of racial prejudice. One black journalist succinctly described the situation by writing, "Mexican emigration fever is rife here."[32]

In December of 1894, another large-scale settlement was attempted. W. H. Ellis, a black businessman, joined forces with the Agricultural, Industrial and Colonization Company of Tlahualilo, agreeing to settle 100 black families in the state of Durango. The terms of the deal seemed advantageous to everyone involved. The families, hailing largely from Georgia and Alabama, were to have most of their transportation costs covered. They were also to receive 60 acres of land, tools, seed, livestock, and a small monthly stipend. In return, the company took 40 percent of each family's cotton and corn yield. Ellis profited by taking a 10 percent share.

Eight hundred blacks undertook the venture.[33] Unfortunately, the reality of life in Durango proved far more difficult than anyone had imagined. Snow greeted the settlers as they arrived on company grounds. Lodging facilities proved substandard, as families of up to 12 individuals were crammed into tight, floorless adobe homes. As winter became spring, unusually torrential downpours exposed scores of leaks throughout their dwellings. Dreams of wealth were further dashed as the colonists discovered that the tools they had been provided were of inferior quality.

To make matters worse, epidemics set in. A mysterious liver disease struck in April, followed by ravaging smallpox in July. Colonists began getting restless, quarreling among themselves. Eventually, they started abandoning the settlement. Of the original 800, just 50 or 60 remained. The rest sought U.S. government support to be resettled in Birmingham, Alabama. By the fall, the death toll of the short-lived colony stood at 148, with 250 missing.[34]

As the colonization attempt in Durango shows, success across the Rio Grande could not be predicted with certainty. Some settlement efforts became great success stories. Others failed. However, during the mid to late nineteenth century, what did seem constant and predictable were the conscious efforts by entrepreneurs to distort the reality of life in Mexico in order to attract and exploit black labor. It wasn't just whites who were engaging in these practices. Black entrepreneurs like Ellis were equally guilty.

Episodes of individual black success in Mexico also served to attract others, while offering a valuable and often more reliable source of information about life across the border. Occasionally, these success stories became matters of legend, magnified when picked up by the black press. When the *Indianapolis Freeman* and the *Washington Bee* ran a letter from Dr. Jesse Mosley (in 1907 and 1915, respectively), they effectively endorsed black migration. Mosely proudly recounted that he was "the private physician to the governor [of Tamaulipas]," and that in Mexico, American blacks were "making money and enjoying life."[35] The readers of the paper, contrasting their lives with his, took notice.

From the Mexican point of view, there were limits to just how open the nation was when it came to accepting tides of black immigrants. Well before the 1860s, some Mexicans dared to oppose the country's open border policy for runaway slaves. Much later, in reaction to the ill-fated 1894 settlement in Durango, a columnist for *El Heraldo* (Guadalajara) wrote that encouraging black immigration "is to toll the bell so that the Negro avalanche will fall on Durango preceding the white." Other reactions followed suit. *El Tiempo* (Mexico City) objected to the settlement by stating that "this way of stopping lynching and helping the United States get rid of a race which the Yankees detest is very harmful and disquieting to Mexico . . . it is preferable that we continue seeing our fields deserted and living with a small population than to admit North Americans of the Negro race." *El Cronista Mexicano* (San Antonio) conveyed fear over the possibility that the blacks would seek to keep their American nationality and lord it over the Mexicans.[36]

Completely unrelated to events in Durango, the Gulf Coast town of Papantla was quite clear in the late nineteenth century that it did not want to host blacks. Interestingly, the town had its own longstanding African heritage, stretching back deep into the colonial period. In fact, it was only one of a handful of places where free people of color had boldly resisted the impositions of royal authority in the eighteenth century. But in the nineteenth century, the town wanted to distance itself from this past. Local officials extended a warm invitation to immigrants of all other races and nationalities, save blacks and Chinese.[37]

In still other contexts, Mexicans were quick to assign blacks a host of negative qualities. Columnists from papers such as *El Monitor Republicano* occasionally labeled blacks as lazy, dissolute, and unintelligent.[38] Words such as "mean, cruel, prone to crime, and perpetual drunkards" were also encountered with some frequency. These descriptions were almost identical to those used to describe blacks and mulattos in the colonial period. Hence, certain racist stereotypes survived independence.[39]

Bitter feelings towards black immigrants had to do with debates over the proper course of progress for the nation. According to the principles of social thought that dominated the nineteenth and early twentieth centuries, the successful development of nations was largely determined by two main criteria. On the one hand were environmental factors. Nations located in hotter, tropical climates were at a disadvantage when compared to those located in temperate zones. Earlier thinkers such as Montesquieu had noted that the environment also affected the operation of human institutions, such as governments and businesses. Climate equally had a direct effect on agricultural production and human performance. Unfortunately, there was little a nation could do about where it was situated. However, the second set of success criteria, a nation's racial composition, could be altered.

The prospects for a nation's fortune were often measured by the inherent talent and capacities of its human resources. Frequently, a nation's human capital was tallied by racial standards. Psuedoscientific theories, rooted in eighteenth century thought, taught that some races were innately superior to others. Whites, in general, were deemed better than blacks, Indians, and Asians. The work of Lamarck and the appearance of the field of biology led to the belief that the inferior qualities of nonwhites were permanently fixed in their physiology and were inheritable from one generation to the next. When Charles Darwin published the *Descent of Man* in 1859, demonstrating that breeding populations adapt over time, his theories, too, were reworked into social thought. The "survival of the fittest" principle was reinterpreted to say that because of natural selection, some races, particularly whites, were "more fit" to survive, and were therefore predestined to dominate other races.[40]

Yet, through carefully managing immigration policy, engaging in limited wars designed to alter the demographic balance of a country, and through adept political maneuvering, a nation could gradually improve its racial stock, and consequently, its prospects for the future. Likewise, intelligent macroeconomic decisions could create the circumstances necessary for improving a nation's social conditions, oftentimes described as an important third factor towards successful national progress. In 1883, the process by which nations consciously chose to selectively breed their populations along these lines became known as eugenics.[41]

In Mexico, these theories matured gradually over time, with complicated variations. As early as the 1820s and 1830s, Mexicans were already expressing concern that blacks and Indians were deadweights on the nation. In 1836, the influential Mexican liberal thinker, José María Luis Mora, shared his views publicly. He prophesied that by mid-century, thanks to vigorous racial mixture, blacks would disappear in Mexico. Indians would enjoy the same fate, but the process would take longer, perhaps a century.[42] The unwritten corollary, at least as far as blacks were concerned, was that for the intermixture to have full effect, black immigration had to be curtailed, even halted.

By the second half of the nineteenth century, two main philosophical camps had emerged. On one side stood the Jacobins and Conservatives, who generally disdained all forms of nonwhite immigration. They even ranked whites by order of preference. They tended to favor "Latins" (Spaniards, Italians, Portuguese, French, and Belgians), since they believed that Latins would marry into the lower classes, could be easily assimilated, and could help the country create a "beautiful native population" that would defend Mexico from the North American menace. On the other side of the philosophical debate stood Mexico's Positivists.[43] Their stance on immigration, particularly that of lower-class migrants, is best summarized in a statement which was popular among them: "*lo que es blanco por fuera puede ser negro por dentro.*" This literally meant that what appeared white on the outside might actually prove black on the inside. Clearly revealed in this thinking is that blackness still bore a negative connotation, but that Positivists called for a deeper examination and assessment of racial worth. Each immigrant needed to be evaluated for their overall work capacity and their ability to contribute to the nation's progress. In some instances, Positivists contended, Mexicans would be surprised to find that blacks and Asians might be preferred.

The 1870s platform of the Secretary of the Treasury, Matías Romero, was in many ways indicative of the Positivists' position. Romero was convinced that black and Chinese immigration was the answer to many of Mexico's longstanding economic problems. In his opinion, both groups were the ideal populations to work the fertile plantations and estates of the nation's lowlands. Furthermore, Article 11 of the Mexican constitution protected their immigration rights.

Romero was not alone in his outlook. By the late 1880s and early 1890s, other Positivists firmly believed that Mexico's immigration policy should stress diversity. Since the country was composed of many different climatic areas, each region deserved special types of attention. Because the science of the day taught that whites thrived in cooler environments, Mexico's temperate central zones could be best exploited by encouraging white immigration. Meanwhile, the hot and humid coasts were perfectly suited for black labor, given their "great muscular strength, extraordinary physiological resistance, and their socially rooted work habits."[44]

Many Positivists, however, were realistic. They were among the first to admit that Mexico could probably never be able to compete economically with the United States and its success in attracting and utilizing floods of white immigrants. Therefore, rather than focusing any significant attention on developing Mexico's temperate zones and cities, they reasoned that the best course was to devote the greatest energy towards exploiting the coasts and countryside, the "great hope of the nation." Under these premises, as late as February 1911 plans were being made by the government of Porfírio Díaz, along with the Development Company of the Southern Lands (*Compañia Desarrolladora Tierras del Sur*), to bring in North American blacks to settle and stimulate the economy of the coastal region of Campeche in the Yucatan peninsula.[45]

In 1895, *El Universal* (Mexico City), among other papers, further stressed that blacks, particularly American cotton farmers, possessed special skills that would be vital for progress.[46] Looking internationally, Positivists noticed how blacks had already proven indispensable in the United States to developing the economy of the South, and were instrumental in underwriting the plantation economy of Cuba. More importantly, the blacks that had already migrated to Mexico had demonstrated a remarkable facility for social integration. They worked hard at learning the language, adapted to the nation's customs, and sometimes even became small landholders. They achieved this integration even better than Anglo-Saxons, who proved difficult to assimilate and often arrived with an air of snobbery. Men like Matías Romero were quick to emphasize that blacks fit almost an ideal immigrant profile. If "Latins" couldn't be attracted to Mexico, then blacks were among the next best thing.[47]

In some senses, the Positivists were trapped in a vicious circle of argument. They believed in getting the best race and nationality for the job. Yet assessing who was "the best" was a function of ranking the worth of a race and nationality based on racist criteria. As a result, it was hard to obtain an objective evaluation of blackness. But of all the social thinkers in Mexico, the Positivist camp probably came closest to a neutral understanding of blackness in the late nineteenth century. Of course, there were also Positivists who looked at the United States' model of progress and blindly sought to import waves Europeans. But even so, on the whole, Mexico's Positivists proved more tolerant than their counterparts.

The competition against their position was stiff. Towards the end of the nineteenth century, an expression circulated throughout Mexico—"all that is not European is nothing more than plague to the issue of immigration." Fears ran that introducing too many blacks would not only bring disorder, but also revolt and bloody rebellion. Elements of the Catholic press mused that blacks were agents in a larger, diabolical plan, designed by the United States to wrest control over Nuevo León and Tamaulipas. In the process, the United States was cleverly getting rid of its own racial "trash." Others feared that Ellis's 1894 settlement in Durango would invite swarms of restless and potentially dangerous North American blacks, escalating into the hundreds of thousands. According to late nineteenth century calculations, stamping out a rebellion of just 10,000 blacks would occupy roughly one-fifth of the national army, roughly 6,000 to 8,000 men.

Whereas some praised the great physical strength that blacks were supposedly bringing to the nation, the *Monitor Republicano* pointed out that blacks were lazier and less intelligent than even the country's indigenous population. One of the major concerns for Mexican social thinkers was finding ways to stimulate the productivity of the overwhelmingly large indigenous sector, which, even in the nineteenth century, outnumbered every other population category. Disparagingly, the Mexican thinker Juvenal wrote that not only were blacks useless for this purpose, but they were also a detriment to the moral fabric of the nation. Others wrote that blacks, when placed in the company of Indians, actually caused them to lose whatever redeeming qualities they once had. Indians acquired a host of black vices instead.

When Abdón Morales submitted a proposal to introduce 100,000 Africans and Asians to Mexico in the 1860s, the president of the Mexican Assembly of

Colonization rejected it, since "ugly" black and Asian blood was deemed unable to "improve the mixture of the race" of Mexico. In 1889, when Lancaster Jones sought to introduce black American mining and agricultural colonies into the states of Veracruz, Oaxaca, Guerrero, Michoacán, and San Luis Potosí, Senator Couttolenc rebuffed him with diatribes on the senate floor. The only time that blacks had demonstrated a viable work ethic in their history was "when they were slaves," he argued. In freedom, all they could demonstrate was their inherent laziness. In nearby Cuba, which was still a slave regime, blacks had to be whipped before they worked effectively, Couttolenc explained. More disturbingly, the black population contributed to the island's degeneracy. If Mexico's efforts to make positive use of Italian immigration was failing, imagine the scope of failure that black immigration would produce. These were people who were "instinctively savages and without any form of religion," he contended. While Congress voted overwhelmingly to offer Jones his contract, Couttolenc's loud dissent had been heard.[48]

The concern with degeneracy was real and pervaded Mexican social thought into the twentieth century. Juvenal wrote that black immigration not only contaminated the culture of the Mexican countryside, but that of its cities as well. Within a matter of years, he warned, lower-class urban neighborhoods would be found adopting black habits. Even North American blacks, normally considered among the most desirable of black immigrants, could be faulted for bringing about degeneracy. When a proposal was passed to introduce 20,000 blacks to cultivate cotton and sugar, *El Tiempo* lamented that the majority of these would be "the corrupt, effeminate, and vice-ridden inhabitant[s] of the U.S. South," as opposed to the "vigorous inhabitant[s] of Africa."[49] By invoking Africa in this way, the newspaper slapped a backhanded comment on all free-blacks born and raised in the New World. When blacks arrived fresh off the boat, as did African slaves, they supposedly proved to be better workers and less debilitating in terms of their social impact.

Other newspaper columnists and intellectuals were more democratic than *El Tiempo* in assigning the label of degeneracy. Mexico had to be wary of all blacks and Asians regardless of nationality, some cautioned, since Mexicans exhibited a natural tendency toward accepting the influx of inferior races without being cognizant of the long-term damage that such immigration caused. If the main purpose for importing blacks was taking advantage of their supposed suitability for working in hot climates, then Mexico would be better off employing the labor of non-black Canary Islanders, who were "equally strong, but harder workers and more honorable."[50]

With all of this said, Mexico's mid to late nineteenth-century perspective on blacks could be rather ambivalent, and members of all camps, including

Positivists, Conservatives, and Jacobins, were prone to crossing lines. *El Tiempo*, frequently a vehement protestor of black immigration, supported it when juxtaposed with the prospect of white "Yankee" immigration to Mexico. Wodon de Sorinee, writing about black immigration in 1900, favored the black presence, but only in small doses. He believed that short infusions of blacks from the U.S. South could jump start the Mexican agricultural export sector. Once the economy started getting into gear, he deemed it prudent to scale back on black immigration before it backfired by producing harmful social results. In 1895, both *El Tiempo* and the conservative paper *La Libertad* ran interesting articles responding to an incident that took place in June at the Hotel Iturbide in Mexico City. Three black Americans had tried to check in but were refused service. Normally hostile to blacks, the two papers rallied to their defense. They pointed out that the event was unfortunate and unwarranted in Mexico. In fact, they argued that throughout Latin America, social privileges should not be doled out according to race, since the members of all social classes possessed some "defects" and "qualities" (read racial mixture). *La Libertad* went on to say that "our cousins [the U.S.] cannot deny that in this respect [race relations] we are much more civilized than they are."[51]

The Mexican press's ability to attack black immigration with inflammatory and discriminatory language on the one hand, but to defend blacks against instances of racism on the other, reveals the complex and multifaceted relationship that Mexico had with the concept of blackness. Blackness quite simply provided a running commentary on the state of the nation. How Mexico dealt with blacks provided a measure of the country's position within the global league of nations. In the eyes of the international community there were times when there was no contradiction between being racist and fighting racism. Why? Because both enterprises could be interpreted as defending the interests of the state, which always took priority over other concerns. Being racist with regards to immigration policy was a method of controlling national destiny to ensure progress. However, fighting racism within one's borders was a means of distinguishing oneself from economically successful, but morally/socially backward nations, like the United States.

In certain calculated circumstances, fighting racism publicly was also a means of defending Mexico's own intricate racial mixture from external criticism. Mexicans were acutely aware that their racial and ethnic composition was remarkably more diverse than either Europe or the United States. Fighting select battles against antiblack racism cast Mexico's particular racial blend in a more positive light. On the one hand, it served to distance Mexico's population from immigrant blackness. In these tussles Mexicans were understood to be "intervening" to defend the rights of black "foreigners." Consequently, one should not confuse Mexico as being a black nation, which North Americans and Europeans often did, if mainly in a metaphorical sense.[52] On the other hand, fighting antiblack racism also validated the principles of equal and fair treatment for subordinate, nonwhite peoples of all colors. Mexico's large *mestizo* and Indian population fell into this category. Periodically exhibiting fraternity with immigrant blacks against racism elevated the self-worth of the people.

While Mexico wrestled with how to handle black immigrants, there were important changes in how the country came to understand and discuss its own African-based population. Arguably, Mexicans have always tacitly acknowledged the existence of pockets of Mexican-born blacks in the nation. The Pacific coastal region of the Costa Chica and the Gulf coast areas of Veracruz have both historically been centers of an Afro-Mexican presence. In 1889, Domingo Orvañanos recorded the nation's black population (including immigrants) to be nearly 250,000 out of a total 11 million people. A few years later, Alfonso Luis Velasco observed that in the Pacific coastal state of Oaxaca, 5 out of 14 districts had appreciable black concentrations, many with a long colonial history.[53]

As has been already noted, after independence, Mexican intellectuals and policymakers placed a premium on emphasizing the shrinking nature of the native black population. By 1901, just over a decade after Orvañanos's population estimate, Alberto Correa recorded that blacks had slipped to barely 100,000. Perhaps more importantly, Correa used his figures to point out what many travelers and social thinkers were indicating at the time. By the turn of the century, the majority of Mexico's blacks were believed to be primarily foreign born, hailing mainly from Cuba, the English-speaking Caribbean, and the United States.[54]

Miraculously, therefore, the pulses of black immigration provided Mexico with the ability to transform its native black population into foreigners, even as they continued living on the land their ancestors had settled centuries ago. Migration statistics could be manipulated to rewrite Afro-Mexican history by displacing them from historical memory. Hence, the long-desired extinction of Mexico's black population was achieved not by race mixture alone, but rather by creatively combining miscegenation with immigration policy.

It helped that many black immigrants arrived to work on labor projects that were well defined and of fixed duration. For example, blacks from throughout the West Indies came to construct Mexico's transoceanic railroad. Three hundred Jamaicans landed in 1882 to work on the railroad line from San Luis Potosí to Tampico. Another three hundred were contracted as miners in Durango in 1905. Blacks from the Bahamas were sent to work on the Central Railroad of Tampico. The fixed nature of these projects meant that when the work was complete, there was always the possibility that the workers would leave. Between 1910 and 1911, of the 2,292 blacks that entered the country, just 768 remained.[55] For those who wanted to make the argument, these figures could be used to demonstrate that the black population that came into Mexico was manageable and under control. More ingeniously still, the data could be used not only to help leach the nation's Afro-Mexican population out of its own history, but to recast whatever black population that remained as migrant workers—a temporary national status.

Marching Toward War

Revolution broke out in Mexico in 1910 as rural peasants and ranchers felt unjustly bound into poverty by the regime of Porfírio Díaz, and as middle-class residents in Mexico City felt alienated from key political and economic circles. The outbreak of World War I further thrust Mexico into the international limelight, as both Germany and the Allied powers vied for the country's support. Domestic and global events directly affected the relationship between the United States and Mexico. As during the period of the Mexican-American War, and even during the American Civil War and the Spanish-American War, conflagrations had a way of accentuating matters of race.

The dismal treatment that blacks received in Jim Crow America created a potentially potent destabilizing force that was magnified by war. Mexico could use this for its own political advantage. In 1898, for instance, during the heat of the Spanish-American War, *El Tiempo* published an article encouraging Mexico to foment rebellion among disgruntled Southern blacks and dispossessed Indians as a means of reclaiming land lost in the Mexican American War of 1848, and to repel further aggressions from their northern neighbor.[56] The plea was never acted upon, but the fear of such an outbreak lingered in the minds of American policymakers. Their suspicions were heightened during the Mexican Revolution. Despite its conflicting goals, the revolution was infused with rhetoric about ending class oppression and promoting social equality. The message was attractive to black Americans, and when speaking in the United States, revolutionaries such as Flores Magón were able to lure blacks into their audiences.[57] In 1911, Magón's party, the PLM (Liberal Mexican Party) even convinced a number of blacks in the region of Mexicali to join a motley crew of international freedom fighters. As an added incentive, the PLM offered 140 acres of land and 600 dollars in cash to their "ideological brothers."[58] Pancho Villa, the legendary revolutionary leader of the northern army, proved attractive, too, not just because of his message but because of his phenotypic features. By some accounts, Villa was thought to have been a deserter from the black U.S. 10th cavalry. Others rumored him to be "the son of a black Baltimore resident and a Hispanic woman."[59] Such credentials, even if untrue, proved helpful in his recruitment efforts. In 1914, Villa counted some 500 men in his legion of foreigners, a smattering of whom were black.[60] After 1916, when international circumstances caused Villa to become more anti-"gringo" in tone, many American blacks supported him even more, believing that he was the only person able to stand up successfully to the abuses of white U.S. power.[61]

As key U.S. black intellectuals, such as Hubert Harrison, threw their support behind the revolutionary cause, concerns grew in Washington over the ramifications and scope of the alliances being forged between U.S. blacks and Mexico's rebels. Discouragingly, several arrests were made during the 1910s of blacks supposedly involved in conspiratorial events related to the Mexican uprising. The *New York Times* ran a story about how the government detained two men in Birmingham, Alabama, one white and another black, for "posing as bible salesmen and ministers of the gospel" while "urging black people to migrate to Mexico on specially provided trains."[62] By the time they were apprehended, they had already visited much of the South, spreading their message in Alabama, Louisiana, Georgia, the Carolinas, and Mississippi. In 1917, Sam Doyle, a black farmer in Texas, was reported to have resisted entry into the draft because he was sure that a Mexican army would soon cross the border to "clean up the whites." Other farmers shared his opinion. They were reportedly storing their crops in anticipation of the day when a Mexican army would come to reclaim lost territory.[63]

World War I added to the American government's fears of sedition. The discord within revolutionary Mexico made it a prime target for the predatory ambitions of Germany and Japan. Both countries had already established links in the country. In addition to its business ties, Germany formalized a relationship with President Venustiano Carranza shortly after the outbreak of World War I, maintaining visibly friendly diplomatic relations despite Mexico's declared neutrality. At various moments during the late nineteenth and early twentieth centuries, the Japanese had attempted to purchase tracts of coastal land, establish colonies, and sell munitions to Mexican forces. From the vantage point of the U.S. government, any union between Germany, Japan, and Mexico could prove lethal to U.S. power and sovereignty, especially when combined with the support of American blacks. Furthermore, the potential alignment of blacks, Japanese, and Mexicans added a unique racial twist in that the challenge of these nonwhite forces threatened the very structure of Jim Crow and its principles of white supremacy.

To an extent, these fears materialized in the form of the "Plan of San Diego," signed in San Diego, Texas in January 1915.[64] Marching under the banner of a red and white flag, a Liberating Army of Races and Peoples composed of blacks, Japanese, and Mexican Americans sought to take control of Texas, Oklahoma, New Mexico, Arizona, Colorado, and California. Beginning at 2 A.M. on February 20, 1915, the conspirators planned to murder every white male over the age of 16 in each state. Then they planned to install a Supreme Revolutionary Congress that would liberate blacks, Indians, and Mexican Americans from racial oppression. Although no direct aid was to come from the Mexican government, once the bloody revolution was over, the rebels were to deliberate if they were going to annex their republic to Mexico. In the meantime, they would subdivide themselves into nations according to their race. Blacks would be amassed into six states of their own, while Indians would populate a republic composed of recaptured ancestral lands seized from the U.S. government.

From the beginning, the plan's prospects for success were slim. Its nine primary conspirators were indicted just months after the document was signed. Then February 20 came and went without war. A revised plan was issued shortly thereafter, known as the Manifesto of the Oppressed Peoples of America. Apart from some episodes of sporadic violence that erupted in the summer and autumn of 1915, this too did not have the sweeping effect that was originally envisioned. While there is a significant amount of debate over the Plan of San Diego's true purpose (some believe that a conspiratorial clique of Americans was privately trying to prompt a war themselves), evidence suggests that the plan was probably a political tool used by competing military factions to exploit racial tensions in the Southwest for the advantage of the Mexican government. The recently installed Carranza regime was reaching out, trying to find ways to bolster itself in Mexico. President Carranza may have hatched the plan to scare the United States into accepting his administration as legitimate. Indeed, not long after, President Wilson recognized the Carranza regime.

The Plan of San Diego, and others like it, did not die an easy death. In 1916, a Mr. Fukutaro (or Fukumatsu) Terasawa was responsible for recruiting Japanese sympathizers in Mexico for war in Texas. With the help of a member of the German propaganda forces, Dr. Jesse Mosley, a black doctor and a member of Carranza's Constitutionalist Army, recruited black rebels for similar aims in the areas of Austin and San Marcos.[65] As late as 1917, stories published in the *New York Times* and the *New York Tribune*, along with intelligence reports from operatives in Alabama, Texas, Tennessee, and Mississippi, urged the U.S. government to take the Plan of San Diego seriously. The *New York Tribune* ran a story on April 4 claiming that German spies had met secretly in Greensboro, North Carolina, as well as in New York City, to discuss and resurrect the Plan of San Diego. Also that month, three men near Jackson, Mississippi were said to have been offering blacks "inducements to go to Mexico and join the germans [*sic*] there." In Memphis, 150 migrant workers were detained to investigate their potential recruitment in a Mexican-German army.[66]

The attraction black Americans felt to the Mexican Revolution and the message of liberation offered by Germany and Japan should not be exaggerated. These were opportunistic times, important years that blacks used for carving their space within their own country. As has been seen repeatedly in history, those on the margins of a society oftentimes find that they are able to work themselves more tightly into the fabric of the nation through military service and loyalty. The shedding of blood dramatically reveals a willingness to defend a nation's principles and advance its goals at the ultimate price. Lost heroes on battlefields, the memory of campaigns—all of this serves to build a mythology that can be invoked by minorities and counterbalanced against the pantheon of the majority. Black Americans in the 1910s were faced with options. Would they work for deeper enfranchisement in the nation by exhibiting nationalism, or would they seek an alternative means of expressing discontent over their plight? The choice was neither obvious nor easy. Evidence shows that whatever support plots like the Plan of San Diego enjoyed, and however many black Americans were seduced by the Mexican Revolution, most were not motivated into insubordination by these schemes.[67]

Instead, a number of blacks took advantage of opportunities offered by the Mexican Revolution to build the credentials of their patriotism. In 1916, when Pancho Villa crossed the border and attacked the town of Columbus, Texas, General Pershing led a punitive expedition into Mexico. Two black units, the 24th Infantry and the 10th Cavalry, were mobilized to help secure Villa's capture. At first, President Carranza welcomed the forces, since he wanted to eliminate his rival and strengthen his hold over Mexico. But quickly, his welcome wore thin. Mexican national pride began to surface when the Carrancistas grew worried that the United States would accomplish what they could not—the defeat of Villa. Moreover, the United States's presence was being interpreted as a sign of Yankee imperialism, and a prelude to a full-scale invasion of Mexico. The uneasy relationship between the United States and the Carranza government became increasingly strained.

The fruitless search for Villa turned sour on June 20, 1916. A detachment of 79 cavalrymen under the command of captains Charles Boyd and Lewis Morey received a tip about the encampment of a large force of Carrancistas near the village of Carrizal in the state of Chihuahua. Acting on this information, the troops marched southward on a reconnaissance mission, with explicit orders to avoid combat. Ignoring the orders his superiors, Capt. Boyd impetuously provoked a conflict between the black 10th Cavalry and the Carrancistas when he proceeded to march his troops into Carrizal, despite warnings from the

Mexican officers not to do so. Fourteen U.S. troops lost their lives, including Boyd. Several others were captured. Facing defeat, the Americans sounded retreat and wandered back to Pershing's camp, but the political damage had been done. Mexico and the United States were brought into diplomatic crisis, with both nations sounding the guns of war. Eleven thousand U.S. troops stood poised and ready to march into Mexico. Meanwhile, the blacks who had fought at Carrizal briefly became vaunted as national heroes. Six were buried in Arlington National Cemetery, honored in a ceremony attended by President Wilson and several members of the House of Representatives.

For their part, the Mexicans had actually been surprised to be confronting black soldiers at Carrizal. Despite the fact that black troops had comprised the stalwart mainstays of U.S. military border forces since the 1870s, rumors circulated that the Carrancistas would easily be able to sway their allegiances to the Mexican side. These ultimately proved unfounded. Even though black soldiers would later criticize Capt. Boyd for his rashness, they remained unwavering in their commitment to their nation.[68]

But was the nation as eager to embrace to them? There are indicators to suggest that the honors blacks received for Carrizal were not progressive in their nature, nor were they long lasting in their impact. Whites briefly celebrated the episodes of black patriotism because they fit nicely within the existing framework of U.S. expansionist policy and its dogma of racial supremacy. In fighting against "brown" Mexicans, blacks temporarily "whitened" themselves in the process, but they did not fundamentally alter their status vis-à-vis the nation's white majority. Blacks, after all, were still blacks.[69] Many black intellectuals became cognizant of this fact, especially as U.S. involvement in World War I escalated. On the heels of a 1917 rebellion of black soldiers in Houston, and in the aftermath of protests arguing against segregation in the military, W. E. B. Du Bois published a powerful editorial entitled "Returning Soldiers" in 1919. Passionately, he wrote "we are cowards and jackasses if now that the war is over, we do not marshal every ounce of our brain and brawn to fight a sterner, longer, more unbending battle against the forces of hell in our own land."[70] Du Bois fully realized that fighting war abroad did not cleanse racial prejudice at home.

Complicated Pathways to the 1960s

Mexico largely forgave black Americans for their aggression at Carrizal. Mexican politicians remained aware of the complexity of black loyalties during the World War I and revolutionary periods, and so were less rigid in blaming blacks for the attack. Perhaps as a result of this implicit understanding, although the era of grand colonization schemes had largely ended during the first decade of the twentieth century, in 1917 the Mexican government endorsed Theodore Troy's plan to found a farming colony called "Little Liberia" near Ensenada. Peaking at 200 settlers in the 1920s, the black colony thrived into the 1960s. Also, the government did not stand in the way when the oil boom in Tampico (1910–1920) brought scores of new black immigrants from New Orleans. However, the high-profile residency of Jack Johnson (1917–1919) probably best demonstrated Mexico's cordiality towards U.S. blacks. Johnson's close friendship with President Carranza and his Cinderella relationship with the elite showed the favorable elements of black American status within Mexico's official circles on the eve of the 1920s.[71]

Even though President Alvaro Obregón (1920–1924) continued meeting with black investors into the early 1920s, a couple of events marked a change in Mexican attitudes. The end of the armed phase of the Mexican Revolution brought forth a second, longer-lasting cultural phase that endured to 1940 and beyond.[72] Weary from years of bloodshed and civil strife, Mexico yearned for a unity that was achieved, in part, through articulating a new racial ideology. Two of the most powerful concepts to emerge from the revolution were those of *indigenismo* and *mestizaje*. *Indigenismo* sought to remedy the alienation of Indian peasants from the Mexican nation by placing them at the center of its cultural and social programs, and by embracing indigenous history as foundational for the expression of Mexican society. Meanwhile, *mestizaje* praised the value of Mexican racial mixture. With his 1925 book, *La Raza Cósmica* (*The Cosmic Race*), José Vasconcelos virtually overturned theories like those of Herbert Spencer, which understood racial mixture to be degenerative to the development of nations. In the process, Vasconcelos, and other proponents of *mestizaje*, opened space in Mexican society for the masses of *mestizos* to participate.[73]

Indigenismo and *mestizaje* were concepts that constantly informed one another. Together, they became hegemonic in Mexican thought. Yet they were also imperfect ideas; although *indigenismo* purported to praise Indian society, what was being really praised was the Indian past, not its present. Therefore, Indian culture and society in the twentieth century was patronizingly seen as being in need of remediation—of needing to be aggressively brought in line with the rest of the nation. *Mestizaje* served as the benchmark for this process. The *mestizo* became the cultural mainstream; Indians were to be realigned into their mold.

Because the type of race mixture celebrated through the ideology of Mexican *mestizaje* was focused intensely and fundamentally on the miscegenation between whites and Indians, blacks were almost irrelevant to the discussion.

There were moments when intellectuals considered incorporating blacks into the broader theoretical debates. A few articles appeared here and there in the early 1920s on the subject.[74] Manuel Gamio, one of the country's leading anthropologists and head of the Demographic Department of the Secretariat of Governance (*Secretaría de Gobernación*), conceived of a project that would investigate all of the heritages of the nation in each of its regions. If correctly realized, the project would have inevitably examined the history of the nation's blacks, but it was never completed.[75] It would not be until the 1940s, with the research of Gonzalo Aguirre Beltrán (encouraged by Gamio), before a Mexican scholar would engage in serious scholarly inquiry into the black heritage. Unfortunately, by this time the valuable opportunity to include blacks in conversations about the national image had passed since the key formative stage of the revolution's cultural phase had already ended.

The combined power of *mestizaje* and *indigenismo* created a climate that was inhospitable towards accepting black immigration.[76] This was accentuated by economic crisis, which struck between 1926 and 1931. In reality, hard times worked to limit all forms of immigration to Mexico, but the government paid special attention to barring blacks, East Indians, Syrians, Lebanese, Armenians, Palestinians, Arabs, Turks, and Chinese from entering the country. As part of a policy designed to protect opportunities for Mexican workers and to "prevent the mixture of races that had been scientifically proven to produce degenerate descendants," entry of each of these groups was restrained in legislation passed on July 8, 1927.[77] The rationale behind the exclusions smacked of racism from the prewar years, the difference now being that the restraints were shrouded under the seemingly liberal theory of *mestizaje*.

The U.S. black press picked up on the negative tenor and ran stories throughout the 1920s avowing Mexico's cool reception of blacks. Among the more damaging articles was one published in a 1929 edition of the *Chicago Defender*. The piece claimed that the Mexican government had gone so far as to ask American officials to deny black travelers their citizenship certificates, which were important documents needed to secure legal entry.[78] Ironically, just a century earlier, it was the U.S. government that had itself unilaterally decided to refuse blacks these papers in order to curtail slave and free-black movement across the border.

Blacks continued encountering barriers to entering Mexico through the early years of the Depression and during the early days of the administration of President Lázaro Cárdenas (1934–1940), Mexico's progressively minded, leftist head of state. Finally, in 1935, the Mexican ambassador in Washington, Francisco Castillo Najera, worked to remove the impediments that kept blacks from acquiring permission to cross.[79] This did not open the floodgates of transborder travel, however, and certain individuals still experienced racism at the hands of Mexican officials, some of it from the ambassador's office itself. On February 13, 1937, W. E. B. Du Bois wrote a letter to Frank Tannenbaum, a professor at Columbia University, urging him to help find a solution to the nagging problem. The previous summer, two of Du Bois's colleagues at Atlanta University had experienced very telling episodes of discrimination en route to Mexico. The first involved a man Du Bois described as "brown . . . of Negro descent, an artist." Arriving at New Orleans, he was detained, hassled, and forced to post a cash bond of 250 dollars before leaving for Mexico. The other black traveler was a "yellow man of Negro descent, a doctor of philosophy from Harvard." He had applied for a border pass at the Mexican consulate in Washington, D.C. but was "put off indefinitely." Complaining to some of his friends in the State Department he was eventually granted permission to cross, although by this time he was already in California. Disparagingly, his tourist pass read: "Permission granted in spite of the fact that the person is of Negro descent."[80] The ultimate insult in the whole affair was that while these two faculty members entered Mexico only with great difficulty, a third Atlanta University professor, a white man, sailed through the border after paying a customary one-dollar tourist tax.

By all measures, the 1920s and 1930s had witnessed serious damage to Mexico's reputation as a racial paradise. With the emergence of Hollywood, some blacks were influenced by the industry's negative stereotyping of Mexico as backwards and uncivilized. Others interpreted the attitudes and actions of Mexican policymakers, particularly in the realm of religion, as profoundly unchristian. They did not want to spend time in what they were increasingly considering to be a heathen nation. Additionally, near the advent of the Depression, Mexicans were crossing the border into the United States in growing numbers. Nearly 600,000 arrived between 1910 and 1930 alone. Along with Mexican immigration came job competition, as Mexicans competed directly with blacks at the bottom rungs of the U.S. economy.[81] Irritatingly, sometimes Mexicans were favored over blacks for certain jobs; a few even enjoyed privileges denied to blacks.[82] This brewed black antagonism, which in turn unfavorably altered their impression of Mexico. Du Bois, in his efforts to improve the ease by which black tourists crossed the border, threatened to harness this antagonism and use it against Mexico. In his 1937 letter to Tannenbaum, Du Bois contemplated urging blacks to join forces with stronger and more vocal opponents to Mexican immigration. By these means, he hoped to secure concessions on black travel. Tannebaum alerted Mexican president, Lázaro Cárdenas, to the political ramifications of Du Bois's plan. Citing Du Bois as one of the premier black intellectuals in the country, he cautioned that not only would new difficulties arise for Mexicans seeking employment in the

United States, but Mexico's "good name" would also be internationally tarnished, while exposing some contradictions with the Mexican Revolution's emphasis on social justice.[83]

To a certain degree, the deteriorating relationship between American blacks and Mexicans was masked in the familiar rhetoric of color blindness. Mexicans denied that they treated blacks any differently than anyone else. As Ambassador Castillo Najera explained in 1943, "racial differences are no longer significant in Mexico . . . social stratification does not correspond any more to ethnic categories but rather to economic levels." Yet, when asked by the black press if any blacks had ever been invited to the Mexican embassy, he responded, "The occasion has not arisen to invite a Negro representative to a reception given at the Mexican Embassy [in Washington] . . . this does not mean, however, that a policy of exclusion is followed."[84] Double-speak of this sort proved endlessly frustrating to black onlookers who were trying to gauge the extent to which Mexicans could be counted upon as friend or foe. How could blacks be considered equal to everyone else, yet never be invited to embassy functions?

Needless to say, it would take much for blacks to reimagine Mexico as a special place of refuge and solace. Artists took some of the initial steps in this regard. Some of the artistic ideas to emerge from the Mexican Revolution became powerfully attractive to a new generation of blacks who sought to use the Mexican model as a means of addressing their own oppression at home. The monumental works of Diego Rivera, David Alfaro Siqueiros, and José Clemente Orozco, among others, demonstrated an appreciation for the Mexican folk tradition and were aimed at crafting poignant social messages in a language that the masses could understand. Between 1930 and 1960, black artists referenced Mexico in patterning their image of the "New Negro." In community centers across the United States, black artists held discussions on how they could infuse their work with the Southern black folk tradition—all while generating powerful social and political messages.[85] Charles Alston, Elizabeth Catlett, Jacob Lawrence, Charles White, Sergeant Claude Johnson, John Wilson, Jon Biggers, and Hale Woodruff were among those taking up the challenge.[86] Catlett was one of the few who relocated permanently to Mexico, acquiring Mexican citizenship in 1962.[87]

In the 1940s, a number of other events transpired that made Mexico become even more alluring. On the cultural front, the brief international popularity of two Mexican songs, *Almas Blancas* ("White Souls") and *Pintame Angelitos Negros* ("Paint For Me Little Black Angels"), as well as a movie based on *Pintame Angelitos Negros*, generated an image of Mexico as a place that understood the subjective predicament of the black condition.[88] Less significantly, in 1948, Mexican scientist Dr. José Baraquiel Calva discovered a chemical that could straighten black hair for months.[89] Giving it the name *Lustrasilk*, his product represented the first major advance in the development of black hair care since Madame C. J. Walker's shampoo-press-and-curl process in 1900. That *Lustrasilk* was developed by a Mexican was not lost upon some observant African Americans.[90]

On the intellectual front, Gonzalo Aguirre Beltrán's research on the African presence in Mexico started gaining notice in the United States. Trained by Melville Herskovits at Northwestern University, and incorporating a methodology that searched for African survivals in New World cultures, Aguirre Beltrán's work represented the first systematic, book-length treatment of the black condition in the history of the nation. *La Población Negra en México 1519–1810* ("The Black Population in Mexico") was published in 1946, followed by *Cuijla, Esbozo Etnográfico de un Pueblo Negro* ("Cuijla, Ethnographic Sketch of a Black Town") in 1957.[91]

Given Aguirre Beltrán's seminal importance to the field of Afro-Mexican studies, and the extent to which his work has been cited by Americans and Mexicans alike, some of his findings are worth mentioning here. Unfortunately, despite its innovative subject matter, Aguirre Beltrán's research did not veer strikingly from the course laid by the proponents of *mestizaje* and *indigenismo*. This is to say that his depiction of the black population fit neatly into the prevailing intellectual climate that emphasized the salience of race mixture in Mexican history. Inadvertently, Aguirre Beltrán's work established a timeline whereby the overwhelming importance of blackness was relegated to the colonial period, where Mexico's blacks were found in their greatest proportions. With the dawn of the national era, he asserted that a wholesale "integration" of blacks had taken place.[92] As a consequence, pure blacks remained only in certain isolated pockets where underdevelopment hindered their broader incorporation into the nation and kept them frozen in time. Essentially, Aguirre Beltrán's research validated and historicized a process of black marginalization that ironically came about through enfranchisement and assimilation. His decision to assign the Afro-Mexican population the label of "*Afromestizos*" (a term that remains unique even within Latin America) underscores his special vision of black integratedness into Mexico.[93]

It took time for Aguirre Beltrán's studies to make an impact in Mexico. In the meantime, *La Población Negra* was reviewed favorably in American academic journals and popular publications such as *The Crisis*.[94] The American media was fascinated to learn that blacks had a long documented history south of the border. Aguirre Beltrán's research further contributed to a phenomenon that one might describe as "Diasporic Blackquest." In dealing with subjugation at home, black Americans throughout the twentieth century frequently sought cultural and racial heroes, as well as empowerment from the experiences of struggle abroad.[95] The Haitian Revolution and the grand figure of Toussaint L'Ouverture were inspirational here, as was the figure of General Antonio Maceo from Cuba's independence wars. To a lesser extent, the political career of Cuba's presidential hopeful Lazaro Peña was followed in the late 1940s for similar reasons.[96]

As elements of the American press acknowledged Mexico's black presence with greater care, a source of racial fraternity developed with Mexico too. As early as 1931, Carleton Beals, writing for *The Crisis*, published an article discussing the history of a small Afro-Mexican village that had been involved in a protracted power struggle against greedy landowners and a corrupt mayor. Where other authors might have omitted discussing the town's African heritage, Beals eagerly provided details about their customs, phenotypic features, and dress. In recounting their troubles and struggle for freedom, he made it easy to infer parallels with blacks in the United States.[97] In 1948, *Ebony* magazine announced that there were as many as 12 million blacks in Mexico, representing no less than half the national population.[98] By applying the U.S. "one drop rule" and taking a liberal interpretation of Aguirre Beltrán's research, the magazine effectively spun the traditional arguments of *mestizaje* in ways that minimized the country's *mestizo* heritage in favor of accentuating its blackness. Even if Mexicans individually chose to deny their African heritage, *Ebony* asserted that thanks to 400 years of interbreeding one could ultimately never escape the reality that "millions of Mexicans have a decided Negro caste to their features."[99] This, then, was the real value of *mestizaje*.

In 1951, the *Negro Digest* ran an article celebrating what it declared was Mexico's first black president—José María Morelos.[100] The article took the liberty of showcasing Morelos's mulatto lineage despite numerous complicated issues surrounding his own racial self-identification. It also reinterpreted the feats he achieved in the name of the nation, as symbolic racial victories that were valuable to blacks throughout the Diaspora. The *New York Age* also ran a story on Morelos, where again, his importance as a member of the black Diaspora was highlighted.[101] Towards the end of the 1950s, *Ebony* revisited the town of Valerio Trujano, first covered by Carleton Beals in 1931.[102] As with Beal's essay, the legacy of black resistance, particularly slave resistance, figured prominently in the *Ebony* piece.

The phenomenon of Diasporic Blackquest certainly piqued new curiosity about Mexico and changed the conversation about what Mexico meant to African Americans. Mexico was becoming conceived as a country where blacks could reconnect with others in the Diaspora. Blacks, however, would not be inspired to travel to Mexico on this score alone. More powerfully, they began to journey there again due to increasing wealth after 1940, major improvements in the Mexican tourist industry, and because of new employment and educational opportunities offered abroad in the post–World War II era.

While the Great Depression eliminated many of the economic gains that American blacks had made during the opening of the twentieth century, they benefited greatly from jobs that opened up in the wartime economy of the industrialized North. Nearly 1.5 million blacks migrated northward during the decade of the 1940s, marking the beginning of 30 years of northbound migration. Even though blacks remained heavily concentrated in low-paying, low-skilled positions, between 1947 and 1953 they experienced a steady climb in their economic power. Median black family income (calculated in 1974 dollars) rose by 28 percent, from 3,560 dollars to 4,550 dollars. Recession struck in 1953–1959, but shortly thereafter, black buying power strengthened. Median family income rose again by 20 percent between 1959 and 1964, and by 36 percent between 1964 and 1969.[103] Overall, black incomes still lagged behind those of whites, but the improvement in black economic status meant that for some, especially members of the middle-and upper-middle classes, greater resources were available to spend on things such as travel.

Advances in Mexico's tourist infrastructure made travel seem more attractive. Between 1930 and 1960 a host of new highways opened, linking virtually all of the country's major cities to the coasts and the U.S. border. In the 1930s and early 1940s, the Mexican Tourism Department conducted an aggressive campaign to construct tourist camps that would provide rest and temporary lodging along the major highways. The efforts were successful. From 1929 to 1939, automobile tourism increased from 2,730 vehicles to nearly 24,000 per year.[104] Air and railway traffic also climbed steadily. By the summer of 1939, over 1,000 tourists per month visited Mexico from the United States by train, and annual revenues by air totaled over 3 million dollars.[105] Substantial investments in the hotel industry and in advertising kept tourists coming. By the middle of the 1930s, a series of affordable and modern, yet traditionally styled lodgings, were springing up throughout the country.[106] With these structures in place, during World War II American tourists traveled to Mexico and Canada instead of Europe, thanks to the insecurities produced overseas by the war. The devaluation of the Mexican peso in 1949 helped tourism further, since Mexico now became a greater bargain for American travelers.[107] They flocked southward in impressive numbers throughout the 1950s, with only minor interruptions from 1952 to 1953, thanks to dislocations produced by the Korean War. Indeed, between 1950 and 1955, well over 350,000 tourists arrived annually, most of them from the United States. Americans continued dominating the Mexican tourist industry, accounting for nearly 90 percent of all travelers from the 1930s into the mid-1960s.[108]

What did this mean for blacks? First, we should note that a significant change began to take place in the pattern of black travel to Mexico. In the nineteenth and early twentieth centuries, blacks arrived on Mexican soil primarily as laborers, fugitives, or solace-seekers searching for relief from Jim Crow. From the 1940s onward, a growing number of blacks participated in leisure travel southward. Magazines that regularly featured articles describing the best places for blacks to travel started including Mexico among their lists.[109] *Color* ranked Mexico among its top three destinations in North America for blacks.[110] Closer than Europe and with a better climate than Canada, it was an ideal getaway. The high-profile visits of celebrities and prominent entreprenurial further cemented Mexico's new status as a black leisure paradise. Mrs. C. J. Walker and Edna C. Wells were photographed in Mexico during trips in the early 1950s along with insurance tycoons like Victor Williams and the Dejois family. Nat King Cole and his new bride, Marie Ellington, honeymooned in the country in August 1948. The attention showered on their wedding (billed as the largest Harlem wedding in a quarter century) naturally generated tremendous enthusiasm and public interest in the honeymoon. Their one-week jaunt through Mexico City and Acapulco was covered in a brilliant photo diary kept by Cole himself. The rationale behind their decision to visit Mexico resonated with other black Americans. Rich enough to travel anywhere in the world, the couple selected Mexico because they felt that only here would they receive "the right kind of treatment."[111] Black Americans immediately knew what that meant.

Quick to capitalize on black tourists were Morris Williams and Leroy Martin, two enterprising African Americans who opened a tourist agency in 1950 that targeted a black clientele. Based in Mexico City, *Williams and Martin Tours* experienced tremendous success. By 1960, the company boasted a constellation of clients, including superstars such as Hazel Scott, Cab Calloway, Willie Mays, Dr. Lucien Brown, Don Newcombe, and Junior Gilliam.[112] In a way, this black-owned agency with its respected profile and top-tier customers assisted in keeping the stream of blacks coming to Mexico.

While the number of black American tourists was on the rise in the 1940s and 1950s, those staying for long periods of time probably decreased from the nineteenth century. By the end of the 1940s, there were roughly 300 blacks known to have settled in Mexico permanently.[113] They ranged widely in their wealth and experiences. Some were simple students; others were bustling entrepreneurs who had made their fortune in Mexico. Among the best known was William Huey "Butch" Lewis, a successful restaurateur and hotel owner who owned one of Mexico City's largest restaurants during the 1930s, a sprawling operation that seated 600 customers. Lewis first arrived in Mexico in 1902, after having logged a career as a Pullman Car "buffet man." Sick and tired of being called "boy," he crossed the border and remained there. Steadily, he built the connections (including a friendship with Pancho Villa) that allowed him to become one of the country's most successful blacks. He had no desire to leave. Privately, he told friends: "I'll die in Mexico if I live long enough." His wife shared his sentiments. Returning to the United States after three years in Mexico, a white insurance salesman congratulated her on returning to "God's country." She retorted: "I just left God's country."[114]

Other black American entrepreneurs included the talented and successful Jones brothers of Chicago, George and Edward, who were rumored to have become millionaires.[115] Ed Jones owned a shop call *Jacqmar* on Avenida Madero, specializing in hand-blocked silks. His wife ran another *Jacqmar* along the fashionable Paseo Reforma in downtown Mexico City.[116] A man named George Brown arrived in Mexico in 1941, establishing a neon-sign manufacturing plant worth 40,000 dollars and employing 40 workers. Another African American, was rumored to have introduced soft-tissue toilet paper in Mexico during the late 1930s and supposedly founded his own company called the Maricopia Paper Company. On a smaller scale, Lee Weaver, who had been a Western Electric radar inspector during World War II, moved to Mexico in 1946 with 1,000 dollars in savings. He proceeded to create Weaver Laboratorios Servicio de Radio, a small but successful radio repair business in the heart of the capital.[117]

The new flurry of short-term black tourism, combined with the success stories of long-term black expatriates, became intertwined with the ideology of *mestizaje* to produce a phenomenon one might describe as the mythos of the "super-black." In short, the super-black was the image of a black American who appeared to be doing everything—living a remarkably productive, sophisticated, yet relaxed and effortless life south of the border. The image, spread by word of mouth and the print media, was part fiction and part true. It could exist because the ideology of *mestizaje* projected a discourse of racial tolerance in Mexico, which, while not entirely accurate, certainly represented an improvement over race relations in the United States. The American press picked up on this. Writers for publications such as *Color*, *The Crisis*, *Negro Digest*, and *Ebony* used the perception of racial tolerance to promote the image of the super-black. Liberated from racial oppression, black Americans, even the most humble among them, could maximize their inner potential, becoming more than they ever thought they could be. Additionally, the economic power they wielded as Americans literally bought them an upper-class passport into Mexico. With the average Mexican worker making just 15 cents a day in 1950, black Americans could bring their savings to Mexico and live like royalty. For just 35 dollars a month they could rent a desirable apartment in Mexico City, and for another 20 dollars a month, they could add the services of a cook and maid. Outside

Mexico City, black money stretched even further. Being able to observe the benefits of U.S. cash in action helped seduce the black press into believing Mexico's message of racial equality, to the extent that they virtually ignored interrogating the reasons why Mexico's own black population almost invariably wallowed in poverty.

Concrete examples of the super-black mythos included William Byers, an ex-navy pharmacist's mate who moved from Washington, D.C. to San Miguel Allende and lived in Mexico during the late 1940s and early 1950s. Nicknamed "Wild Bill," he chose to relocate in order to study art at the school of *Bellas Artes* in Guanajuato. Here, he began his meteoric ascension to super-black status. Byers quickly became one of the most popular students in his school, in addition to being captain of the soccer team, the organizer of a boxing team, a baseball player, one of the best dancers in town, and a "mean saxophone player." For clothes, Byers boasted a wardrobe of exquisitely tailored fabrics, which he wore with flair when escorting local beauties to the town's fiestas. If he had wanted to, it was rumored that he could have spent every night of the week carousing the town. As if this were not enough, he traveled vigorously and reportedly knew every inch of the country within a 200-mile radius of San Miguel. For more cosmopolitan experiences, Byers made monthly trips to Mexico City. Beyond this, his creative energies flowered in Mexico. He filled sketchbooks and painted scores of canvasses that incorporated the colonial landscape of his surroundings. Impressively, his artistic talents were honed further under the direction of the great, extremely left-wing muralist David Siquieros. Relaxing in his comfortable nine-room home, complete with a patio, studio, corral, and garden, Byers was the model of black success.[118]

The phenomenon of the super-black was by no means limited to men. Arriving in 1946, Bernice Maxwell found the conditions in Mexico perfect for completing a master's degree in Spanish literature and for undertaking a Ph.D. in romance languages. Gladys Wells traveled to Mexico and became the head housekeeper of the millionaire racetrack boss Bruno Pagliai. This was a lucrative position that placed six servants under her charge. Mable Sanford Smyth settled with her husband in the mining town of Taxco and proceeded to live a patrician lifestyle in a splendid two-bedroom home with servants and a cook. It is unclear whether she studied, but she certainly traveled extensively throughout the country and made acquaintance with Taxco's high society. Perhaps the crowning accomplishment of her super-black lifestyle was that she was happily married to a white American. The marriage, scandalous in the United States, did not evoke a word amongst her social peers in Taxco.[119]

In some ways, the image of the super-black replicated many stereotypes about African Americans. In Byers's case, his athletic, artistic, and sartorial accomplishments were overemphasized. In the case of Wells and Smyth, domestic achievements were accentuated. Regardless, as knowledge about these lives spread, more blacks became interested in finding retreat in Mexico.

Mexico City emerged as one of the primary sites of choice for black expatriates.[120] The black American community here consistently numbered between 50–100 individuals between 1948 and 1952. While blacks tended generally to know of one another, they were too dispersed throughout the city to comprise a tightly knit group. According to William Somersille, the longer that some blacks resided in Mexico City, the less sensitive they became towards race. This was one of the attractions of being there. Black Americans didn't have to live their skin everyday: "Living in Mexico dulls your senses to racial problems to the point [that] you only occasionally think about the situation that existed in the States . . . the identities [of blacks in Mexico City] were really not apparently Afro-American, but rather brothers of life without any particular racial identity."[121]

By and large, the majority of black Mexico City residents were professionals, artists, and students, interspersed with a few bohemian types, entertainers, athletes, and escapees from the McCarthy era communist scare.[122] Of the permanent black residents, a substantial number were males and females who had arrived single. Many eventually took a Mexican spouse or married whites from the larger international expatriate community. Of the few black couples, pensioners were a factor. Dudley and Gertrude Woodard, for example, were retired educators who spent half the year in Mexico City studying literature at the National University (UNAM). There was also a younger crowd of black couples, among them Jack and Irma Wertz. He was a pre-med student, while she worked on a master's degree, both at the UNAM.[123]

The opening of Mexico City College turned out to be a significant event in attracting blacks to the capital. Founded in 1940, it was the first school of its type—an American-style liberal arts college in Latin America. The school offered a wide range of subjects, but was particularly strong in archaeology, art, and anthropology. Advanced degrees in creative writing and foreign trade rounded out its curriculum. The student body hailed from all over the world, including Central and South America, the Caribbean, Canada, East Asia, Europe, and the Philippines. From the United States, World War II and Korean War veterans came to comprise a staple portion of the student body thanks to educational opportunities offered under the G.I. bill.[124]

By 1955, blacks constituted 3 percent of the student body of 975 students. Many were exchange students who typically spent a quarter or two learning Spanish before returning to the United States. Given the college's broad international student representation and the diverse composition of its faculty, it acquired a reputation for racial tolerance that was appealing to many American blacks. Moreover, many classes were conducted in English, appealing to those still struggling with the Spanish language. The UNAM, of course, remained a popular option for those seeking affordable alternatives to American higher education, especially for medical students, but Mexico City College came to be regarded as a special place for blacks and was featured repeatedly in popular publications, including *Ebony* magazine's cover story in June 1955.[125]

Despite all of the fanfare surrounding the progress blacks achieved in various entrepreneurial, artistic, and educational endeavors, not all was perfect in paradise. Imperceptibly, under the radar, there were instances of racism and racial rejection. Often, given the previous experiences of individual blacks with race relations in the United States, African American expatriates did not always recognize the signs in Mexico. Sometimes, misinterpreting the nuances of foreign language and culture itself prevented a full understanding of Mexican-style racial branding. But episodes still occurred.

Backlash hit the pages of the black press in 1952, as a headline sprawled across the *Pittsburgh Courier* read: "Loud Mouth Tourists Hurting Interracial Attitudes in Mexico." The article itself contained some alarming passages:

> Offensive Negroes from the States are definitely hurting the reputation of the race in this country [Mexico]. Of the possibly fifty U.S. Negroes in this city [Mexico City], around thirty are known to frequent Communist meetings. Many of these colored visitors try to "make" every English-speaking Mexican girl, and even go so far as to violate national custom by deliberately visiting a girl's home. This is unthinkable here without first having parents' permission. When warned against it they cry "discrimination."[126]

The article, penned by a Mr. Lorenzo de Aber,[127] proceeded to categorize black visitors indiscriminately as "drug users and underworld characters." American blacks proved so problematic in their behavior that, reportedly, the black hotel owner of Butch's Manhattan refused to allow other black customers into his establishment: "He reached his decision after his place became a hangout for dope fiends, broken-down prize fighters and outright criminals who drove away both white and respectable tourists."[128] At an American embassy party, the article said, a daring black stood up at the table and launched into a diatribe about discrimination and how "Negroes needed communism."

Aber's article essentially blamed blacks for causing discrimination in a Mexico that was otherwise free of racial prejudice. It proceeded to justify that discrimination by lauding it as a proper response to offensive black behavior that was not just criminal, but subversive. Even with Mexico's postrevolutionary socialist tendencies and the host of communists who found refuge within the nation's borders, American blacks were pushing the envelope too far.

On July 26, 1952, a Mr. Warren E. Blanding published a rebuttal in the *Courier*.[129] A long-time resident of Mexico City, he was appalled at Aber's gross caricature of black behavior. It was well known, he argued, that drug traffickers were white, not black. If Aber sought evidence, he needed only to review the police records of the most recent drug-related arrests in the capital. As for the moral character of black expatriates, according to Blanding's notes, their credentials were impeccable. Providing a list of 57 persons, he demonstrated that nearly all were upstanding community members, including a city councilman, an assistant U.S. district attorney, several medical professionals, writers, entertainers, and businessmen. This was certainly not the profile of the rabble alluded to by Aber, and probably not a nest of communists. Furthermore, blacks, he argued, represented "a new and virtually untapped gold mine" for Mexico, not a detriment to the nation.[130] If discrimination existed in Mexico it was not the fault of blacks, but of geography. Mexico's borders were too close to Texas and the U.S. South, making it easy for racist southerners to cross over, carrying their attitudes with them. While Mexicans resisted this racism, they could never prevent it from surfacing in their country completely.

Footsteps from Prejudice

The Civil Rights movement initiated important changes in the American social scene that had grand implications for race relations. The gradual death of legal and racial discrimination opened new possibilities for blacks domestically. Concomitantly, the flow of black travel to Mexico became less influenced by racial problems at home. The growing consumerism seen in black travel across the border in the 1940s and 1950s continued exuberantly into the 1960s and 1970s. Joyce Bailey, who lived in Mexico City for a year (1960–1961) with her best friend and dog, perhaps summed it up best: "We did not go to escape racism or to study; we went simply because we wanted to, had the time, and the money to do it!"[131]

After the 1960s, black and white patterns of travel to Mexico grew more closely aligned than ever before. Retirees sought inexpensive, relaxing living conditions in comfortable and friendly settings. Professionals built business connections in urban and semi-urban environments, bringing their families or marrying into the Mexican middle class. Artists sought inspiration from Mexico's history of conflict, from its Pre-Columbian and colonial heritage, and from its modern masters. Students flocked to an increasing array of classes, to the bustling resorts and beaches, and to the ancient ruins and colonial buildings. Through it all, blacks continued commenting on their unusually warm acceptance and treatment, as well as on the lingering differences in racial attitudes between the United States and Mexico. In 1972, retired World War II merchant seaman William Ferguson breathed a sigh of relief after living for some years in Guadalajara, "Everybody is the same here."[132] But the urgency of racial struggle, intertwined with a conscious understanding of black involvement in U.S.–Mexican politics, was beginning to fade from his, and everyone else's, memory.

Notes

Introduction From the Eyes of an Historian

1. The black Diaspora (or African Diaspora) is an academic term that is gaining prominence in the field of African American studies. It most commonly refers to the study of black peoples and their dispersion around the globe. Its increasing popularity as an intellectual concept is due to the importance of globalization and interconnectivity in contemporary society, the rearticulation of diversity as a more pluralistic concept (no longer limited to just "black" and "white"), as well as new research and understanding about the global flows and migratory patterns of black peoples, beyond movement associated with slavery. An excellent, comprehensive article on the subject is Kim D. Butler, "Defining Diaspora, Refining a Discourse," *Diaspora,* 10, no. 2 (2001): 189–217.
2. "Mexico: A Haven for Disabled Vets," *Ebony*, Jan. 1972, 31–40.
3. Apart from fighter pilots, there were many more "Tuskegee Airmen," including ground crews and bomber pilots. Near the end of World War II, there were over 6,000 blacks in the Army Air Forces, of which only 563 were pilots. See Lynn M. Homan and Thomas Reilly, *Black Knights, The Story of the Tuskegee Airmen* (Gretna, Louisiana: Pelican Publishing Co., 2001), 215.
4. "Ex-GI Starts Haiti Airline, Vet Sees Good Business Opportunity for U.S. Negroes," *Ebony*, Feb. 1948, 28–29.
5. Interview with Walter Palmer, Sept. 12, 2003, Indianapolis, Indiana.
6. Interviews with Jack Willis and Bill Jackson, Jan. 22, 2003, Puerto Vallarta, Mexico

1 *Virgil*: Before the War

1. In actuality, cotton prices experienced a steady increase in 1912–1920. The price drop did not take place until 1921, well after Armistice Day (Nov. 11, 1918). See: U.S. Bureau of the Census, *Historical Statistics of the United States, Colonial Times to 1970, Bicentennial Edition, Part 1* (Washington D.C.: U.S. Government Printing Office, 1975), E-123–124.
2. Wiley College was founded in 1873 in conjunction with the Freedman's Aid Society of the Methodist Episcopal Church. Its charter noted: "the object … is to establish and perpetuate an institution of learning wherein may be afforded opportunities to all, without distinction of race, condition, sex, or religious antecedents, to acquire a liberal education." This mission statement was expanded in 1920 with the clause that the goal was to provide a place for "young Negro men and women of the Southwest to obtain a liberal Christian education that will fit them for leadership." By 1933, under the energetic and inspired leadership of its president, Wiley became widely recognized as one of the best black colleges in Texas, with a faculty that included three Ph.D.s and twelve M.A.s.

See Michael R. Heintze, *Private Black Colleges in Texas, 1865–1954* (College Station, Texas: Texas A & M Univ. Press, 1985), 23, 42, 59, 100.

3. Dr. Dogan, the son of slaves, was president of Wiley from 1896–1942. Apart from being an exceptional administrator who developed the school's physical plant and intellectual environment, he was also well known for displaying tremendous acts of generosity and kindness towards his students. He constantly found ways to help them learn to help themselves. His assistance to Richardson in getting a scholarship, admitting him to college, and later in getting a job, were very typical. Heintze, *Private Black Colleges*, 98–101.
4. In the late 1800s Wiley students wore uniforms, although they were not formally obliged to do so. Females wore blue flannel dresses with gold trim around the collar, and cuffs with gold braids. White male students wore blue flannel as well, but with brass buttons. The incorporation of uniforms in these early years was intended to encourage "economy, uniformity and the 'appearance of students as a body.' " Uniforms were abandoned in the 1920s, but very formal attire was expected. Women attended class only in dresses. Men wore ties, white shirts, and even dress coats. See: Heintze, *Private Black Colleges*, 160–61.
5. A leading activist in the 1960s, Farmer's life is perhaps best recounted in his autobiography: *Lay Bare the Heart, An Autobiography of the Civil Rights Movement* (Fort Worth: Texas Christian University Press, 1998); see also Robert E. Jakoubek, *James Farmer and the Freedom Rides (Gateway Civil Rights)* (Brookfield, Connecticut: Millbrook Press, 1994).
6. James L. Farmer was the son of slaves and one of the first black Ph.D.s in the state of Texas.
7. Tolson taught at Wiley from 1924 to 1947, taking a year off 1930–1931 to pursue a Master's degree at Columbia University. It was after his year in New York that his first poetry was published. Some of his pieces became memorable contributions to the *Washington Tribune* in the late 1930s and early 1940s. It was in 1947 that Tolson was asked to compose the centennial ode to Liberia and became that country's poet laureate. However, perhaps his best-known body of work, "A Gallery of Harlem Portraits," was not published until the 1970s. See Melvin B. Toslon, *A Gallery of Harlem Portraits*, ed. Robert M. Farnsworth (Columbia, Missouri: University of Missouri Press, 1979). For more information see Joy Flasch, *Melvin B. Tolson* (New York: Twayne, 1972), and Robert M. Farnsworth, ed., *Caviar and Cabbage: Selected Columns by Melvin B. Tolson from the Washington Tribune, 1937–1944* (Columbia, MO.: University of Missouri Press, 1982).
8. Calverton was a respected Marxist intellectual of the "Old Left" who founded the *Modern Quarterly*, wrote the column "Cultural Barometer" for *Current History*, and edited the *Anthology of American Negro Literature*, among numerous other activities. It was through the anthology that he became aware of Tolson, eventually leading to his decision to publish Tolson's work in the *Modern Monthly*. See Farmer, *Lay Bare the Heart*, 137; and Leonard Wilcox, *V.F. Calverton: Radical in the American Grain* (Philadelphia: Temple Univ. Press, 1992), 1–11, 224.
9. More details about Calverton's visit can be found in: Farmer, *Lay Bare the Heart*, 137–140.
10. The Works Progress Administration, created in 1935, focused on providing jobs during the years of the Depression for scores of unemployed Americans. Three of the numerous projects that fell under its administration were the Federal Art, Writer's and Theater Projects, which gave struggling artists the chance to practice their craft in times of scarcity. Many of the Federal Theater Project's performances were free to the public.
11. V.F. Calverton actually died in 1940, two years after this incident. However, the man who answered the door apparently did not want to assist Virgil. Later, in the summer of 1938, James Farmer would also travel to visit Calverton in Greenwich Village. His

meeting was far more successful, since he actually received an audience with Calverton himself. Farmer noted that Calverton claimed to have gotten Richardson a role in a Little Theater production, and that they would soon see if he was as talented as he appeared in Wiley's production of *Damascus*. Virgil, however, does not have any recollection of physically meeting Calverton after graduating from Wiley College. Farmer's account can be found in Farmer, *Lay Bare the Heart*, 140–141.

12. Lee's boxing career ended in 1933, just two years after receiving the blow that damaged his retina. Along the way, he had been the lightweight amateur champion and had won 200 professional fights after turning pro in 1926. He took up acting once he realized that the blind spots produced by his failing vision impaired him from fighting professionally. It was in 1936 that he starred in Orson Welles' stirring, all-black performance of *MacBeth*, the first major Shakespearean drama production to have an all-black cast. The play was innovatively set in Haiti, a rousing political commentary that tapped into the nation's popular imagination—just two years had passed since the United States had removed its Marines from the island. Lee's performances in *MacBeth* and Du Bois's *Haiti* were powerful statements of the strength and capacity of the black population as political figures and as cultural icons. The Shakespearean tragic figures in *MacBeth* remain among the greatest characters created in theater history. Similarly, the protagonists of *Haiti* were among the greatest political leaders of their age. Christophe's real life story, however, was as tragic as the play in which Lee starred. Having participated in the liberation of Haiti from the French in the 1790s, Christophe went on to become one of the early presidents of the new nation. In the process, he became ever more autocratic and declared himself king. He eventually committed suicide.
13. Virgil Richardson was actually referring to Claire Booth Luce's 1936 play, *The Women*.
14. *Night Must Fall* was actually written by Emlyn Williams. Information on the play, including a full synopsis, director's report, and script can be found in *National Archives and Records Administration (NARA)*, College Park, Maryland, Record Group 69, Works Progress Administration, Records of the Federal Theater Project, Bound Federal Theater Project Bulletins, 1936–1939, Night Must Fall—Old Autumn, Box 463.
15. Information on the plot of the play comes from The Schomburg Center for Research in Black Culture Manuscripts, Archives, and Rare Books Division, New York City (Schomburg Center Archive), American Negro Theater Alumni Collection, Virgil Richardson File, " 'Hell's Half Acre, Negro Drama Against Lynching."
16. All "trains" refer to the New York City subway system.
17. Konstantin Stanislavski, a cofounder of the Moscow Art Theater in 1897, developed the first acting "system." The "Stanislavski Method" became perhaps the single most important influence on modern stage and screen acting. He indirectly affected such important acting schools as the Actors Studio and the Group Theater. He laid the foundations for modern opera and can be credited with helping to catapult the careers of Maksim Gorki and Anton Chekhov. Stanislavski died the year Virgil arrived in New York. The American Negro Theater attempted to integrate his repertory style for their productions, forming a core group of 25 permanent actors that were trained in his techniques. See Sonia Moore, *The Stanislavski Method; The Professional Training of an Actor. Digested from the Teachings of Konstantin S. Stanislavski* (New York: Viking Press, 1960); William B. Worthen, *The Harcourt Anthology of Drama* (Fort Worth: Hartcourt College Publishers, 2002); Schomburg Center Archive, American Negro Theater Records, "The American Negro Theater—(Behind the Scenes)."
18. This information is acquired from examining a description of Nadya Ramanov's acting courses in the mid-1940s. See Schomburg Center Archive, American Negro Theater Records, "American Negro Theater School of Drama Announcement for the Season 1947–48."

19. Born in Washington, D.C. in 1900, Hayes' career was truly illustrious. She started acting when she was only five years old. By age nine, she was already starring on Broadway in the play *Old Dutch*. Nicknamed "The First Lady of American Theater," her career on stage and screen lasted for nearly 80 years until her death in 1993. See Helen Hayes, with Dody Sandford, *On Reflection; An Autobiography* (New York: M. Evans, 1968); and Helen Hayes, with Katherine Hatch, *My Life in Three Acts* (San Diego: Harcourt Brace Jovanovich, 1990).
20. These items from Virgil's résumé can found in the Schomburg Center Archive, American Negro Theater Records, "The American Negro Theater Presents On Striver's Row," Sept. 11, 1940. The written record also notes that Mr. Richardson used his speaking voice on a radio program called *Five Star Final*. During our interviews and conversations, however, Mr. Richardson does not recall being on this particular program.
21. More on Abram Hill can be found in: Loften Mitchell, *Voices of the Black Theater* (Clifton, New Jersey: James T. White & Company, 1975), 113–51; and Harold Bloom, *Black American Poets and Dramatists* (New York and Philadelphia: Chelsea House Publishers, 1995), 60–72.
22. Information on the Federal Theater Project and black participation is drawn from Ronald Ross, "The Role of Blacks in the Federal Theatre, 1935–1939," in *The Theatre of Black Americans*, ed. Errol Hill (New York: Applause Books, 1987); and Anita Gonzalez and Ian Granick, "Federal Theater Project," 2001, http://www.igranick.com/portfolio/website/african/navigation.html.
23. In the June 5 meeting that actually established the ANT, some accounts note that there were 18 original members; others say that there were 29 members. However, Virgil asserts that there were just six original founders. See Schomburg Center Archie, American Negro Theater Alumni Collection, Virgil Richardson File, Letter from Richardson to Fred O'Neal, Sept. 21, 1987, Mexico City. He was probably incorrect, and there were 8 original founders prior to June 1940, and then 21 additional charter members joined on June 5.
24. Much of the information on the structure and goals of the American Negro Theater comes from Schomburg Center Archive, American Negro Theater Records, "Constitution and by-laws of the American Negro Theater," and Schomburg Center Archive, American Negro Theater Records, "The American Negro Theater," by Claire Leonard.
25. Schomburg Center Archive, American Negro Theater Records, "The American Negro Theater Presents the First Variety Show."
26. "On Striver's Row" ran until Feb. 1, 1941, with a record 50 performances, the first time that a noncommercial theater group had been able to have such a run. Thousands of people saw the play throughout New York City. By December 21, 1940, over 5,000 tickets had been sold. The play also reached many by radio. On Sunday mornings at 11:15 A.M., excerpts from "Striver's Row" could be heard on WLTH. While some critics did not understand the play, "Striver's Row" was still a hit, and during its initial run the play was rumored to have been considered for Broadway production. See: *New York Amsterdam News (NYAN)*, Dec. 7, 1940, Theater Section; *NYAN*, Jan. 18, 1941, Theater Section.
27. In December 1940, the New York Amsterdam News reported that roughly 22 percent of the audience was drawn from Harlem. Interestingly, the participation of blacks as patrons and audience members for ANT productions was three times greater than that for shows given by the Federal Theater. See *NYAN*, Dec. 21, 1940, Theater Section.
28. This description of the play's plot comes from *NYAN*, Dec. 10, 1940, Theater Section.
29. The World's Fair was held from 1939 to 1940.

30. *Natural Man* was another tremendous success for the American Negro Theater and can be credited with catapulting the career of Stanley Green. World War II however, took a toll on the ANT's membership. By 1944, of the 30 "cooperative" members of the group, 10 were at war. See Schomburg Center Archive, American Negro Theater Records, "The American Negro Theater" by Claire Leonard, 1943–1944.

2 In the Army Now

1. Most likely, Richardson is referring to the incident that occurred in 1917, when the 24th Infantry (an all-black unit) responded to racial violence against one of its members by taking up guns and fighting whites. Taking place in Houston, this was one of the bloodiest incidents of racial violence led by blacks against whites since Nat Turner's rebellion. Whites lived in fear for their lives afterwards. In the wake of the episode, 19 of the soldiers were hanged and at least 50 more were sent to prison for life.
2. Born in St. Croix in the 1883, Hubert Harrison became one of the leading black writers, orators, and critics of the 1910s and 1920s. He has been dubbed the "father of Harlem radicalism," and was one of the most important figures of the Harlem Renaissance, before his death in 1927. See Jeffrey B. Perry, ed., *A Hubert Harrison Reader* (Middleton, Connecticut: Wesleyan University Press, 2001).
3. Benjamin O. Davis, Sr. joined the army in the Spanish American War (1898). Born in Washington, D.C. and trained at Howard University, Davis went on to become a colonel in 1930. In addition to his military positions he also held teaching posts in military science and tactics both at Tuskegee and Wilberforce. Roosevelt appointed Davis to the rank of brigadier general. He retired in 1948.
4. Virgil's unit was shipped overseas in February 1942. See NARA, Box 177, R.G. 107, "Air Corps Departmental," Aida Harrison to Judge William H.Hastie, June 23, 1941.
5. An adjutant's post is equivalent to that of a secretary to the commanding officer of a battalion, usually a colonel.
6. Between the months of February and June 1942, Virgil underwent many more hardships regarding his eligibility for Tuskegee. In April, he was asked to retest for Air Corps qualification. He successfully passed, but was dismayed since he had already cleared the tests in September. He promptly applied for a 30-day furlough. Virgil was aware that aviation cadets were not allowed furloughs of any significant length once they began training, so he wanted to take one now. His superior officers responded by telling him that he would not hear about the furlough until he was notified that he was qualified to enter Tuskegee. Virgil protested vociferously, again stating that he had already received word in September. But according to the official in charge, Virgil's paperwork was unavailable since his previous unit, the 394th, had been shipped overseas (along with Virgil's records). These events soured Virgil's stay in California. See NARA, Box 177, R.G. 107, "Air Corps Departmental," Aida Harrison to Judge William H. Hastie, June 23, 1941.
7. AWOL refers to an unauthorized absence from military duty, which constitutes a serious, punishable offense. Also, it appears that Virgil would have married Aida earlier, but he was required to remain a bachelor until Dec. 20, 1941, for the purpose of entering the Army Air Corps.
8. Aspects of Virgil's experience in England can be found in the Schomburg Center Archive, American Negro Theater Alumni Collection, Virgil Richardson File, "Tuskegee Cadet Anxious to Go Back to England for Air Crack at Nazis." Although this was a published article, the clipping in the archive does not disclose the publisher's information.

3 Days at Tuskegee

1. Throughout the 1930s, Chicago was an important site for black aviation. While blacks flew from several airfields in the area, the field located on Harlem Avenue in the suburb of Oaklawn was especially important. This was not a Jim Crow airfield; both white and black pilots interacted frequently. Cornelius Coffey, a black flight instructor, was especially well known and respected by black and white students alike. He provided many army pilots with their initial civilian training. In 1939, the National Airmen's Association (a black organization) and various newspapers put political pressure on Washington to establish a non-college pilot training program in the Chicago area, open to both blacks and whites. This was successfully launched under the direction of Miss Willa Brown, a black woman. With such a strong black flying tradition, Chicago sought to be the primary training ground for potential black military aviators. The Chicago Urban League participated in this effort. Some felt that blacks should not be limited to military flight instruction in a Jim Crow environment, but be integrated with whites, as had been successfully accomplished in Chicago. Tuskegee, however, was a segregated flight-training environment. Source: NARA, R.G. 10, Box 178, Air Corps General, LOL 390/10/13, Entry 91, Howard D. Gould to Mr. William H. Hastie, Nov. 15, 1940.
2. For more on the life of Daniel "Chappie" James see James R. McGovern, *Black Eagle: General Daniel "Chappie" James, Jr.* (Birmingham, Alabama: University of Alabama Press, 1985); and J. Alfred Phelps, *Chappie: America's First Black Four Star General: The Life and Times of Daniel James, Jr.* (Novato, California: Presidio Press, 1991). For a complete survey of Virgil's flying record and grade sheets at Tuskegee, as well as a list of some of his instructors see NARA, R.G. 18, Box 2, Academic Records, Tuskegee Army Air/Army Flying School, Virgil Richardson Final Grade Sheet. Apparently, Virgil finished Tuskegee with satisfactory grades in primary, basic, and advanced flight training, and with an 84 average in ground school, including courses in chemical war defense, armament, identification of naval forces, photo interpretation, airforces, and aircraft identification.
3. NARA, R.G. 18, Box 2, Academic Records, Tuskegee Army Air/Army Flying School, Brigadier General W.W. Welsh to Major W. Stone, June 29, 1943. In Virgil's graduating class, out of an original 31 cadets, only 25 finished. Two of the graduates were holdovers from previous classes. See: NARA, R.G. 18, Box 2, Academic Records, Tuskegee Army Air/Army Flying School, Cpt. Roy Morse, May 6, 1943.

4 From Tuskegee Back to War

1. Richardson noted that during World War II, men like Tresvel received their commissions in three years instead of four from West Point. Their fourth year was spent as air cadets at Tuskegee.
2. Paradise Valley was a ghetto on the East Side of Detroit comprising roughly 60 square blocks, and with nearly 200,000 black residents. The stiffness of segregation in the city kept blacks largely relegated to this area.

5 Atlantic Sound

1. This is Virgil's impression based upon his experience. I have not confirmed this as a situation that was generalized throughout the war.

2. Lee "Buddy" Archer probably became the country's first black ace in World War II, having flown with the 332nd and 302nd fighter squadrons. He is officially recorded as having 4 victories, but he probably had many more that remain "unconfirmed." He was a supremely confident pilot, but never too comfortable in the air, since he believed arrogance inspired sloppiness. See Gail Buckley, *American Patriots: The Story of Blacks in the Military from the Revolution to Desert Storm* (New York: Random House, 2001), 293. Lt. Hall did receive the Distinguished Flying Cross for being the first black to shoot down a German aircraft. According to some sources, however, Hall only shot down a total of three planes. See United States Airforce Fiftieth Anniversary of World War II Commemoration Committee, "Tuskegee Airman Fact Sheet" (Washington, D.C.: HQDA, SACC, Pentagon, 1995).
3. "Merlin Powered" P-51s could climb over 40,000 feet. They were equipped with a Packard-built, Rolls Royce "Merlin" V-1650 engine, with 1,520 horsepower, and a 2-stage, 2-speed supercharger. The "Allison Powered" P-51s had a ceiling of 30,000 feet, but were powered by an Allison V-1710, liquid cooled, 1,200 horsepower, 12-cylinder engine. The P-51 also weighed 9,500 pounds, as compared to 13,500 pounds for the P-47.
4. On December 15, 1944, Richardson was one of the formation/flight leaders that took off from Ramitelli to Innsbruck, Germany. This appears to have been one of the only flight missions in which he served as a flight leader. The narrative mission report can be found in NARA, R.G. 18, Records of the Army Air Forces, World War II Combat Operations Reports, 1942–1946, 332nd Fighter Group, Narrative Mission Reports, July 1944—April 1945.
5. In 1940, after the German invasion of France, the Franco-German armistice divided the country into two zones. Some Frenchmen believed that if they supported Hitler, they would be able to eliminate the communists and socialists who had assumed power in the government. These Frenchmen, many of whom were part of Vichy France, were responsible for shipping thousands of Jews to death camps, for being political collaborators with the Nazis, and for sending countless numbers of their fellow citizens to jail. One of the seminal works on the subject remains Robert O. Paxton, *Vichy France Old Guard and New Order* (New York: Columbia University Press, 1972).

6 A Soldier's Homecoming

1. Richardson's participation in the ANT from 1945–1949 can be traced in the surviving records and minutes from the period. Most meetings took place at night when members of the ANT were at home from work. In the late 1940s, meetings were even held past midnight. Richardson presented bills, lobbied to take people to court, and suggested fines, amongst other activities. See Schomburg Center Archive, American Negro Theater Records, MG 70, Box #1 (1946–1949).
2. "A Voice is a Voice" was a real breakthrough. Up until 1945, the only black radio actor who played roles of all colors was Juan Hernandez. "A Voice is a Voice," launched in September 1945, diversified considerably the parts open to black talent on the air. In the summer of 1946, even opera was introduced regularly into the programming format. In newspaper interviews, Ted Cott mentioned that "nothing could more prejudice the listener than to present [A Voice is a Voice] as a formula Negro show." He sought out the ANT to do radio both for its talent and its "outstanding versatility." The show was "conceived as a proving ground to develop directors, writers, producers, sound-effects men and allied technicians" who were black. For the show's actors, Cott noted: "the microphone is the most democratic of the arts—it draws no color line." "The American Negro Theater over WNEW has presented the Negro as Scotchmen, Irishmen, French waiters,

American bankers, doctors, lawyers, and even Indian . . . chiefs." Source: Schomburg Center Archive, American Negro Theater Scrapbook, "Heard and Overboard," *P.M.* (New York City), Sept. 1945, and July 11, 1946.

3. Roi Ottley, *"New World A-Coming"; Inside Black America* (Boston: Houghton Mifflin Company, 1943).
4. Samuel Hynes, Anne Matthews, Nancy Caldwell Sorel, Roger J. Spiller, eds., *Reporting World War II*, vol. 1 (New York: Library of America, 1995).
5. There were only two or three places in the United States where blacks could study law at a historically black institution. In 1949–1950, Texas established a black law school operated by UT Austin (The School of Law for Negroes), but it had just three teachers, three classrooms, and two students. It was precisely here where Virgil was being groomed to teach. The school was designed to operate under the "separate but equal" rule, with whites studying at UT's main law school. However, in June 1950, Howard Sweatt, a black law student, raised a lawsuit against UT Austin that was upheld by the Supreme Court. His victory forced UT Austin to open its doors to blacks in an integrated setting. Sweatt became the first black law student at UT's traditionally white campus.

7 Bienvenidos a México

1. Mexican pilots flew during World War II, in a unit known as "The Aztec Eagles." Mexico declared war on Germany after two of its oil tankers were sunk in 1942. Although no ground or naval troops were sent into combat, in July of 1944, 38 elite, volunteer Mexican pilots were trained at Foster Field in Texas, along with 250–260 ground crew in Long Island. Overcoming discrimination, they flew dive-bombing missions against the Japanese and provided air support for American ground units stationed in the Philippines. They returned to Mexico City in 1945 as victorious heroes. See Robert Huddleston, "They Also Served: Mexico's Fliers," *The News and Observer* (Raleigh, N.C.), November 11, 2002; and Daniel Borunda, "Aztec Squadron 201 Eagles, Mexican Fighter Wing Soared in WWII," *The Brownsville Herald* (Brownsville, TX), November 14, 2002.
2. An interesting but in many ways controversial tome on the black ancestry of Vicente Guerrero is Theodore G. Vincent, *The Legacy of Vicente Guerrero, Mexico's First Black Indian President* (Gainesville: University. of Florida Press, 2001).
3. The word "*mestizo*" has acquired many meanings. It's primary usage, however, refers to the racially mixed population (typically white and Indian mixture) that dominates the demography of Latin America. A still timeless classic on the subject is Magnus Mörner, *Race Mixture in the History of Latin America* (Boston: Little, Brown and Company, 1967). However, *mestizo*, in a broader sense, could refer to racial mixture in various manifestations, including a person of mixed black, white, and Indian ancestry. This is the spirit of Virgil Richardson's usage of the word. A foundational work in discussing the African mixture in the racial heritage of Mexico is Gonzalo Aguirre Beltrán, *La población negra en México, Estudio Etnohistórico*, 3rd ed. (Mexico City: Fondo de Cultura Economica, 1989). In English, see also, Beltrán, "The Integration of the Negro in the National Soceity of Mexico," in *Race and Class in Latin America*, ed. Magnus Mörner (New York: Columbia University. Press, 1970).
4. Not only is Guerrero and the Costa Chica region (just south of Acapulco) considered to be among the blackest areas in contemporary times, but the region was also heavily black in the colonial era. See Ben Vinson III, "The Racial Profile of a Rural Mexican Province in the 'Costa Chica': Igualapa in 1791," in *The Americas (TAM)*, 57, no. 2 (October 2000): 269–82.

Note also that the estimated population for blacks in Mexico in the late 1980s and early 1990s was about half a million individuals. See Organization of Africans in the Americas, *Quest for Inclusion: Realizing Afro-Latin American Potential* (Washington, D.C.: Organization of Africans in the Americas, 2000), 16.

8 From Tourist to Resident—Being Black in Mexico City during the 1950s

1. Teotihuacan (literally meaning "where the gods lived," in Nahuatl) flourished between 200 and 500 A.D., and may have had a population of nearly 200,000 during its zenith. The existing archaeological site, long believed to have been a ceremonial center, has shown significant signs of habitation. Sprawling apartment complexes, royal residences, and lower-class dwellings reveal an intricate, socially stratified society.
2. Morris Richardson is Virgil's second-youngest brother. Like Virgil, he had served in the army during World War II, even being stationed in England while Virgil was there. The two brothers were unaware, however, of each other's whereabouts at the time. Morris's first visit to Mexico was with his wife. They spent part of their honeymoon in Virgil's company, making use of the opportunity to visit Teotihuacan.
3. Standing at 213 feet tall, the Pyramid of the Sun is the third largest pyramid in the world.
4. Virgil's observations here are speculative and there isn't any definitive proof that I have seen which links the basic Latin dances to slavery in this fashion, although it is an interesting possibility.
5. Along with Diego Rivera and David Alfaro Siqueiros, José Clemente Orozco was a member of the vanguard of Mexican muralists who revolutionized the nation's artistic tradition beginning in the 1920s.
6. The Virgin of Guadalupe is a unique, Mexican manifestation of the Virgin Mary. On the morning of December 9, 1531, a recently baptized Indian named Juan Diego crossed a hill (Tepeyac) on his way to mass. It was here that a vision appeared—a dark-skinned woman who called Juan Diego "my son." She claimed that she was the Virgin Mary, the mother of Jesus, and that she wanted a church to be built for her on the hill. This apparition has been a powerful event in Mexican Catholicism, with many faithful devotees. The Virgin of Guadalupe, the name given to this apparition of Mary, was instrumental in converting thousands of Indians in colonial Mexico.
7. UNAM is currently located on a relatively centralized campus along the southern extremities of Mexico City.
8. When the 1936 Spanish elections brought to power a left-wing regime, revolts were launched against the government by conservative and fascist forces. Their coalition, called the Nationalists, fought against the Republicans in a bloody struggle that lasted until 1939. During the struggle, Nazi Germany and Italy supported the Nationalists, providing them with weapons, troops, and supplies. Meanwhile, Russia supported the Republicans. Other international forces became involved and sided with the Republicans through the all-volunteer "International Brigade." Americans supported the war with their Abraham Lincoln Brigade (in which some blacks fought). The Republicans were eventually defeated, ushering in the dictatorship of Franco, which lasted until 1975. See Pierre Vilar, *Historia de España* (Barcelona: Editorial Crítica, 1989), 142–71.
9. The Bellas Artes building, built in the nineteenth century under the dictatorship of Porfirio Diaz, is located in the heart of Mexico City, not far from the central square (*Zócalo*).

10. Evans managed to fight on the provincial bullfighting ring circuit and was always moving throughout the country. He may not have lived in Mexico for much more than one year. Source: Letter from Lew Louderback, July, 2002.
11. Using intricate blue and white tilework, the "House of Tiles" or "Casa Azulejos" was originally built in 1596 for the Marqués del Valle de Orizaba. It has since become a landmark and home to one of Mexico's most famous restaurant chains, *Sanborns.* During the Mexican Revolution (1910–1921) the House of Tiles also doubled as a meeting place for insurgents.
12. For more on the Hollywood Ten see Richard M. Fried, *Nightmare in Red, The McCarthy Era in Perspective* (New York and Oxford: Oxford University Press, 1990), 73–78.

9 Livin' and Workin' the Mexico City Scene

1. Started in June 1940, Mexico City College took off as an institution in the summer of 1945, boosted by the enrollment of returning war veterans. In 1947, the school had over 126 students. Many of these came from schools in the United States and studied subjects such as "Latin American Culture." The first bachelor's degrees were awarded in 1947. By 1955, some 745 students had graduated with their B.A. and another 207 had received master's degrees. The college's unique mission to provide "intercultural cooperation" and multiracial education made it unique among institutions of its kind, especially those in the United States. According to Richardson, the Writing Center was funded in part by the Rockefeller Project, which paid not only tuition for some students (specifically, Mexican authors), but also a 200-dollar monthly stipend for students to work with Margaret Shed. For more on Mexico City College see Raymond Arthur Young, "The Mexico City College Library: Its History and Its Role in International Education," (Ph.D. diss., University of Washington, 1955).
2. Virgil mentioned that one of Margaret's teaching assistants (who may or may not have come with her from Berkeley) was George Bennett, an African American who spent a number of years in Mexico. George changed his name to Hal and authored several books, including *This Passionate Land*, a work about the experience of slavery. Unfortunately, I have not been able to locate this book or find any additional details on George's life.
3. Instituto Mexicano de Cinematografia, *La Fabrica de Sueños, Estudios Churubusco 1945–1985* (Mexico City: Estudios Churubusco Azteca, S.A., 1985), 174.
4. Of the 26 episodes that aired, the record shows that Virgil starred in at least two of the films, *Trade of the Killer* and *Eyes of the Idol.* Since credits were not given to all actors, it is possible that Virgil starred in more of these movies.
5. In Latin America the word "licenciado" refers to someone holding a bachelor's degree. As with the prefix "Dr." in the United States, "Licenciado" is a commonly used title to denote someone of the educated, professional class. Given that there are far fewer people holding a bachelor's degree in Mexico than in the United States, the title carries significant social meaning.
6. Originally an Aztec palace, the Castle of Chapultepec was rebuilt by Cortés as a fortress in the 1500s. In the late eighteenth century it became the home of the Mexican viceroy, and in the 1800s it served as a military academy. The castle went on to become one of Mexico's major landmarks when a group of young cadets plunged to their deaths here during the Mexican-American War (1841). Between the 1860s and the mid-1940s, the castle served as the primary residence of Mexican heads of state.
7. Charles Richardson, Virgil's son, did note that Virgil returned to New York briefly in 1956. Interview with Charles Richardson, March 22, 2003.

10 New York Interlude

1. James Peck, *Freedom Ride* (New York: Simon and Schuster, 1962). There were 16 original Freedom Riders who, in 1947, went on a two-week trip through the states of North Carolina, Kentucky, and Tennessee.
2. Charles actually never attended his prom. He did meet Judy Richardson, however, at a party thrown by the brother of one of his friends. The family lived across the street. Meeting Judy was the first time Charles had seen a member of Virgil's branch of the family since the early 1950s. The lack of contact came about because Virgil's siblings had moved to Queens, whereas Charles and his brother still lived with their mother in the Bronx. Interview with Charles Richardson, March 22, 2003.

11 Transitions—Back in Mexico during the 1960s

1. The PRI stands for the Party of the Institutionalized Revolution, which, until recently, held a virtual lock on the Mexican presidency. A vast political machine with roots stemming back to the end of the Mexican Revolution (1921), the PRI offered an alternative to bloody opposition politics by being able to integrate dissent within a one-party framework. Not all politically inspired violence was contained, however.
2. Excellent recent treatment of Cantinflas and his times can be found in Jeffrey M. Pilcher, *Cantinflas and the Chaos of Mexican Modernity* (Wilmington, Delaware: Scholarly Resources, 2001).
3. Some of the Tarzan movies were filmed in Brazil, as well as in Mexico, and aired on NBC (7:30 p.m. Eastern) for two seasons between 1966–1968. There were 31 episodes that aired during the first season (1966–67). Another 26 episodes aired during the second season (1967–1968). In the surviving record, I have found that at least 7 of the episodes in which Virgil starred. Virgil can be found in *The Prisoner* (starring as Nahnto), *Tarzan's Deadly Silence* episodes 1 and 2 (starring as Tabor), *The Day of the Golden Lion* (starring as Notu), *Jungle Dragnet* (starring as Chief M'Boru), *Thief Catcher* (starring as Yaga), and *The Last of the Supermen* (starring as the Leader).
4. The show had at least four different producers in two seasons.
5. Mexico City received a facelift prior to the Olympic games. An efficient and modernized subway was installed that rivaled the French system upon which it was modeled. Construction projects changed the skyline as middle-class neighborhoods cropped up from nowhere and as hotels were furiously built. Mexico flexed its economic muscle like never before in an effort to show the world how successful it was and to attract foreign investment. But at the same time, lurking behind modernization was the problem of uneven development. Not all of the country experienced success equally. The poor barely saw a real change in their situation. Even the middle class, who had benefited greatly from years of economic progress, felt removed from politics. Crime escalated, as did numerous other social problems. So close to the Olympics, the government overreacted to these events, trying to subdue all hints of civil disorder. In the summer of 1968, tens of thousands of university students took to the streets in protest. Demonstrators were punished with tear gas, torture, and bullets in the "Massacre at Tlateloco." For more on the general situation of Mexico City in the 1960s see Diane E. Davis, *Urban Leviathan: Mexico City in the Twentieth Century* (Philadelphia: Temple University Press, 1994), 137–218. For information on race and the Olympics see Amy Bass, *Not the Triumph but the Struggle: The 1968 Olympics and the Making of the Black Athlete* (Minneapolis: University of Minnesota Press, 2002).

12 Border Crossings

1. *After Hours*, a drama about extortion, may have been first produced in 1972, with an all-black cast.
2. While German participation in the slave trade was less than the involvement of England or France, Germany did have colonial possessions in Africa, especially German East Africa (Tanzania) and Namibia. Germany acquired its African colonies relatively late in comparison to other European powers (in the late 1800s) and had to relinquish control over its holdings after the conclusion of World War I.
3. During the Boxer Rebellion in 1900, a Chinese secret society called "Boxers" launched an effort to eradicate foreign rule within their country. The rebellion was crushed, but peasant discontent with British overlords did not cease.
4. The Opium Wars refer to a series of trading wars between the British and the Chinese in the nineteenth century (1839–1842 and 1856–1860). In the second struggle, the French were also allied with the British. Western nations exported opium to China in order to create a more favorable balance of trade with this country, which had traditionally believed the West had nothing to offer in terms of material goods.
5. As the French attempted to maintain control, the battle of Dien Bien Phu proved decisive during the first Indochina wars (1946–1954). Dien Bien Phu showed the resolve and resilience of the population in the face of tremendous adversity, and proved instrumental in precipitating the end of French rule over the country.

13 Black American Yankees on Montezuma's Soil

1. *Mexico This Month*, April 1960, 24.
2. Vincent, *The Legacy of Vicente Guerrero, Mexico's First Black Indian President* (Gainesville: University of Florida Press, 2001), 263.
3. Johnson was on the run for having been convicted for violation of the Mann Act, which forbade the transportation of white women from one state to another for purposes of prostitution. The woman that Johnson happened to be "transporting" was his own wife, Lucille Cameron.
4. Jack Johnson and these ideas are explored in Gerald Horne's forthcoming book, *Black and Brown: African Americans and the Mexican Revolution* (New York: New York University Press, 2005), especially chapter 2.
5. Aguirre Beltrán, *La Población Negra*; Matthew Restall, *Seven Myths of the Spanish Conquest* (New York: Oxford University Press, 2003), 44–63; Colin Palmer, *Slaves of the White God: Blacks in Mexico, 1570–1659* (Cambridge, Massachusetts: Harvard University Press, 1976); Herman L. Bennett, *Africans in Colonial Mexico: Absolutism, Christianity, and Afro-Creole Consciousness, 1570–1640* (Bloomington and Indianapolis: Indiana University Press, 2003); Ivan Van Sertima, *They Came Before Columbus* (New York: Random House, 1976).
6. For one of the best surveys see Jane Landers, *Black Society in Spanish Florida* (Urbana and Chicago: University of Illinois Press, 1999).
7. The life of James Forten is best captured by Julie Winch, *A Gentleman of Color, The Life of James Forten* (New York: Oxford University Press, 2002). For the Santanders and other information on free-colored labor, see Vinson, *Bearing Arms for His Majesty: The Free-Colored Militia in Colonial Mexico* (Stanford: Stanford University Press, 2001), 60, and chapter 3. A leading assessment of the caste system remains Robert Douglas Cope,

The Limits of Racial Domination: Plebeian Society in Colonial Mexico City, 1660–1720 (Madison: University of Wisconsin Press, 1994).

8. The free-black and mulatto Mexican population numbered roughly 300,000 upon the eve of independence. The free-black population in the United States numbered roughly 60,000 in the 1790s.
9. Patrick Carroll has made the important argument that blacks were an important force in bringing together the Spanish and Indian sectors. See Patrick Carroll, "Los Mexicanos Negros: El Mestizaje y los Fundamentos Olvidados de la 'Raza Cósmica,' Una Perspectiva Regional," *Historia Mexicana* 44, no. 3 (1995), 403–38. An important work on integration is Aguirre Beltrán, "The Integration of the Negro." However, the arguments about integration have tended to be overblown in Mexican historiography. Still, for comparative purposes, the argument is a useful one.
10. This subject is treated masterfully in Peter Linebaugh and Marcus Rediker, *The Many-Headed Hydra: Sailors, Slaves, Commoners, and the Hidden History of the Revolutionary Atlantic* (Boston: Beacon Press, 2000), 211–47.
11. The true racial status of Morelos is a question of debate. There are many who describe him as a *mestizo* (mixture of Spanish and Indian). I am persuaded by the literature that includes in his heritage some traces of African ancestry, making him either a mulatto or *pardo* (mixture of black, Indian, and even Spanish ancestry). What is more important than his race, however, was his strong commitment to the advancement of the lower social classes, including Indians, *mestizos*, mulattos, and blacks.
12. In Acapulco alone, for instance, blacks and mulattos outnumbered whites and *mestizos* by a factor of 20 to 1 in the late eighteenth century. See Aguirre Beltrán, *La Población Negra*, 226.
13. *Ibid*, 21–27.
14. Quoted in Felipe Tena Ramírez, ed., *Leyes Fundamentales de México, 1800–1976* (México, City: Editorial Porrúa, S.A., 1976), 30; Hidalgo and Rayon's documents found on pages 21–27.
15. Buckley, *American Patriots, The Story of Blacks in the Military from the Revolution to Desert Storm* (New York: Random House, 2001), 4–5. Note that some historians feel that Buckley's numbers for blacks serving in the Continental Army are exaggerated.
16. *Ibid.*, 16–17.
17. I do not want to take this argument too far. Very little research has been conducted as to whether aspects of Mexico's independence struggle had a "black agenda," or even if this is a fair characterization of the multiclass, multiregional, and multiethnic struggle that took place. We do know that in many instances, regional, familial, and personal agendas directed many lower-class individuals to rebel, perhaps more so than an encompassing racial consciousness. Nevertheless, the question needs to be pursued by more scholarship. One of the best recent treatments examining the discrete goals of the lower social and racial classes is Eric Van Young, *The Other Rebellion, Popular Violence, Ideology, and the Mexican Struggle for Independence, 1810–1821* (Stanford: Stanford University Press, 2001). He refrains from presenting a "race-based" analysis, yet he uncovers many complexities and nuances in the nature of rebellion that will prove foundational for the field for years to come. Also of importance is Peter Guardino, *Peasants, Politics, and the Formation of Mexico's National State, Guerrero, 1800–1857* (Stanford: Stanford University Press, 1996).
18. The 1812 constitution was based on the new Spanish constitution and aspired to undercut the strength of the insurgency.
19. Alvaro Ochoa Serrano, "Los Africanos en México antes de Aguirre Beltrán (1821–1924)," in *Publication of the Afro Latin American Research Association (PALARA)* no. 2 (1998), 80.

20. Martha Menchaca, *Recovering History, Constructing Race: The Indian, Black and White Roots of Mexican Americans* (Austin: University of Texas Press, 2001), 163.
21. Brian Hamnett perceived racism to be a major tension in the early national period in terms of politics. See Hamnett, *Roots of Insurgency, Mexican Regions 1750–1824* (Cambridge: Cambridge University Press, 1986), 12–13. Concrete examples of how Afro-Mexicans ascended to political power in the area of Jalapa can be found in Patrick Caroll, *Blacks in Colonial Veracruz: Race, Ethnicity and Regional Development* (Austin: University of Texas Press, 1991), 134–41.
22. Rosalie Schwartz, *Across the Rio to Freedom: U.S. Negroes in Mexico* (El Paso: Texas Western Press, University of Texas at El Paso, 1974), 10–11.
23. *Ibid.*, 18–19. The situation is reminiscent of that in Spanish Florida.
24. Menchaca, *Recovering History*, 230.
25. Ronnie C. Tyler, "Fugitive Slaves in Mexico," *Journal of Negro History* 57, no. 1 (January 1972), 3, 6; Ruthe Winegarten, *Black Texas Women: 150 Years of Trial and Triumph* (Austin: University of Texas Press, 1995), 30.
26. Schwartz, *Across the Rio*, 29. Note that my discussion on blacks from 1820 to the 1860s draws heavily from Schwartz's work.
27. The immigration papers of blacks can be studied for the year 1839 in some detail, thanks to a series of documents surviving in the Mexican National Archives. See Archivo General de la Nación (AGN), Grupo Documental 129, Movimiento Marítimo, Pasaportes y Cartas de Seguridad, Registro nos. 243969, 243974, 244042, 244532, 244535, 244536, 245274, 245277. Many of these contain information about blacks from New Orleans en route to Tamaulipas.
28. Benjamin Lundy, *The Life, Travels and Opinions of Benjamin Lundy, including his Journeys to Mexico; with a sketch of contemporary events, and a Notice of the Revolution in Haiti* (New York: Negro Universities Press, 1969).
29. More details can be found in Kenneth Porter, "The Seminole in Mexico, 1850–1861," *The Hispanic American Historical Review (HAHR)*, 31, no. 1 (February 1952), 1–36.
30. The years 1880–1884, coinciding with the presidency of General Manuel González, were particularly important for North American immigration to Mexico. Indeed, by 1884, 20,000–100,000 Americans had migrated south of the border. By the middle of the 1890s, there were as many as ten large foreign colonies in Mexico. See Alfred W. Reynolds, "The Alabama Negro Colony in Mexico, 1894–1896," *Alabama Review* 5, no. 4, (October 1952), 243.
31. Moisés González Navarro, *Los Extranjeros en Mexico y los Mexicanos en el extranjero, 1821–1970*, vol. 2 (Mexico City: El Colegio de México, 1994), 123, 132.
32. Arnold Shankman, "The Image of Mexico and the Mexican–American in the Black Press, 1890–1930," *Journal of Ethnic Studies* 3 (Summer 1975), 43.
33. There are several different estimates of the actual number of blacks who arrived. By some estimates there were 764 in residence, by others 900, 850, or 825. See González Navarro, *Los Extranjeros*, vol. 2, 235.
34. The account of the colony comes from the *Journal Of Negro History*, but a more detailed and careful study of the colony can be found in Reynolds, "The Alabama Negro Colony," 243–268; and Reynolds, "The Alabama Negro Colony in Mexico, 1894–1896," *Alabama Review* 6, no. 1 (January 1953), 31–58. The colony was refounded after the initial colonization attempt failed. By 1907, there were nearly 9,000 inhabitants there, producing cotton valued at 420,000 pesos per year. See: González Navarro, *Los Extranjeros*, vol. 2, 236.
35. Shankman, "The Image of Mexico," 45. Quotes taken from *The Washington Bee*, December 11, 1915, and *The Indianapolis Freeman*, September 28, 1907.

36. Quotes taken from Reynolds, "The Alabama Negro Colony," 260–261; and González Navarro, *Los Extranjeros*, vol. 2, 235. See also *El Tiempo*, February 16, 1895.
37. González Navarro, *Los Extranjeros*, vol. 2, 152.
38. Marco Polo Hernández Cuevas, "The 'Afro-Mexican' and the Revolution: Making Afro-Mexicans Invisible Through the Ideology of Mestizaje in La Raza Cósmica," *PALARA*, 4 (2000), 73.
39. More examples of negative reaction towards blacks can be found in the Mexican serials, "Conflicto Internacional," *El Chisme, Diario de la Tarde*, April 19, 1899; and "Los Colonos Negros," *México*, March 10, 1895. In the article "Los Colonos Negros," it was mentioned that more than 1,000 blacks were ready in the train station of Atlanta, Georgia to come to Mexico. In the article "Conflicto Internacional," it was reported that a "legion of U.S. blacks" had arrived in the capital.
40. Of course, there was considerable variation that had to be accounted for, even within the races. Not all whites were created equal. For example, widely cited thinkers, such as Gobineau, upheld the superiority of "Aryan" (Germanic) whites over Iberians and Celts. Some historians and sociologists were even tempted into rewriting European history, and by extension, world history, as an endless power struggle between the inferior Celts and their white rivals. See Ricardo Garcia Granados, "La Question de Razas e Inmigracion en México," *Boletín de la Sociedad de Geografia y Estadistica*, 5a época, tomo 3 (1908), 327–39.
41. Peter Wade, *Race and Ethnicity in Latin America* (Chicago: Pluto Press, 1997); and Nancy Lays Stepan, *The Hour of Eugenics: Race, Gender and Nation in Latin America* (Ithaca and London: Cornell University Press, 1991).
42. José María Luis Mora, *México y Sus Revoluciones* (Mexico City: Fondo de Cultura Económica, 1986).
43. The differentiation between Mexico's Positivists and Conservatives comes from González Navarro, *Los Extranjeros*, vol. 2, 163. There are many interpretations of Positivists and Conservatives, some of which may differ from what is presented here. I have chosen to follow González Navarro's model.
44. González Navarro, *Extranjeros en Mexico*, vol. 2., 166–67.
45. *Ibid.*, 153, 236.
46. Sentiments expressed in 1895 in the Mexico City newspapers—*El Universal* and *Two Republics.* See Reynolds, "The Alabama Negro Colony," 260.
47. González Navarro, *Los Extranjeros*, vol. 2, 153, 166–67.
48. Information in the preceding three paragraphs, including quotes and statistics, from González Navarro, *Los Extranjeros*, vol. 1, 186–88, 506; and idem., *Los Extranjeros* vol. 2, 250.
49. González Navarro, *Los Extranjeros*, vol. 1, 186.
50. Quotes come from González Navarro, *Los Extranjeros*, vol. 1, 186; and idem., vol. 2, 185–92.
51. Quotes come from González Navarro, *Los Extranjeros*, vol. 2, 189, 266.
52. For some visual images of this see John J. Johnson, *Latin America in Caricature* (Austin: University of Texas Press, 1980).
53. Ochoa Serrano, "Los Africanos," 86–87.
54. *Ibid.*
55. *Ibid.*, 86–9; González Navarro, *Los Extranjeros*, vol. 2, 278.
56. James A. Sandos, *Rebellion in the Borderlands: Anarchism and the Plan of San Diego, 1904–1923* (Norman: University of Oklahoma Press, 1992), 79.
57. Benjamin Heber Johnson, "Sedition and Citizenship in South Texas, 1900–1930" (Ph.D. diss., Yale University, 2001), 86.

58. González Navarro, *Los Extranjeros*, vol. 2, 436. The PLM's "ideological brothers" included all foreigners willing to support the cause.
59. Friedrich Katz, *The Life and Times of Pancho Villa* (Stanford: Stanford University Press, 1998), 75. See also, James N. Leiker, *Racial Borders: Black Soldiers along the Rio Grande* (College Station: Texas A&M University Press, 2002), 153.
60. González Navarro, *Los Extranjeros*, vol. 3, 51.
61. Leiker, *Racial Borders*, 153, 158.
62. Mark Eltis, *Race, War and Surveillance: African Americans and the United States Government During World War I* (Bloomington: Indiana University Press, 2001), 6–7.
63. *Ibid.*, 28.
64. Preceding the Plan of San Diego, the German consul in Monterrey was accused of organizing a rebellion of blacks and Indians against the regime of Porfírio Díaz. See Gonzalzo Navarro, *Los Extranjeros*, vol. 3, 127.
65. Sandos, *Rebellion in the Borderlands*, 143.
66. Eltis, *Race, War and Surveillance*, 22–23; William G. Jordan, *Black Newspapers and America's War for Democracy, 1914–1920* (Chapel Hill: University of North Carolina Press, 2001), 68.
67. Leiker, *Racial Borders*, 160, 173.
68. *Ibid.*, 163–67.
69. These ideas adapted from Leiker, *Racial Borders*, 171.
70. As quoted in Leiker, *Racial Borders*, 175, n. 7.
71. The best treatment on Jack Johnson is Horne, *Black and Brown*. See also Vincent, *The Legacy of Vicente Guerrero*, 262–64; and Leiker, *Racial Borders*, 177.
72. An excellent examination of the currents of the revolution's cultural phase is Gilbert Joseph, Anne Rubenstein, and Eric Zolov, eds., *Fragments of a Golden Age: The Politics of Culture in Mexico Since 1940* (Durham: Duke University Press, 2001). This book questions the boundaries currently imposed by historiography with regard to when cultural elements of the revolution began and ended.
73. Good treatment of some of these concepts can be found in Alan Knight, "Racism, Revolution, and Indigenismo: Mexico, 1910–1940," in *The Idea of Race in Latin America, 1870–1940*, ed. Richard Graham (Austin: University of Texas Press, 1990); Bobby Vaughn, "Race and Nation: A Study of Blackness in Mexico" (Ph.D. diss., Stanford University, 2001); Benjamin Keen, *The Aztec Image in Western Thought* (New Brunswick, New Jersey: Rutgers University Press, 1971), and Hernández Cuevas, "The Afro-Mexican and the Revolution," 59–83.
74. One example is that of Lic. Alfonso de Toro, written in 1920, entitled "Influencia de la raza negra en la formacion del pueblo Mexicano." See Ochoa Serrano, "Los Africanos en México," 86–89.
75. Guillermo de la Peña, "Gonzalo Aguirre Beltrán: Historia y Mestizaje," in *Historiadores de México en el Siglo XX*, ed. Enrique Florescano and Ricardo Pérez Montfort (Mexico City: Fondo de Cultura Económica, 1995), 192–193.
76. The Mexican government rejected a proposal to settle 50,000 U.S. blacks in the Isthmus of Tehuantepec in the 1920s because they believed it would complicate the country's ethnic problem. See: Stepan, *The Hour of Eugenics*, 152.
77. González Navarro, *Los Extranjeros*, vol. 3, 34–35.
78. Shankman, "The Image of Mexico," 45–46.
79. Sue Bailey Thurman, "How Far from Here to Mexico," *The Crisis*, September, 1935, 267, 274.
80. AGN, Presidentes, Lázaro Cárdenas, 548.1/1, Febrero 13 de 1937.

81. Shankman, "The Image of Mexico," 49–50.
82. This is a complicated issue with a complex history. How blacks and Mexicans (and to some extent, black Mexicans) were treated in legislation is best treated by Menchaca, *Recovering History*. In short, sometimes Mexicans were processed as blacks, to their detriment. At other times, blacks were favored over Mexicans (and vice-versa) in U.S. legislative circles, especially in key matters such as schooling.
83. AGN, Presidentes, Lázaro Cárdenas, 548.1/1, Febrero 16 de 1937.
84. Secretaría de Relaciones Exteriores (SRE), Clasificación III-655-2, Embajada de Mexico, Preguntas de la Afro-American News Agency y respuestas del Embajador de Mexico. Francisco Castillo Najera. Washington, 23 de Julio de 1943.
85. The creation of the Works Progress Administration's (WPA) Public Works of Art Project in the 1930s was helpful in giving money to black artists and stressing the importance of producing work for the common man. After 1935, the expansion of the Communist Party's popular front against fascism brought about a flurry of interest in creating art that exposed the injustices of capitalism. The Chicago Renaissance, a counterpart to the Harlem Renaissance (which emphasized black pride), saw blacks engaging in this message and linking racial injustice with class oppression. For more see Melanie Anne Herzog, *An American Artist in Mexico, Elizabeth Catlett* (Seattle and London: University of Washington Press, 2000), 27–28.
86. Lizetta LeFalle-Collins, "The Mexican Connection," *American Visions* 11, no. 6, (December 96/January 97), 20–28.
87. One of the best books on Elizabeth Catlett is Herzog, *An American Artist in Mexico*.
88. The lyrics of *Angelitos Negros* were based on a poem by the Venezuelan author Andrés Eloy Blanco. The words of the song (adapted by Manuel Maciste) ran: "Painter, why do you always paint angels white? Why don't you sometimes paint little black angels?" Maciste also wrote *Almas Blancas*, after witnessing a white man beating up a black girl in Philadelphia. He wrote: "Because my skin is dark, the white man despises me. I don't know why . . . my body is black but my soul is white. Their body is white but sometimes their soul is black—fatal contrast." Unfortunately, the movie adaptation of *Angelitos Negros*, released in 1948 and starring Pedro Infante, was filled with racist stereotypes. An outstanding critique of the *Angelitos Negros* craze is Hernández Cuevas, "*Angelitos negros*, a Film from the 'Golden Epoch' of Mexican Cinema: The Coding of 'Visibly' Black Mexicans In and Through a Far-reaching Medium," *PALARA*, no. 5 (2001), 49–62. An example of the positive press received by *Angelitos Negros* can be found in: Gina Cerminara, "Little Black Angels," *The Crisis*, April 1950, 221–25, 266–67.
89. "New Hair Culture Discovery, Mexican Chemist Claims Process to Make Negro Hair Straight, Silky," *Ebony*, June 1948, 58–59.
90. Less noticed that either *Lustrasilk*, *Angelitos Negros*, or *Almas Blancas*, was the release of a Mexican comic book called *Memín Penguín*, which boldly depicted blacks in wild caricature and upheld scores of racial stereotypes. Had black Americans in the 1940s and 1950s noticed it, it might have produced more backlash. Marco Polo Hernández Cuevas, "Memín Pinguín: Uno de los Cómics Mexicanos Más Populares Como Instrumento para Codificar al Negro," *Afro-Hispanic Review* 22, no. 1 (Spring 2003), 52–59. Note that the comic book still circulates today. The story lines are the same as from the original run of the series in the 1940s to 1970s. This is a commentary on how the comic has literally frozen the black image in time for twenty-first century consumption by Mexican (and now the international) audiences. See www.mundovid.com for web-based information.
91. Aguirre Beltrán published a series of important articles in English before the appearance of *La Población Negra*. These include: "Races in 17th Century Mexico," *Phylon* 6

(1945), 212–18, "The Slave Trade in Mexico," *HAHR* 24, (1944), 412–31; and "Tribal Origins of Slaves in Mexico," The *Journal of Negro History* 31 (1946), 269–352.

92. Aguirre Beltrán, "Integration of the Negro."
93. Bobby Vaughn, "Race and Nation."
94. "Negroes in Mexico," *The Crisis*, March 1948, 90.
95. A glance at the popular press in the 1930s and 1940s reveals these concerns abundantly. Two articles from the mid-1940s that deal specifically with Latin America are: "Gold & Silver, Panama Canal Zone has Strange Jim Crow Setup," *Ebony*, June 1946, 20; and "The Truth About Brazil, Starving Negroes Find they Can't Eat Racial Equality," *Ebony*, November 1945, 36–37.
96. "The Negro Who Could be Cuba's President," *Ebony*, August 1947, 32–35.
97. Carleton Beals, "Valerio Trujano: Black Joy," *The Crisis*, May 1931, 153–54, 174.
98. "Mexico, U.S. Negro Migrants Find a Racial Oasis South of Dixie," *Ebony*, October 1948, 13–17.
99. *Ibid.*, 13.
100. Peter B. Hammond, "Mexico's Negro President," *Negro Digest*, May 1951, 10–14.
101. "Jose Maria Morelos—Mexican Benefactor with Negro Blood," *New York Age*, January 24, 1959, M-2. The black press discussed other racial heroes, besides Morelos, such as Vicente Guerrero. See J.A Rogers' column, "Your History," *Pittsburgh Courier*, June 25, 1960.
102. "Valerio Trujano. All-Negro Village Discovered in Mexico," *Ebony*, April 1957, 91–94.
103. U.S. Department of Commerce, Bureau of the Census, *The Social and Economic Status of the Black Population in the United States: An Historical View, 1790–1978* (Washington D.C.: U.S. Census Bureau, 1978), X, 25.
104. "Tourist Camps," *Modern Mexico*, December 1939, 3; "Auto Tourists," *Modern Mexico*, February 1940, 3; "Stepping on the Gas in Mexico," *Modern Mexico*, April, 1937, 5–9; "Mexico City by Car," *Modern Mexico*, August 1936, 7–8; "Rolling South of Rio Grande," *Modern Mexico*, May 1936, 24; "Mexico on Wheels," *Mexico This Month*, May 1959.
105. "Railroad Tourists," *Modern Mexico*, December 1939, 3, "Air Travel," *Modern Mexico*, December 1939, 3.
106. "Mexico's Hotels Lead the World," *Modern Mexico*, November 1938, 16–17.
107. Another important devaluation took place in 1953, reducing Mexican wages by about one-third relative to the strength of the dollar.
108. Gonzalez Navarro, *Los Extranjeros*, vol. 2, 236–39; "Tourism—Mexico's $500,000,000 Baby," *Mexico This Month*, May 1958, 9, 25. Note that U.S. tourists numbered 40,000 in 1933, but may have numbered over half a million in 1956. More on the Mexican tourist industry can be found in Alex Saragoza, "The Selling of Mexico, Tourism and the State, 1929–1852," in *Fragments of a Golden Age*, 89–115.
109. Two interesting examples of *Ebony's* coverage of tourist destinations include: "Vacation in Haiti," *Ebony*, July 1948, 52–4; "Where to go Vacationing," *Ebony*, July 1947, 14–17.
110. "How Negroes Fare in Mexico," *Color*, October 1953, 13–15.
111. "King Cole's Honeymoon Diary," *Ebony*, August 1948, 24–28.
112. "Daring Negroes Open Tourist Bureau in Mexico," *Color*, July 1950, 25–27; "Izzy Rowe's Notebook—Morris Williams Jr. and Hazel Scott Powell," *Pittsburgh Courier*, June 25, 1960.
113. For comparative purposes, the total number of Americans in Mexico (including whites) numbered several thousand by 1960. See: "The American Colony," *Mexico This Month*, April 1960, 21–24.
114. "Mexico, U.S. Negro Migrants Find a Racial Oasis South of Dixie," *Ebony*, October 1948, 15.

115. Virgil Richardson remembered the Jones brothers as having been involved in the numbers racket prior to leaving Chicago. When Dutch Schultz (1902–1935), the notorious gangster, took over the numbers game, he supposedly had one of the Jones brothers killed. The remaining two (Ed and George) fled to Paris and lived there off of their money until the outbreak of World War II. When the Germans invaded France, the brothers took what was left of their fortune and moved to Mexico. I have heard versions of this story told by other African Americans who lived in Mexico City.
116. Sue Bailey, "Letter from Mexico," *Negro Digest*, October 1950, 78–82.
117. "Mexico, U.S. Negro Migrants Find a Racial Oasis South of Dixie," *Ebony*, October 1948, 14. Information on "El Negro," taken from personal correspondence with William Somersille, August, 2000, Mexico City. Somersille may have confused "El Negro" with Oswald Harris, an extremely successful West Indian who owned an auto repair shop and filling station with 60 employees. He was reportedly worth over half a million dollars in 1948.
118. "Negro Migrants Find a Racial Oasis," *Ebony*, 14–15; Minor Neal, "Paradise Down South," *The Crisis*, April 1950, 231–34.
119. Bailey, "Letter from Mexico," *Negro Digest*, 78–82. Note that a number of black Americans decided to move to Mexico because of marriages they had with whites.
120. Mexico City consistently ranked as one of the favorite destinations for U.S. tourists, white and black alike. Around 1940, roughly half of all U.S. tourists stopped in the capital.
121. Letter from William Somersille, August 2000, Mexico City. The same sentiments expressed by Somersille were shared by Bill Jackson, a former Tuskegee Airman who moved to Mexico in the 1980s. He did mention, however, that from his experience roughly half of the African Americans he knew had their racial sensitivities lessened—the other half remained attuned to race. Interview with Bill Jackson, January 22, 2003, Puerto Vallarta, Mexico.
122. During World War II, the U.S. government entered into an agreement with Mexico that allowed Negro League players to play in Mexico in exchange for Mexican workers who were contracted to assist America in preparing for war. A few of these players stand out in memory. Alfred Pinkston, the six-foot-five, 215-pound slugger, demolished Mexican pitchers in the Mexican League and held the all-time Mexican League record career batting average of .372. Ray Dandrige, one of Mexican baseball's two greatest shortstops, was an African American who could hit, catch, and throw as well as anyone, and was a genius infielder, able to play any position. James "Cool Papa" Bell (.367) and Willie Wells (.347) were other standouts. Black players continued playing throughout the country after World War II, and continue to do so today. See: William F. McNeil, *Baseball's Other All-Stars: The Greatest Players from the Negro Leagues, the Japanese Leagues, the Mexican League, and the Pre-1960 Winter Leagues in Cuba, Puerto Rico and the Dominican Republic* (Jefferson, North Carolina, and London: McFarland and Company, 2000), 154–67; and Phil Dixon and Patrick J. Hannigan, *The Negro Baseball Leagues, A Photographic History* (Mattituck, New York: Amereon House, 1992).
123. "Negro Migrants Find a Racial Oasis," *Ebony*, 14–15.
124. "Mexico, Negro Students Play a Scholarly Tune South of the Border," *Color*, April 1954, 50–53.
125. Apart from the April 1954 issue of *Color* see: "Negro Students in Mexico," *Ebony*, June 1955, 88–92; "Siesta, Fiesta, American Students and Death in the Afternoon," *Color*, August 1950, 40–43. For more information on the college scene in Mexico during the 1950s and 1960s, see the annual summer school review article in *Mexico This Month*. Some key articles from the same magazine include: "Student Summer," May 1955, 8, 22;

"Live and Learn," May 1956, 16–19; "School in Mexico," March–April, 1961, 6–9, 25–31; and "Summer Schools: A Capsule Guide to Universities, Art Institutes and Other Study Programs," March 1964, 8–11. Note that the UNAM, like Mexico City College, offered summer school programs. The UNAM was the pioneer here, opening its doors to summer students in the 1920s. In the 1940s, it offered its "summer" classes on a year-round basis. Summer courses were targeted at American and foreign students who had limited experience with Spanish. At first, language teachers made up the bulk of the student body—mainly from Texas and California (including many women). But as the program matured and became more diversified, students were enrolling to pursue an intricate range of courses related to completing the bachelor's, master's, and Ph.D. degrees. By 1963, as many as 10,000 foreign students were enrolling in "summer courses" in Mexico City alone.

126. "Loud Mouth Tourists Hurting Interracial Attitudes in Mexico," *Pittsburgh Courier*, May 24, 1952, 3.
127. "Mr. Aber" may have been a fictitious name.
128. "Loud Mouth Tourists," *Pittsburgh Courier*, 3.
129. "Americans in Mexico Are Mad About the Courier Story," *Pittsburgh Courier*, July 26, 1952, 2.
130. *Ibid.*
131. Letter from Joyce Bailey, March 14, 2003, Lagunitas, California.
132. "Mexico: A Haven for Disabled Vets," *Ebony*, January 1972, 31–40.

Selected Bibliography

Archives and Manuscript Collections

Archivo General de la Nación (AGN), Mexico City (Mexican National Archives and official state papers).

Grupo Documental 129, Movimiento Marítimo, Pasaportes y Cartas de Seguridad.

Presidentes, Lázaro Cárdenas, 548.1/1.

National Archives and Records Administration, College Park, Maryland.

Record Group 69, Box 463, Works Progress Administration, Records of the Federal Theater Project.

Record Group 107, Box 177, Air Corps Departmental.

Record Group 10, Box 178, Air Corps General.

Record Group 18, Box 2, Academic Records, Tuskegee Army Air/Army Flying School.

Record Group 18, Records of the Army Air Forces, WWII Combat Operations Reports, 1942–1946.

Secretaría de Relaciones Exteriores, Mexico City Embassy Records.

Clasificación III-655-2, Embajada de Mexico.

The Schomburg Center for Research in Black Culture Manuscripts, Archives, and Rare Books Division (New York City).

American Negro Theater Alumni Collection.

American Negro Theater Records.

American Negro Theater Scrapbook.

Published Government Documents

U.S. Airforce 50th Anniversary of WWII Commemoration Committee. *Tuskegee Airman Fact Sheet*. Washington, D.C.: HQDA, SACC, Pentagon, 1995.

U.S. Bureau of the Census. *Historical Statistics of the United States, Colonial Times to 1970, Bicentennial Edition*. Washington, D.C.: U.S. Government Printing Office, 1975.

U.S. Department of Commerce, Bureau of the Census. *The Social and Economic Status of the Black Population in the United States: An Historical View, 1790–1978*. Washington, D.C.: U.S. Census Bureau, 1978.

Interviews

The following oral history interviews were conducted by the author:

Jackson, Bill. January 22, 2003, Puerto Vallarta, Mexico.

Palmer, Walter. September 12, 2003, Indianapolis, Indiana.
Richardson, Charles. March 22, 2003, Los Angeles, California.
Richardson, Virgil. Multiple Interviews, 1999–2003, West Columbia, Texas.
Willis, Jack. January 22, 2003, Puerto Vallarta, Mexico.

Letters

Correspondence received by the author with the following dates:
Bailey, Joyce. March 14, 2003, Lagunitas, California.
Cruse, Harold W. July 16, 2002, Ann Arbor, Michigan.
Deaver, Kirsten J. July 9, 2002, New York, New York.
Krangle, Mark Lee. October 10, 2002, Brooklyn, New York.
Louderback, Lew. July 9 and November 5, 2002, Staten Island, New York.
Malley, Barbara. July 2, 2002, New York, New York.
Somersille, William. August 15, 2000, Mexico City.

Newspapers and Magazines

Brownsville Herald (Brownsville, Texas)
Color
Crisis (NAACP)
Ebony
Mexico This Month
Modern Mexico
Negro Digest
New York Age
New York Amsterdam News
News and Observer (Raleigh, North Carolina)
Pittsburgh Courier

Books, Dissertations, and Journal Articles

Aguirre Beltrán, Gonzalo. *La población negra en México, Estudio Etnohistórico*. 3rd ed. Mexico City: Fondo de Cultura Economica, 1989.

——. "Races in 17th Century Mexico." *Phylon* 6 (1945), 212–218.

——. "The Integration of the Negro in the National Soceity of Mexico." In *Race and Class in Latin America*. ed. Magnus Mörner, 11–27. New York: Columbia University Press, 1970.

——. "The Slave Trade in Mexico." *Hispanic American Historical Review* 24 (1944), 412–31.

——. "Tribal Origins of Slaves in Mexico," *Journal of Negro History* 31 (1946), 269–352.

Bailey Thurman, Sue. "How Far from Here to Mexico?" *The Crisis*, September, 1935, 267, 274.

Beals, Carleton. "Valerio Trujano: Black Joy." *The Crisis*, May 1931, 153–54, 174.

Beil, Gail K. "Looking for Dr. Farmer." Unpublished paper delivered at the Texas State Historical Association Meeting, March, 1998.

Bennett, Herman L. *Africans in Colonial Mexico: Absolutism, Christianity, and Afro-Creole Consciousness, 1570–1640*. Bloomington and Indianapolis: Indiana University Press, 2003.

Bloom, Harold. *Black American Poets and Dramatists*. New York and Philadelphia: Chelsea House Publishers, 1995.

Buckley, Gail. *American Patriots: The Story of Blacks in the Military from the Revolution to Desert Storm*. New York: Random House, 2001.

Butler, Kim D. "Defining Diasproa, Refining a Discourse." *Diaspora* 10, no. 2 (2001): 189–217.

Caroll, Patrick J. *Blacks in Colonial Veracruz: Race, Ethnicity and Regional Development*. Austin: University of Texas Press, 1991.

——. "Los Mexicanos Negros: El Mestizaje y los Fundamentos Olvidados de la 'Raza Cósmica,' Una Perspectiva Regional." *Historia Mexicana* 44, no. 3 (1995), 403–38.

Cerminara, Gina. "Little Black Angels." *The Crisis*, April 1950, 221–25, 266–67.

Cope, Robert Douglas. *The Limits of Racial Domination: Plebeian Society in Colonial Mexico City, 1660–1720*. Madison: University of Wisconsin Press, 1994.

Davis, Diane E. *Urban Leviathan: Mexico City in the Twentieth Century*. Philadelphia: Temple University Press, 1994.

Dixon, Phil and Patrick J. Hannigan. *The Negro Baseball Leagues, A Photographic History*. Mattituck, New York: Amereon House, 1992.

Eltis, Mark. *Race, War and Surveillance: African-Americans and the United States Government During World War I*. Bloomington: Indiana University Press, 2001.

Farmer, James. *Lay Bare the Heart, An Autobiography of the Civil Rights Movement*. Fort Worth: Texas Christian University Press, 1998.

Farnsworth, Robert M., ed. *Caviar and Cabbage: Selected Columns by Melvin B. Tolson from the Washington Tribune, 1937–1944*. Columbia, Missouri: University of Missouri Press, 1982.

Flasch, Joy. *Melvin B. Tolson*. New York: Twayne, 1972.

Fried, Richard M. *Nightmare in Red: The McCarthy Era in Perspective*. New York and Oxford: Oxford University Press, 1990.

Garcia Granados, Ricardo. "La Question de Razas e Inmigracion en México." *Boletín de la Sociedad de Geografia y Estadistica* 5a época, tomo 3 (1908): 327–39.

Guardino, Peter. *Peasants, Politics, and the Formation of Mexico's National State, Guerrero, 1800–1857*. Stanford: Stanford University Press, 1996.

Hammond, Peter B. "Mexico's Negro President." *Negro Digest*, May 1951, 10–14.

Hamnett, Brian. *Roots of Insurgency, Mexican Regions 1750–1824*. Cambridge: Cambridge University Press, 1986.

Hayes, Helen, with Katherine Hatch. *My Life in Three Acts*. San Diego: Harcourt Brace Jovanovich, 1990.

——. with Dody Sandford. *On Reflection; An Autobiography*. New York: M. Evans, 1968.

Heber Johnson, Benjamin. "Sedition and Citizenship in South Texas, 1900–1930." Ph.D. diss., Yale University, 2001.

Heintze, Michael R. *Private Black Colleges in Texas, 1865–1954*. College Station, Texas: Texas A & M Univ. Press, 1985.

Hernández Cuevas, Marco Polo. "*Angelitos negros*, a Film from the 'Golden Epoch' of Mexican Cinema: The Coding of 'Visibly' Black Mexicans In and Through a Far-reaching Medium." *Publication of the Afro Latin American Research Association* no. 5 (2001), 49–62.

——. "Memín Pinguín: Uno de los Cómics Mexicanos Más Populares Como Instrumento para Codificar al Negro." *Afro-Hispanic Review* 22, no. 1 (Spring 2003), 52–59.

——. "The 'Afro-Mexican' and the Revolution: Making Afro-Mexicans Invisible Through the Ideology of Mestizaje in La Raza Cósmica." *Publication of the Afro Latin American Research Association* no. 4 (2000), 59–83.

Herzog, Melanie Anne. *An American Artist in Mexico, Elizabeth Catlett*. Seattle and London: University of Washington Press, 2000.

Hill, Errol, ed. *The Theatre of Black Americans*. New York: Applause Books, 1987.

Homan, Lynn M. and Thomas Reilly. *Black Knights, The Story of the Tuskegee Airmen*. Gretna, Louisiana: Pelican Publishing Co., 2001.

Horne, Gerald. *Black and Brown: African-Americans and the Mexican Revolution 1910–1920*. New York: New York University Press, 2005.

Instituto Mexicano de Cinematografia, *La Fabrica de Sueños, Estudios Churubusco 1945–1985*. Mexico City: Estudios Churubusco Azteca, S.A., 1985.

Jakoubek, Robert E. *James Farmer and the Freedom Rides*. Brookfield, Conn.: Millbrook Press, 1994.

Johnson, John J. *Latin America in Caricature*. Austin: University of Texas Press, 1980.

Jordan, William G. *Black Newspapers and America's War for Democracy, 1914–1920*. Chapel Hill: University of North Carolina Press, 2001.

Joseph, Gilbert, Anne Rubenstein, and Eric Zolov, eds. *Fragments of a Golden Age: The Politics of Culture in Mexico Since 1940*. Durham: Duke University Press, 2001.

Katz, Friedrich. *The Life and Times of Pancho Villa*. Stanford: Stanford University Press, 1998.

Keen, Benjamin. *The Aztec Image in Western Thought*. New Brunswick, New Jersey: Rutgers University Press, 1971.

Knight, Alan. "Racism, Revolution, and Indigenismo: Mexico, 1910–1940." In *The Idea of Race in Latin America, 1870–1940*, ed. Richard Graham, 71–113. Austin: University of Texas Press, 1990.

Landers, Jane. *Black Society in Spanish Florida*. Urbana and Chicago: University of Illinois Press, 1999.

Lays Stepan, Nancy. *The Hour of Eugenics: Race, Gender and Nation in Latin America*. Ithaca and London: Cornell University Press, 1991.

LeFalle-Collins, Lizetta. "The Mexican Connection." *American Visions* 11, no. 6 (December 96/ January 97), 20–28.

Leiker, James N. *Racial Borders: Black Soldiers along the Rio Grande*. College Station: Texas A&M University Press, 2002.

Linebaugh, Peter and Marcus Rediker. *The Many-Headed Hydra: Sailors, Slaves, Commoners, and the Hidden History of the Revolutionary Atlantic*. Boston: Beacon Press, 2000.

Lundy, Benjamin. *The Life, Travels and Opinions of Benjamin Lundy, including his Journeys to Mexico; With a Sketch of Contemporary Events, and a Notice of the Revolution in Haiti*. New York: Negro Universities Press, 1969.

McGovern, James R. *Black Eagle: General Daniel "Chappie" James, Jr.* University, Alabama: University of Alabama Press, 1985.

McNeil, William F. *Baseball's Other All-Stars: The Greatest Players from the Negro Leagues, the Japanese Leagues, the Mexican League, and the Pre-1960 Winter Leagues in Cuba, Puerto Rico and the Dominican Republic*. Jefferson, N.C. and London: McFarland and Company, 2000.

Menchaca, Martha. *Recovering History, Constructing Race: The Indian, Black and White Roots of Mexican Americans*. Austin: University of Texas Press, 2001.

Mitchell, Loften. *Voices of the Black Theater*. Clifton, New Jersey: James T. White & Company, 1975.

Moore, Sonia. *The Stanislavski Method; The Professional Training of an Actor. Digested from the Teachings of Konstantin S. Stanislavski*. New York: Viking Press, 1960.

Mora, José María Luis. *México y Sus Revoluciones*. Mexico City: Fondo de Cultura Económica, 1986.

Mörner, Magnus. *Race Mixture in the History of Latin America*. Boston: Little, Brown and Company, 1967.

Navarro Moisés, González. *Los Extranjeros en Mexico y los Mexicanos en el extranjero, 1821–1970*. 3 vols. Mexico City: El Colegio de México, 1993–1994.

Neal, Minor. "Paradise Down South." *The Crisis*, April 1950, 231–34.

Ochoa Serrano, Alvaro. "Los Africanos en México antes de Aguirre Beltrán (1821 1924)." *Publication of the Afro Latin American Research Association*, no. 2 (1998), 79–91.

Organization of Africans in the Americas. *Quest for Inclusion: Realizing Afro-Latin American Potential.* Washington, D.C.: Organization of Africans in the Americas, 2000.

Ottley, Roi. *'New World A-Coming;' Inside Black America.* Boston: Houghton Mifflin Company, 1943.

Palmer, Colin. *Slaves of the White God: Blacks in Mexico, 1570–1659.* Cambridge, Mass.: Harvard University Press, 1976.

Paxton, Robert O. *Vichy France Old Guard and New Order.* New York: Columbia University Press, 1972.

Peck, James. *Freedom Ride.* New York: Simon and Schuster, 1962.

Perry, Jeffrey B., ed. *A Hubert Harrison Reader.* Middleton, Conn.: Wesleyan University Press, 2001.

Phelps, J. Alfred. *Chappie: America's First Black Four Star General: The Life and Times of Daniel James, Jr.* Novato, Cal.: Presidio Press, 1991.

Pilcher, Jeffrey M. *Cantinflas and the Chaos of Mexican Modernity.* Wilmington, Del.: Scholarly Resources, 2001.

Porter, Kenneth. "The Seminole in Mexico, 1850–1861." *The Hispanic American Historical Review* 31, no. 1 (February 1952), 1–36.

Restall, Matthew. *Seven Myths of the Spanish Conquest.* New York: Oxford University Press, 2003.

Reynolds, Alfred W. "The Alabama Negro Colony in Mexico, 1894–1896," *Alabama Review* 5, no. 4, (October 1952), 243–68.

——. "The Alabama Negro Colony in Mexico, 1894–1896." *Alabama Review* 6, no. 1 (January 1953), 31–58.

Sandos, James A. *Rebellion in the Borderlands: Anarchism and the Plan of San Diego, 1904–1923.* Norman: University of Oklahoma Press, 1992.

Schwartz, Rosalie. *Across the Rio to Freedom: U.S. Negroes in Mexico.* El Paso: University of Texas at El Paso Press, 1974.

Shankman, Arnold. "The Image of Mexico and the Mexican-American in the Black Press, 1890–1930." *Journal of Ethnic Studies* 3 (Summer 1975), 43–56.

Tena Ramirez, Felipe, ed. *Leyes Fundamentales de Mexico, 1800–1976.* Mexico City: Editorial Porrúa, 1976.

Tyler, Ronnie C. "Fugitive Slaves in Mexico." *Journal of Negro History* 57, no. 1 (January 1972), 1–12.

Van Sertima, Ivan. *They Came Before Columbus.* New York: Random House, 1976.

Van Young, Eric. *The Other Rebellion, Popular Violence, Ideology, and the Mexican Struggle for Independence, 1810–1821.* Stanford: Stanford University Press, 2001.

Vaughn, Bobby. "Race and Nation: A Study of Blackness in Mexico." Ph.D. diss., Stanford University, 2001.

Vilar, Pierre. *Historia de España.* Barcelona: Editorial Crítica, 1989.

Vincent, Theodore G. *The Legacy of Vicente Guerrero, Mexico's First Black Indian President.* Gainesville: University of Florida Press, 2001.

Vinson, Ben III. *Bearing Arms for His Majesty: The Free-Colored Militia in Colonial Mexico.* Stanford: Stanford University Press, 2001.

——. "The Racial Profile of a Rural Mexican Provice in the 'Costa Chica': Igualapa in 1791." *The Americas* 57, no. 2 (October 2000), 269–82.

Wade, Peter. *Race and Ethnicity in Latin America.* Chicago: Pluto Press, 1997.

Wilcox, Leonard. *V.F. Calverton: Radical in the American Grain.* Philadelphia: Temple University Press, 1992.

Winch, Julie. *A Gentleman of Color, The Life of James Forten*. New York: Oxford University Press, 2002.

Winegarten, Ruthe. *Black Texas Women: 150 Years of Trial and Triumph*. Austin: University of Texas Press, 1995.

Worthen, William B. *The Harcourt Anthology of Drama*. Fort Worth: Hartcourt College Publishers, 2002.

Young, Raymond Arthur. "The Mexico City College Library: Its History and its Role in International Education." Ph.D. diss., University of Washington, 1955.

Index